MENTAL ILLNESS RECOVERY SERIES X PSYCH2GO

Michelle Gaston

Cover Artist:
Alexandra Garlick

Editors:
Bianca Quinaln
Yasmin Sadiq
Mira Chipongian
Halimah Auleear
Ryan Parr
Saira Tariq
Vanessa Rogers
Michelle Truong

ISBN: 1974396940
ISBN 13: 9781974396948

QUOTE FROM THE AUTHOR

"Mental Illness isn't something you should feel ashamed of. Nor should you feel alone. Millions of people worldwide battle with it. The problem with mental disorders is that it distorts your reality affecting every aspect of your life. It lies to you, making you believe in all sorts of delusions. Once you are sucked in by it, it seems impossible to overcome it, but the truth is you can live a happy and fulfilling life with your mental disorders by discovering your inner strength."
~ Michelle Gaston

ACKNOWLEDGEMENTS

I would like to thank each one of you, who supported and followed this series since the very beginning. I deeply appreciate all 100 people who shared their stories with me. I am also grateful for Tai and the Psych2go Team, who gave me a safe and supportive place to write. And a special thanks to my parents Mytzi Gaston and Luis Rodriguez who supported me through this journey and reminded me to never give up.

TABLE OF CONTENTS

STORY # 1

DEPRESSION, ANXIETY DISORDER & INSOMNIA

Cassidy (Cas for short) was born in New Mexico and currently resides in Arizona. She enjoys writing stories, songs and poems. Cas is a painter and sells her art. At the moment, she is going to school to learn how to produce music. Her goal 5 years from now is to have graduated and find work as an audio engineer.

Cassidy was diagnosed on April of this year with depression, anxiety and insomnia after being admitted to a mental hospital for trying to commit suicide. Cassidy suspects her mental disorders stem from post-traumatic stress disorder (PTSD). Her doctor was unsure, but prescribed her medication for bipolar disorder and she was referred to other psychiatrists and therapists. Cas does not have good medical insurance and due to this she has not been able to seek adequate help.

She had to deal with horrible symptoms such as, recurring nightmares with sleeping and appetite changes. Cas would stop eating for long periods of time. She also had mood swings and would become angry for no apparent reason. Cassidy lost interest for the things she cherished most. Her insomnia spiked out of control with little to no sleep. She also had severe panic attacks that had no explanation.

Because of this her daily life was affected tremendously. Cassidy pushed everyone she loved away. Losing a bunch of friends in the process. She kept those who truly cared about her away by purposely being mean and picking fights with them. Not only that, but during her high school years and first year in college she failed her courses because she did not have any motivation whatso ever.

Feeling empty Cassidy became addicted to cocaine while she did other drugs such as acid, ecstasy and mushrooms just to feel something. On April 24, 2015 after taking ecstasy Cassidy tried to commit suicide. Her boyfriend found her still conscious on the bathroom floor. He started crying and screaming at her. The neighbors heard his screams calling an ambulance thatsaved her life. This made Cas feel desperate because she wanted to calm her boyfriend, and yet die in his arms. This created a huge tear in their relationship, her boyfriend still hides her pill bottles and has taken control of her medication.

Till this day Casidy still feels terrible for putting him through that. Her turning point to overcome her mental disorder was at the mental hospital after the incident. Cassidy hasn't fully recovered yet. She said, "I will always be in recovery from these and I will always have to work hard to not let them control me, it is a lifelong disorder that you learn to live with." She copes with this by keeping herself busy with puzzles, writing, painting, school work, and reminds herself every day that she is loved. Even on days she doesn't find the motivation to do anything she makes herself take a shower, put on new clothes and do the dishes. By doing this she feels accomplished. Her boyfriend has helped along the way as well by helping her quit drugs and reminding her she can talk to him.

This ordeal has taught her that she is loved and now her outlook in life haschanged. She no longer feels like dying and now she looks up to the future. Whenever she feels like relapsing she confides in her boyfriend or her best friend of 3 years. She is happy with her life and is on track now, she also has her own apartment she paying for and is passing school.

This is Cassidy's advice for those struggling:

"I would like to tell you all that No matter what your dealing With, somebody will listen, somebody cares, and even if you just get up and shower it still helps you feel accomplished and if that's the best you can do that day then do it, I am proud of you, and tomorrow try doing a little more, maybe shower and clean or write a new chapter to your book, or read, or take your dog on a walk, it helps trust me."

STORY # 2

BIPOLAR TYPE 1, SCHIZOAFFECTIVE DISORDER, ANTISOCIAL PERSONALITY DISORDER & POLYSUBSTANCE ABUSE DISORDER

Charles Owens from Roseville, Michigan and enjoys eclectic music. He does not stick to a certain music genre, but he prefers to listen to songs that have a deep meaning he can relate to. His music preferences vary from classic rock, alternative rock, rap and hip hop, etc. He also is fond of reading although he doesn't read often. Charles does not find the energy or interest to develop any hobbies due to his mental illness and drug addiction.

Charles is going to start classes at the end of August of this year. He decided to certify as a plumber pipe fitter because he enjoys working with his hands and detests repetitive jobs. His goal is to eventually become a master and work his way up in the commercial and industrial area, alongside engineers.

Owens has seen different health professionals which is the reason why he has been given different diagnosis. He has either bipolar type 1 with psychotic features or is schizoaffective. He has also been diagnosed with antisocial personality disorder, along with polysubstance abuse disorder. He has been on and off different medications for the past 10 years and has been suggested therapy, but doesn't stick too long with it. Charles is still struggling with recovery; his bipolar disorder has not gone away. He has been having a hard time staying clean and has relapsed in various occasions. Now, Charles has been clean for a month and a half.

He has struggled with extremely difficult symptoms throughout his life. Owens has considered and longs for suicide as an escape. Due to his bipolar disorder, he has times of acceptable emotions, but when his mania hits he has difficulty sleeping, has high energy and talks fast. Not only that, but in moments of stress he will have auditory and visual hallucinations.

Charles has had a hard time maintaining a job because of his lack of attendance. When the depressive side of his mental illness would hit he would isolate himself completely to the point that he does not answer his phone or hangout with friends. He would also self-harm and attempt suicide. When his manic side overcomes him, his friends become distant due to his high energy levels and aggressive behaviors towards others, often picking fights. Many have had a hard time relating to Charles because they either view his behavior as call for help, which made him become more isolated, or they felt pity over him making him more distant because he did not want to be constantly looked over.

He has been able to control his illness by taking 3 different medications to manage his symptoms. When he attends therapy, he receives coping skills that helps him deal with the stresses of his daily life. He also attends narcotics anonymous meetings and has a sponsor who has a father suffering with mental illness who he can confide in. Charles shared, "My sponsor, he has helped me apply some principles from the narcotics anonymous program to my life of dealing with mental illness, and how I need to stay medication compliant, because knowing that I have this, it'd be insane to go off my meds and let this illness wreak havoc on my life."

His ordeal with mental illness has taught him that he is resilient and that he can deal with more than he previously thought. He has become less aggressive and has an easier time letting go of things that bothers him. Charles has decided to prevent a huge mess by speaking out, staying on medication and attending NA program. This is his advice to other struggling with mental illness:

"Stay on your medications regardless of anything else. Anyone suffering from addiction, please get help, you are worth it. We can live clean, sober and enjoy a nice life."

STORY # 3

DEPRESSION

Justice is from Waynesboro, VA, and she enjoys drawing and painting. She also lifts weights with her step-dad and runs in varsity cross-country and track in her high school. Her future goal is to major in architectural engineering at Virginia Tech.

Justice was diagnosed with depression 6 months ago, although she has been struggling with it for about three years and a half. Justice suspects her depression to be hereditary and stem from unresolved feelings from her parents' divorce. Not only that, but she has been bullied physically, verbally and sexually. She also struggles to understand her sexuality. She was diagnosed by her primary physician and went to professional counselling for about a year. The counselling did not work for Justice because her counsellor seemed less than interested and always looked at the clock instead of focusing on her. So, Justice decided to go to the lay counsellor at her church, she instantly connected with her and till this day they are friends.

Justice had deal with horrible symptoms of depression. She explained, "I was nothing. I wasn't worth the dirt beneath my feet. I always felt hopeless. I didn't belong. I believed that no one wanted me around. Who would want to be friends with someone like me?"

This affected her daily life because she constantly beat herself up and didn't want to let anyone down. It was difficult for her to get out of bed and maintain good grades. Justice attempted suicide twice and self-harmed by cutting and bruising herself. Her depression made her push everyone she loved away and those who cared about her did not want to be around her because they did not want to be responsible if she killed herself. Justice felt in agony, sharing, "I felt alone. I felt unloved. Nothing I could say could truly convey how alone and unloved I felt."

The turning point to help control her depression was the day before September 20th. On this day, Justice was going to commit suicide, but she went to a cross country meet where she ran into a friend from her church. Justice stopped going to church, so her friend invited her back to the youth group. By connecting with god, true friends and her counsellor she is here today fighting to overcome her depression. Justice constantly stays in touch with people she trusts, who keeps her accountable, and loves her. Her best friend Hannah, despite being far from her always texted, spoke the truth, and encouraged Justice when she needed it the most.

This ordeal taught her to be strong. Justice revealed, "I was put through this storm so I could be a light to others and help them through their struggle. That's why I am not ashamed of my story." This experience changed her outlook, she now loves her life. She prevents this from happening again by being a devout Christian and being in prayer for strength. This is her advice to others struggling with similar mental conditions:

"Don't be afraid to reach out! That's the hardest part, but it's also the most important. If you can't talk to your parents or your parents are part of the problem reach out to an older friend (not your peers but maybe a college age friend). Be honest with your struggles and sadness. You are not alone!"

STORY # 4

DEPRESSION & ANXIETY DISORDER

Amanda is from Western, PA and she enjoys reading, listening to music and archery hunting. She is currently starting school to become a pastor. Her goal 5 years from now is to be either pastoring at church or starting her own ministry.

Amanda suffers from anxiety and deep depression since she was a child, although her depression was stronger as a young teen. She is still struggling with both disorders. Amanda believes her mental illness stems from childhood verbal and mental abuse, along with genetics.

Amanda saw a psychologist for a while, who diagnosed her with a severe case of depression and anxiety. Her psychologist worked with her by using mental imaging and techniques of distraction to help her calm down. She had to deal with terrible symptoms. Her depressive side dealt with sadness, loss of interest and complete numbing with constant fatigue. Amanda admitted, "I preferred to stay in bed all the time than to participate in life." She felt anger and aggression towards the people she loved most for unrealistic reasons and thought no one loved her. Her anxious side dealt with irrational fears such as, loved ones dying and could not leave the house without having a panic attack. When she managed to leave the house she couldn't drive the interstate for years due to the anxiety.

Because of this Amanda's life was a disaster. Her mental illness provoked her to have gastrointestinal distress, which made her miss school a lot for being sick. She was unable to leave the house for various days and that didn't help her depression because she was alone for most of the time. She explained, "I was in such a dark place, constantly convinced that I wasn't good enough, that no one cared for me or loved me. I was undeserving." She also added, "Everyone would be better off without me", which made her want to move far away.

Although Amanda had depression and anxiety she did no attempt to hurt herself or anyone else. The turning point to recover from her mental illnesses was taking medication and finding relief through her faith in Jesus. Her loving and supportive husband also help her stay afloat through dark times. Amanda said, "My husband is my biggest cheerleader and support. He lets me talk it out when I'm having some anxiety and he knows when I need space or for him to just hold me tight when my world is crashing down around me. He also takes over caring for the kids when he can tell I just need to go be alone for a while and regroup."

This ordeal taught Amanda that if she lets her mental illness consume her it will win. She understands that she needs to fight every day of her life with depression. This experience changed her outlook in life. She now appreciates the little things and joys of life. This is Amanda's advice for others struggling:

"Don't give up. There are going to be hard days, there are going to be days where you'll say, "what mental illness?", and there are going to be days where the weight of this illness is just too much and you won't think you'll be able to take it any longer. Just know you are stronger than this, there are people who do love you, who do care, and do understand. When you hit rock bottom, there is nowhere to go but up."

STORY # 5

DEPRESSION & SOCIAL ANXIETY DISORDER

Lauren is from Utah and she loves listening to the Australian pop punk band 5 Seconds of Summer and writing romantic stories. Lauren's future goal is to become a nurse to help others. She suffers from depression and social anxiety. Her mental illnesses stem from family problems and the bullying she went through as a child. She has been seeing a mental health professional for the past two years and it has been the best decision she has made to overcome her mental disorders.

Lauren suffered symptoms that disrupted her daily life. Her depressive symptoms made her feel low on energy and she slept all the time. Additionally, never wanted to go out anywhere. Her anxiety symptoms made her constantly hyperventilate, while she focused on negatively. This behavior made her think everyone saw her flaws, which are fundamentally the symptoms of social anxiety.

Because of this Lauren couldn't walk down the hallways without feeling like everyone was staring and thinking bad of her. Lauren disclosed, "I always thought that I was pathetic and that I wasn't worth anything." Lauren considered suicide and to run away from her home a few times. She did self-harm, but she is grateful her scars went away.

This affected Lauren's relationships with her friends and family because she became dependent on their opinions and help. She also made them feel bad because she was upset. Lauren said, "I felt very angry with myself because I didn't want to seem like a burden on anyone. I also felt extremely upset and defective as if something was wrong with me."

The turning point to overcome her mental disorders was when she focused on her problems such as, low self-esteem and her desire to give more to others. Lauren copes with her anxiety by taking medication that helps with dopamine release. Not only that, but she uses techniques she has learned to control her panic attacks. Her friends and family help her by allowing Lauren to vent out even if it didn't make any sense.

This ordeal taught Lauren that when things get tough, it is to teach her valuable lessons. She also has learned that mental illness isn't something she needs to be ashamed of. This is Lauren's advice to others struggling though similar situations:

"Do not be afraid to get help. Do not be ashamed to deal with this. Like many people have physical illnesses, others deal with mental illnesses and that's okay. Just know that it gets better and it's okay to deal with it with help. You don't have to be alone."

STORY # 6

DEPRESSION

Anonymous is from the United States and she enjoys reading and writing. Her favorite book is A Tree Grows in Brooklyn by Betty Smith, but she also is fond of John Green and Toni Morrison books. Her goal is to be financially self-sufficient and to be happy. In five years from now she wants to either be in graduate school or working at a job she loves.

She still is struggling with depression since middle school and started showing symptoms of anxiety in high school. Even though her depression was informally diagnosed, she knew she had it. She went through various treatments such as Cognitive Behavioral Therapy (CBT), Group Dialectical Behavioral Therapy and medication.

The symptoms she still deals with affect her immensely. She revealed, "I felt empty and constantly exhausted. I overthought everything and hated myself. I either slept too much or not at all. Same goes for eating." This affected her life, she constantly struggled keeping up at her school. When she felt emotionally worse she resorted to self-harm at the age of 14, stopped and started again at 16. Then she became suicidal, but thankfully she was too afraid to attempt it.

The only relationship that was not affected was with her best friend, this ordeal made them closer. But her relationship with her parents became difficult and quickly deteriorated after she asked them for help. She shared, "I felt judged, misunderstood, and ultimately rejected." This made her feel angry and frustrated with her parents over the last couple of years. Her parents handled the situation poorly making her feel trapped and isolated.

The turning point for overcoming her depression was the realization that it is an everyday battle. The strategy she used to cope with her illness was learning that there will always be bad days. She focused on creative outlets and practiced self-care to cope with her illness. Not only that, but her best friend and school teacher helped her along the way.

This ordeal taught her many aspects about herself and now her outlook in life has changed. She said, "I am almost a completely different person than I was when I started high school 4 years ago. I've become cynical and distrustful, but I've become so much more open-minded and empathetic." She now makes a greater effort to keep toxic people out of her life.

This is her advice to those still struggling with depression:

"Reach out. Learn self-care. Mental health before everything else. Home isn't always a place and family isn't always your mother(s) and/or father(s); your best friends can be your family. Hang in there. Relapse doesn't equal failure. You deserve to happy because you have worth and you have worth simply because you are."

STORY # 7

MAJOR DEPRESSIVE DISORDER, POST-TRAUMATIC STRESS DISORDER, GENERALIZED ANXIETY DISORDER & DERMATILLOMANIA

K at is from California and she loves art, printmaking history, graphic design, makeup and clothing. Kat's future goal is to have built an independent skill set and income, as well as a strong mental foundation. She still suffers from major depressive disorder (MDD), Post-Traumatic Stress Disorder (PTSD), Generalized Anxiety Disorder (GAD) and Dermatillomania, also known as skin-picking disorder.

Her mental disorders stem from genetic history, verbal and emotional abuse, physical abuse she witnessed in her household, and from being a passenger in two nearly fatal DUIs accidents at the ages of 8 and 9. Kat was diagnosed by a professional only for the MDD and PTSD. Her GAD was made without a formal diagnosis and she took cognitive behavioral therapy for a limited time.

Kat had to deal with terrible symptoms. She had severe panic attacks three to four times per week. She constantly felt paranoid and insecure. This affected impacted her life to the point that she frequently used pot in order to attend her classes in college. Kat admits, "I am sober now, but I have frequent self-sabotaging and self-disparaging thoughts paired with lack of work ethic and limited motivation." When her MDD strikes, she sleeps 14+ hours per day.

Kat began to self-harm at the age of 13, that occurred during extreme cases of anxiety and/or depression. Her dermatillomania still remains active as a source of instant soothing. Her relationships with other has been affected, she disconnected with others who did not know how to empathize and loved ones who insisted that she overcome her symptoms. This made Kat feel terrible because she feared to fulfill the roles her parents assumed she should achieve.

The turning point for Kat to overcome her mental illnesses is that she does not want her present family to see her the way her biological family did. The strategies she uses to cope with her illnesses is using fear as a motivator along with antidepressants and a clear mindset. She confesses, "I try (and usually fail) to harness anxiety as motivation to improve. I also try to slow my somewhat manic expectations and calm my depressive feelings using benefits of ASMR." Kat also embraces her sexuality in a positive way and pushes her physical limits.

Kat has learned that there is no substitute for hard work. She does not feel any stronger yet, but she hopes that these experiences will create a well-rounded woman. Kat believes her illness won't ever fully leave, but she will keep fighting until there are more benefits than stressors. This is her advice:

"The sensitivity we inherit through mental illness is a superpower! It's different for everyone- think of superman, who has more limits than anyone! One can easily take him down if they know his vulnerabilities, but he's worked hard enough so that his strength overpowers even his more obvious weaknesses."

STORY # 8

DEPRESSION & DISSOCIATIVE DISORDER

Tori is from Bangladesh, but currently lives in New Jersey. Tori loves music, drawing and art. Her future goal is to move away and find a job. Tori was diagnosed by a counselor and psychiatrist with depression and dissociative disorder, although her doctors did not quite understand her dissociation. Tori's mental disorders stem from family and economic problems. Tori and her mother moved to the United States with her step-father, whom she considers her dad. Because of this her family was not making much money and the financial burden created verbal and psychical fights between her parents. Tori reports, "The fights began when I was 6 or 7. My parents argued about money and had a lot of problems. Some days I heard screaming at 1 am and it didn't stop till 7am. It was scary, I was so scared that my mom was going to get divorced again. I didn't want anything bad to happen to her, and she was all I had. Some nights the fights would get physical and I would try to come downstairs to make it stop. I tried, but all I could do was cry."

Tori had to deal with terrible symptoms such as, extreme fatigue, weight gain, social anxiety and frustration. Tori added, "My grades dropped, I slept a lot, I stopped talking to friends." Tori wanted to disappear because even living was exhausting for her, but she did not want to kill herself. Her distraction was school and her friends, she said, "The thing that got me by was school. I LOVED school. Going to school made me forget all my troubles at home, also since I lived in an apartment complex I always came home, finished homework and played with all the other kids till sun set."

Tori's depression skyrocketed during 8th grade because she had to move to another town leaving all her friends behind. She mentioned, "The people there were different. I couldn't relate to anyone and no one accepted me for my personality or for who I was. I just couldn't find anyone who I was in-synch with." This made Tori feel frustrated because school used to be fun for her and now it's become a drag. When Tori got to high school she was able to make new friends, although it was extremely difficult for her because this meant a new type of hangout as in sleepovers, movies, and hanging out at the mall. Her parents never allowed her to go out with friends. She explained, "This continued all throughout my life till end of high school. The older I got, the more I fought my parents to let me go places. All my friends would hang out and I never got to. I told myself that I didn't need to socialize outside of school, and that I would be able to maintain my relationships." Tori remembers having a folder full of birthday invitations she couldn't go to.

Because of this Tori fell into deep depression. She slowly distanced herself from most of her friends keeping only one or two friends around. She no longer wanted to make people laugh, or relate to anyone. She constantly struggled to find peace with her lifestyle and by junior year Tori gained a lot of weight. At the age of 16 Tori really liked a boy, the two became close and talked every day on the phone, but one day he became and distant broke off their friendship.

Tori's parents obligated her to watch Bengali TV series with them. She hated watching it because most of the series were about how women in Bangladesh would get harassed, beaten or forced into marriage. One day, while Tori was watching TV with her parents she 'snapped'. Stating, "I was suddenly not in the room with my parents but in my head just thinking. I lost all awareness of my surroundings and was just day dreaming in my head. I got up and went to my room after the show ended, and I felt so numb, yet it felt like I had gained a new super power. An ability to leave my current environment, go somewhere else, into my head. I could ignore anything bad that would happen to me, and didn't have to feel it. If my parents forced a situation on me, I could just be there, but not be there mentally. I could sit in one place and think for hours and I would never get bored. Really I had lost all sense of awareness and the ability to feel the outside world."

When Tori got into University, she had more freedom and a car to go to University with. It was at that moment when she realized how different she had become. Tori could not feel anything, she would move her hands and it felt like it wasn't hers. Not only that, but even if she looked at herself in the mirror she could not recognize herself. So, Tori visited her university's psychiatrist, took therapy and medication. It was an uphill battle for her, constantly going back and forth. Till one day while Tori was walking to visit a friend of hers, she realized how lonely she felt, and instantly she felt a burst of happiness to feel.

Although Tori, has not been able to feel things like she used to, she is not letting this situation bring her down. Currently her parents are putting stress on her because in the South Asian community, Tori is getting old and running out of time. Her parents want her to get married immediately otherwise no one will want her. A frame of mind which is typical of the south asian culture. At the moment Tori is working hard to find a stable job, so she can move out and get the freedom she wants.

STORY # 9

DISSOCIATIVE IDENTITY DISORDER, DEPRESSION, ANXIETY DISORDER, POST-TRAUMATIC STRESS DISORDER & PHOBIAS

Jess is from Northwest Indiana, USA and she has Dissociative Identity Disorder (DID), for approximately 14 years now. Her different identities suffer from depression, anxiety, Post-Traumatic Stress Disorder (PTSD) and phobias. Her group name is Rheeshmyu. Rheeshmyu enjoys hobbies such as, DIYs, drawing, writing, molding and cooking. Not only that, her group is a self-published author and their goal five years from now is to focus on writing and to publish the stories they are working on.

Jess was diagnosed by a mental health professional and the therapy she received was focused on helping her accept her other identities. Teaching Jess what upsets and satisfies Rheeshmyu. Before the therapy her identities were separate causing a lot of problems for Jess. Jess had to deal with terrible symptoms, for example memory blackouts, night terrors, sleep paralysis, extreme social anxiety and felt useless.

This affected her daily life because she could not remember what she learned during college. Due to this Jess had to drop out and has difficulties maintaining jobs. It's difficult for Rheeshmyu because some of her identities have a hard time being around strangers. Jess had to move out of her home because her relationship with her parents was unhealthy. She did this despite of the fact she could not afford to live on her own. In the past six months Jess has moved four times.

Some of her identities has attempted self-harm and suicide (Jess has a semi colon tattoo to support others who struggle with suicidal thoughts) because of this Jess relationships with others are affected. Although she currently has two friends and is in a poly-relationship, living with one of her boyfriends. Her group feels sad because they have to hide their true nature in public. They also feel angry for being judged and frustrated when others think they are ill and in need of help. Jess and her other identities said, "I feel trapped sometimes, because this isn't how I should look. I feel angry that I feel useless. I feel sad that I can't handle school or a job. We have panic attacks and night terrors when we're awake. We're a mess, but we're better than we were before. The boyfriend that we live with has been vital to our happiness, he's the first one to show such strong support for us."

Jess does not want to overcome this because she does not want to be alone and feels happy sharing her body with Rheeshmyu. The turing point for the group was her two boyfriends who helped point out the way. Her identities shared, "We wake up smiling some days now. In my entire life, I honestly never thought I'd be waking up smiling. It's amazing what true, unconditional love and support can do for us."

Rheeshmyu used therapy to maintain control and wrote journals to help them along the way. They also confined in drawing as well. Jess would like to share this message:

"I want to tell the world that just because you're not what society says is 'normal' doesn't mean that you're not healthy! Do not get hung over on what others think of you. They're not you, they don't know your mind like you do. You know yourself best. So, stop listening to others who want you to believe otherwise.

STORY # 10

DEPRESSION

Nicholas is from Switzerland and his favorite hobbies are skiing and acting. His goal five years from now is to have graduated from acting school and to be able to perform in various plays. Nicholas would be happy if he gets to work with wonderful people while acting. He has struggled with depression for three years, but has now recovered.

His depression was caused by pressures at school and the environment he was in before. Nicholas ended up suppressing his emotions. Before the summer of 2014, Nicholas did not seek professional help, which caused him to spiral downward. He later decided to consult a professional and was diagnosed.

Nicholas felt very little, mostly empty although sadness was the most he felt. This affected his daily life. It was difficult for him to complete any homework; Nicholas procrastinated a lot. He was in a constant state of numbness, and he lacked motivation to do things even on weekends. He neglected his body by working out excessively and eating too little. Nicholas almost fell into alcoholism, he ended up every other night grabbing a couple of beers to watch television with before bed.

When he felt anger, he would become self-destructive to control himself from hurting his family. This lead him to self-harm. Nicholas did not cut much because he relied on his scars to remind him of the pain. Once the scars started to heal he would cut to keep the reminder. Thankfully he received help from friends and this kept him from not committing suicide. Although he thought a lot about death, he cared too much for his friends to hurt them that way.

His depression made him a kinder person because he tried to see the pain behind others. Due to this Nicholas had to leave from more than one social gathering due to the fear of breaking down. He stopped responding to text messages because he couldn't maintain a joyful image. His depression made him feel terrible, Nicholas said, "Depression in all its miserable glory I think always holds a component of lack of freedom. Anger is an emotion I have control over and it never slips beyond my control, sadness overcomes me on occasion and I get lost in it unable to function and that can be caused by a range of things, from seemingly insignificant things to world crushing things."

His turning point was at a five-week summer camp, it was the best time of his life. This helped him tremendously because whenever he felt the need to cut, he couldn't because Nicholas did not have access to a knife. He was not aware he was beating his depression, until he overcame it. Nicholas shared, "One of the things I learned is the validity of emotions, and to let them come and go is not a bad thing. I remember on the last day everyone was in tears, but I couldn't cry and I was fine with it because I knew my emotions were just as valid and just as powerful as everyone else's." He became committed to not hurt himself again, and started to express himself freely with friends he trusted, while he concentrated on positive things.

His friends helped him by listening and challenging him. Nicholas added, "I remember on one occasion I was talking about something rather personal and my friend responded by making me look him in the eye and not fiddle with objects." Nicholas learned a lot about self-care, that pain is relative and that he is the only one that can save himself from depression. This changed his outlook in life; he is now a kinder person, for example he now offers food to the homeless and completely listens to others speaking. He explains, "It has also made me much more self-aware and offered a great appreciation for the deep and lovely dark because without it we wouldn't be able to see the stars."

He now uses a support system to express himself by writing poetry, listening to music, hanging out with friends, playing games, and exercising. To prevent himself from falling into depression again he would like to drop out of school. His advice to others is: "Please don't go, don't forget to breathe and hold onto something."

STORY # 11

DEPRESSION, SOCIAL ANXIETY DISORDER, GENERALIZED ANXIETY DISORDER, PANIC DISORDER & AGORAPHOBIA

B ailey is from British Columbia, Canada, and she enjoys her wonderful family. She is fond of reading and animals. Her goal five years from now is to learn a musical instrument or language. She sees herself working hard to support her growing family and being active within her community.

Bailey was diagnosed with depression, social anxiety disorder, generalized anxiety disorder (GAD), panic disorder and agoraphobia. She still struggles with depression, but is able to control it well. Thankfully, she no longer has agoraphobia. She has received counselling and cognitive behavioral therapy with different medications.

She has dealt with difficult depressive symptoms such as; feeling numb, crying often, not eating, and sleeping a lot with no energy. Bailey constantly felt self-hatred and developed bad hygiene; she stopped showering, brushing her hair, and would wear the same pair of pajamas for days.

Her social anxiety disorder made her feel alarmed in social situations. She also felt useless most of the time and feared that others were constantly judging her. Bailey was consistently over-thinking things, causing her immense stress.

"I felt very angry that I couldn't seem to function like 'normal' people", Bailey said. As a result, she ended up isolating herself.

Bailey always felt sick due to her generalized anxiety disorder. She had bad thoughts that repeatedly played on a loop. Bailey would feel panic and terror, with weakness and muscle spasms. Her panic disorder did not allow her to focus on anything and she had a tough time verbalizing. When she felt overwhelmed, her heartbeat would elevate and she would start to sweat, while her face, hands, and feet would go numb.

Her agoraphobia made her feel frightened. "I was scared all the time but being in my house (my room especially) made me feel safer", Bailey said. If she wasn't at home, she felt out of control which provoked her panic attacks.

"I never felt like anything was real. It often felt like I was outside my body looking in at myself. It felt like I was always dreaming and things looked 'too real'", Bailey mentioned.

All of these difficult symptoms affected her daily life. Bailey felt she was simply not living. Her depression started when she was 11 years old, and by the time she became a teenager, she stopped eating and began to cut herself.

"I would feel numb for long stretches of time and then have short intense bouts of anger. I didn't know how to cope with it," Bailey shared.

Bailey still struggles with social anxiety, and according to her, it is taking a toll on her daily life.

"I want to be able to go out and have fun like everyone else. I want to feel relaxed at work and not constantly be on edge because I'm scared of who might talk to me. I feel really stupid because I feel like I'm lacking something very basic. It makes me very angry and I have times where I really think of myself critically. People think I'm very calm under pressure but I would trade in feeling calm in a stressful situation so I could relax around people, talk comfortably and not feel so isolated."

Thankfully, Bailey did not try to commit suicide, though she did wish to die in an accident simply because she did not want others to know how sad she felt. She also did not want her friends and family to think they could have saved her. Bailey ended up not leaving her house for three months which resulted in her being clingy with her mother. She felt she wasn't only ruining her life, but her family's as well. Her friends thought she didn't want to be around them, making her feel alone.

After being inside her home for months, she went to a doctor's appointment. She was prescribed antidepressants, but Bailey refused to take them. Her mother pleaded for her to take it. Upon refusal of taking the prescribed medication, Bailey's mother shared the following story:

"One day there was a huge flood and many people drowned, while others remained in serious danger. There was a man sitting on his roof, praying for god to send him a boat. Suddenly, a man in a raft rowed close by. The man in the raft said to the man on the roof, 'I have some room. You should come with me and we'll find safety.' unto which the man on the roof replied, 'No thank you. God is going to send me a boat.' The man in the raft went on his way. This happened two more times and both times the man on the roof declined. Eventually, the water level got higher and higher, and the man drowned."

Bailey's mother then asked her, "What if this is your boat? Please get on the boat. I don't want you to drown."

Bailey felt a powerful mix of love and despair coming from her mother, so she decided to take her medication. Eventually, things got better. The strategies she used to control her mental disorders were to use the tips she learned during therapy. Bailey would also challenge herself, and try to do something new and speak within a group of people. She gave herself credit no matter how small her victory was. She also surrounded herself with close family and friends that gave her love and support.

Bailey learned a lesson throughout her ordeal;

"No matter how hard things get, you need to keep going. 10 years ago I wasn't sure if I'd even be alive today. Now I'm married with two kids, I have a job I love, and a lot of new things I am passionate about. When I think about these experiences I don't feel scared and weak. I actually feel quite strong and powerful. I made it."

Bailey refuses to get back to the point she was in. If she notices she is staying inside her house too much, she challenges herself to go for a walk or to the mall, even if she does not want to socialize. In fact, sharing her story is a challenge she put up for herself, and I want to thank Bailey for taking such courage to share her story with us.

STORY # 12

GENERAL ANXIETY DISORDER & PANIC DISORDER

Jenna is from Ohio and she enjoys listening to music and singing. She loves to spend time with friends and family. Her favorite movies are Iron Man, The Hobbit and The Lord of The Rings trilogy. Jenna's goal five years from now is to hopefully be studying psychology to become a therapist.

She was diagnosed with general anxiety disorder (GAD) and panic disorder at 16 years old, and still struggles with it to this day. Jenna first saw a therapist and later on visited a psychiatrist who confirmed her diagnosis. She had always been an anxious child, though it became more evident through an attack that happened one day during Spanish class. She experienced a panic attack with an elevated heartbeat, light-headedness, sweats, and shallow breathing. This provoked Jenna to isolate herself; she did not want to leave her house, not even to go visit her grandmother. She also stopped eating, losing approximately 15 pounds.

Jenna started to feel hopeless, and felt like she was a burden due to her stubbornness. Her parents became concerned because every time Jenna had a panic attack, she would leave. Thankfully

Jenna never considered suicide, but she did want to disappear and live somewhere isolated. Her behavior affected her relationship with her parents because they could not understand what was happening to her. Jenna also grew distant from her friends because she did not want to spend time with them.

This made Jenna feel a wide range of emotions, except for happiness. She felt confused, angry, and sad because she couldn't understand why this was happening to her. Jenna also felt desperate because she thought she would live like this for the rest of her life. Because of this Jenna begged her parents to see a therapist. Since this did not help her, she decided to see a psychiatrist. Jenna was prescribed medicine that helped her in some days and she eventually learned to cope with her disorders. She is getting better day by day.

She is determined to live her life fully. Jenna does not want her life to be ruled by her anxieties. "I'm not going to let it get in the way of what I want to do, who I want to be, and I sure wasn't going to let it steal my happiness away," she said.

Jenna used the techniques her therapist taught her to deal with anxieties. She also bought herself a few self-help books that helped her tremendously. The strategies she used were to maintain distraction by listening to music, watching television, doing chores, and using the computer. She also surrounded herself with close friends and family that stuck with her through thick and thin, giving her the help she needed.

This is what she learned from this ordeal:

"I actually have more courage and strength than I thought. This was definitely the darkest time of my life, but I never gave up no matter how hard it became. My life was never over because of this, even though it seemed like it did at the time."

This experience changed Jenna in many ways. She said:

> "I'm definitely more empathetic for people who struggle with this or any mental illness. It's not easy living with a mental illness, but I believe anyone can get through it. It has given me a more positive outlook on life, to keep going even when times get tough."

This is her advice for others struggling through similar situations:

> "First of all, don't be ashamed to get help. If you need to see a therapist, go to one. They are so helpful and they will not judge you. Also, if you think medicine will help, I would recommend it if therapy isn't helping 100%. Lastly, never ever give up. You are a lot stronger than you think you are and I know you can get through this tough time. Keep yourself around people you love and always have a positive attitude. I have faith in you."

STORY # 13

DEPRESSION & ANXIETY DISORDER

This is an anonymous story of depression and anxiety from Langley, BC, Canada. Within a year, Anonymous sees herself in college, but does not know what to do or where she will be. She has a passion for writing and digital art, although it has diminished due to her depression. She would love to do something in psychology, but she fears to get too emotionally invested affecting her mental health.

She was diagnosed in the spring of 2012 by a professional who prescribed Cipralex for her depression and anxiety. She used to have an eating disorder, but thankfully she has recovered. Additionally, she shows strong signs of OCD and PTSD, but has not been diagnosed with that. She believes her depression and anxiety could be due to genetics because it runs on her mother's side of the family. When she developed her eating disorder, her depression got out of control, making her world spiral downwards. She has friends whom she loves like family, and they had their fair share of struggles contributing to her depression and anxiety. Her possible PTSD could be caused by an ex-boyfriend, who sexually harassed her making her feel humiliated among other things.

Her depression has made her feel hopeless and heavy. Most days she has little to no motivation to do anything. She says, "Sometimes, it feels like I have a weight on me preventing me from moving."

This is what Anonymous says about her hopelessness; "The hopelessness comes into play when I feel like I'll never get better and that sometimes makes me feel so hopeless that I get suicidal." Ever since she broke up with her boyfriend, she feels emotionally numb and detached from the world.

In the summer of 2011, she started self-harming. Thankfully, she has not self-harmed since December 3rd of 2014, although she still struggles with the urges to do so. She has felt suicidal, but hasn't attempted it due to her fear of dying. Her mental illness has affected her relationships with others because she feels like she can't tell her loved ones how she feels at times, making her feel trapped. She disclosed, "I feel like I can't live my life freely, and I feel like I won't ever be able to make it in this world by myself. If I think about it, it makes me feel trapped."

What motivated her to recover were Demi Lovato's story and her song "Skyscraper". Her parents helped her journey to recovery by allowing her to see a counsellor. She has a strong coping system, it being her family and especially her friends. She distracts herself by watching interviews of her favorite bands, television shows, and reading manga and books.

This is what she has learned from her ordeal:

"Life isn't always rainbows and butterflies. Sometimes life is a sharp blade that stabs you in chest. People will betray you, but your true friends will be there to help you get over your heartbreak. Even with your friends, no one can fix you other than yourself."

This experience has changed her in many ways, she has matured, and has stopped being carefree like she used to be. She is now careful in life. She says, "I now know that you need to watch out for yourself, and that sometimes, you have to be the one to save yourself. There's not always going to be a Prince Charming to save you from your despair."

This is her suggestion for others struggling with similar situations:

"I would tell them that, above all, a strong support system makes the most difference. Even so, it's important to remember that no one can "fix" or "cure" you other than yourself."

STORY # 14

DEPRESSION

Callie is from Gautier, MS and she enjoys watching anime, playing video games and reading books. She is also fond of animals, especially horses. Callie hopes to become a veterinarian, or to work helping animals. She was diagnosed with depression by a doctor, but Callie also self-diagnosed herself with anxiety. She visited a therapist regularly after cutting herself. Callie spent a couple of weeks in a mental health facility, but became worse due to the treatment she received.

The staff members made Callie and the other patients stay up till four in the morning, drawing out blood. Callie believes the other patients did not have a mental disorder; they seemed to be delinquents with drug addictions. She does not remember much of the symptoms.

"I've had it for so long it's kind of a blur. The main thing with my depression was the numbness and sadness; I couldn't seem to obtain joy from anything I did," Callie mentioned. Her insomnia made her feel terribly exhausted, leaving her with no energy to do anything.

"The fact that I placed high expectations on myself meant I wore myself out getting A's and B's at school; the constant bullying and difficulties making friends just made my self-esteem plummet, adding to my personal hell," Callie added.

Callie's depression and anxiety stemmed from her stepdad's verbal abuse. She would constantly get scolded for not taking initiative to do anything, such as taking out the trash. Even when Callie decided to take initiative, like doing the dishes, her stepfather still scolded her for washing a plate he didn't finish using. This made Callie feel scared because she was afraid to do anything.

"My stepdad's abuse only reinforced the poor view I had of myself. Most of my years living with my stepdad led me to be anxious and scared in my own home. I was scared I would be yelled at or hit for the slightest mistake," Callie mentioned. Even through all of this, Callie managed to get good grades at school.

Callie only self-harmed to feel something aside of numbness, but she stopped when she saw how upset her mother became. She had a hard time making friends, which was an added difficulty to her lack of energy. Even though her stepfather changed, Callie feels the damage has already been done.

Her turning point was at college after having a nervous breakdown. Her mother gave her Zoloft and being on campus, gave Callie access to a counsellor. Little by little she started to improve, and began to feel happy. In college she was able to meet all kinds of people allowing her to create new friendships and socialize with her classmates that had the same interests.

In order to prevent herself from falling back she keeps herself busy with art and videogames. Callie relies on her mother's love and dedication. She also repeats to herself the quote from Harry Potter, 'Happiness can be found even in the darkest times if one only remembers to turn on the light.'

This experience has made Callie appreciate happiness, but this has also made her not to want children of her own because she uses too much energy on herself, and is also afraid her children would inherit her depression.

This is Callie's advice to others struggling through similar situations:

"Everyone's case is different; if you can find a true friend, hold onto them dearly. People who love you, keep close to you. Find something like puzzles or videogames to keep your mind focused on something, even for a little while. You exist on your own terms, and you don't exist to necessarily please anyone else but yourself."

STORY # 15

DEPRESSION & BORDERLINE PERSONALITY DISORDER

A oife is from Ireland and she enjoys keeping herself busy by learning new languages, exercising, watching movies, and listening to music. She is currently working full time in retail, and is trying to save money. Five years from now, Aoife hopes to have a joint degree in political science and psychology. She would love to work for an organization that helps promote awareness of mental health issues that women and children face in developing countries.

Aoife was diagnosed at the age of 15 with depression, and at 18 with borderline personality disorder. She still struggles with her BPD, but she has learned to cope with it. Aoife believes that the stigma of having depression, the attitude of others towards her and being in an abusive relationship contributed to her disorder. Due to this, Aoife has had difficulty maintaining relationships, and has found that she goes through a lot of different "best friends".

She visited a therapist that specialized in dialectical behavioral therapy. Aoife was given lithium, to help motivate and regulate her mood. This led her to experience terrible mood swings and to feel intense emotions that did not require a trigger.

"I really struggle to control the anger- I can lash out at people or throw things," Aoife said. "My mood swings are very frequent - I can wake up feeling happy and motivated, but by midmorning I can feel depressed and apathetic. I struggle with my own identity and I don't have a strong sense of who I am, which means that my goals and aspirations for the future, and the type of person I want to be changes every day. I can sometimes feel very empty and lonely, especially if I haven't reached out to anyone or have fallen behind on a goal. I can occasionally act on impulse, with massive spending sprees completely emptying my bank account, and restrictive eating as well as drinking heavily."

This has greatly impaired Aoife's life. Her depression has occasionally given her suicidal thoughts and she has self-harmed. Thankfully, this does not happen often. Moreover, Aoife has difficulties maintaining stable relationships. She only has a small group of friends and her family has been with her throughout her diagnosis. When she loses a friend, Aoife tends to become so angry, she tries to best them in ways such as obtaining a higher score on a test.

The turning point to gain control over her BPD was explaining to her close friends about her mental disorder and the symptoms associated with it. Her friends ended up giving her a lot of support. The strategies she used were to take her medicine, go to therapy and surround herself with supportive people. Her friends help her by listening, or distracting her with activities such as baking or watching a movie.

This experience has changed her outlook on life.

"I've learned that it is important to see yourself and your emotions as being valid, and that it is okay to feel upset and angry and that all negative feelings will pass eventually. I've also learned that it is important to focus on the good memories and positive emotions, and to really treasure them," Aoife said.

She continues with her treatment in order to prevent going back to how she was before. Aoife hopes to soon come off her meds because she does not want to depend on it. This is her advice to others struggling with similar situations:

"I would suggest that if you feel in any way that you might also have BPD, to talk to your doctor and be put in touch with a mental health professional. They can offer you help and support systems so that you do not have to struggle alone. For anyone currently diagnosed with BPD, I would like them to know that they are not their illness. Of course, there will be bad days and good days, but don't let the bad days and negative feelings take over you. It's important to not repress your emotions and act on them in safe ways."

"Having BPD is kind of like a journey. The beginning is rough and tumultuous, and you don't really know what the destination is, just that you want to be happy. What really counts is how you get there."

STORY # 16

ATTENTION DEFICIT DISORDER, DEPRESSION, ANXIETY DISORDER & IDENTITY ISSUES

Chris/Maeve is from Boston, MA. She enjoys Lord of the Rings, video games and iced coffee. She would like to become an industrial designer or engineer, a career were her art can be part of everyday life. Chris's identity issues are due to her depression, anxiety and problems with people. Her severe insomnia is caused by her ADD. Chris believes her depression began because of bullying and the loss of her mother.

Chris received 4 to 5 years of therapy before she received medication for her condition. She takes Clonidine for her anxiety and sleep, and Adderall for her ADD. Her mental illnesses took a toll on her life. Chris started to have panic attacks and while unaware of what was happening to her, she became frightened, which provoked more panic attacks. Chris felt exhausted all the time, constantly fighting to get out of her bed. She had continuous headaches and back pain; she also could not sleep and when she did, nightmares would take over.

Chris was not able to focus in class, lowering her grades. She almost failed the 7th grade. She also became friends with a girl and their friendship became toxic. Chris began self-harming, was irritable all the time and her eating habits changed drastically. She would eat enough for two days and starve for three. Chris repeated this pattern.

Sadly, while in the 8th grade, Chris tied a hoodie string around her neck in an attempt to hurt herself. Thankfully no damage was done, though she was left with a scar. She has written three suicide notes in the past years that she has ripped up. Since her relationship with her father and sister wasn't healthy, she allowed her toxic friend to take over her life.

"I was submissive enough to let my bad friend take over my life. I had no close friends beyond her at one point. Teachers couldn't get through to me and I couldn't form close relationships in the last 5 years," Chris mentioned.

Chris managed to leave the toxic friendship and started walking home from school to exercise. She convinced her father to let her take medication and found the strength to get better. Chris said, "I found the strength in myself I didn't know I had. I still struggle but it's getting better."

In order to control her mental disorder Chris used different strategies. Whenever she felt like panicking, she would ask herself questions. For example she'd ask if there was a reason behind her feelings, is she could identify it and whether there was anything she could do to help herself. These are additional tips she used to help control her mental illness:

"I used a method called a 5-1 senses. You choose a sense (sight, smell etc), and identify/describe a number of things picked up with that sense. For example, identify 5 things you can hear and describe the sounds. 4 things you can smell, 3 things you can taste. That kind of thing. It's grounding, calming, and helps with disassociation.

The last things I have for recovery are general tips to help with the urges to self-harm.

1) Rub ice cubes on the area you would self-harm on. The feeling bites but doesn't harm you, which helps.
2) Grab a sharpie and draw on the place you want to self-harm (no, ink poisoning isn't a thing and as long as it doesn't get into open wounds it's ok). This will discourage you from hurting yourself (because you don't want ink inside you) and plus, you get to draw a picture.
3) Make a playlist of your favorite music, funny videos, and cute dog videos and train yourself to start the playlist when you feel yourself slipping.
4) Load something like a knock off Minecraft (Lunacraft works as an app) and build. It makes you use your brain and keeps your hands busy, and it's something to do. Build a world and don't stop until you feel better."

This ordeal has strengthened and taught Chris many lessons. She created a helpful group with her friends, to go to in time of need. Chris also has her therapist to go to. She now avoids toxic people and has learned to help others from self-harming.

STORY # 17

DEPRESSION & SOCIAL ANXIETY DISORDER

Courtney is from Northern Ireland and she loves photography, cinematography and all kinds of music. She is currently studying psychology at her University. Her goal is to get a doctorates degree possibly in clinical psychology. She wants to move with her boyfriend and her two dogs to the bay area in America and work with a mental health care facility.

Courtney's therapist named Susanne, diagnosed her with depression and social anxiety which she developed during her first year in University. She still struggles with it, but she has improved a whole lot.

"I was an 87 on the scale that my therapist used (out of 130 I think) and by my last session, it had dropped to the last forties," Courtney said. She believes her mental illness was due to trauma that neither she nor her therapist can pinpoint to a specific event. It took Courtney a while to accept her depression because she has a great boyfriend, family and education. She thought others had it a lot worse than she did. Her therapist gave her CBT and psychotherapy with a focus on mindfulness.

Courtney was constantly on the verge of tears, but she never really expressed it.

"I just became notably quiet. I put on weight from comfort eating. I felt too nervous to leave my room. Everything felt like I was looking at it through a long dark tunnel. I lost passion in everything, I became a kind of blank canvas (which is not me at all, I'm a very opinionated person). I hated seeing people, I hated going to lectures because I'd panic about the friends I'd sit with." Courtney shared. "I can remember one occasion when I was putting on makeup to go out and I had to correct it so many times because my hands were shaking so badly. I was crying and it felt worse than waiting for a dentist to drill a hole in your tooth – constantly. It felt like I was rotting on the inside."

This affected Courtney's life tremendously. She was convinced that everyone hated her, so she never talked to anyone, which made people think she didn't like them. She would stay in bed for hours, instead of going to lectures. Courtney was penalized for not being friendly to costumers at her work and she stopped talking to her best friend of seven years. This affected many of her friendships, but she and her boyfriend became closer. Her parents felt on edge whenever Courtney felt down because they didn't know what to do.

Thankfully Courtney never attempted suicide, but she did think a lot about falling asleep and never waking up. She felt entirely alone.

"I had created this little prison in my mind and that's where I was for 9 months. I got angry that I couldn't tell anyone. I got angry that they probably wouldn't understand," she said. The turning point for Courtney was when she moved out of University student accommodation to move back to her home. She also got a puppy as well. It was the help she needed.

The strategies she used to help stop negative thoughts, was stopping it before it took hold. For example; Courtney would reassure herself that the person has no reason to dislike her, so she shouldn't assume they do. She also accepted her illness by telling herself, "I thought I didn't have the criteria for depression because my life was actually pretty good. But brain chemicals don't care about that."

Her boyfriend, therapist and parents helped her enormously.

"I think having someone who's nice, non-judgmental and on my side helped. My boyfriend honestly coped with how I was so well – I was not the same person I was when we started out together so I admire him endlessly for sticking with me. My parents helped by loving me unconditionally, and doing anything they could to help."

Courtney learned not to listen to her head all the time. She realized her thinking could be so far from the truth and that those thoughts aren't always right. She is much quieter now, although she is pushing herself all the time. She gets stressful a lot now, even when it comes to posting a Facebook comment. In order to prevent herself from falling again, she does not isolate herself in her head.

This is her advice for others struggling with similar situations:

"Get help – even if you think you don't need it. It doesn't matter how great your grades are or how nice your house is – depression is depression and anxiety is anxiety and they don't care about those things. Don't judge people on how they seem. There could be a lot going on underneath."

STORY # 18

GENERALIZED ANXIETY DISORDER, SOCIAL ANXIETY & CLINICAL DEPRESSION

Ciara is from Kildare, Ireland and she loves to read a lot, stating, "I love to read. In fact, I am a huge bookworm. I started reading from a very young age and just fell in love with the possibilities that the next chapter could bring. Reading, for me, was a great form of escape." She also enjoys art, especially clay modeling, though she hasn't been able to do it lately because of a skin condition on her hands. Her goal is to wake up feeling excited each day and to feel satisfied with whatever she has done. Ciara would love to move out of her parents' house, and to have a home she can call her own.

Ciara was diagnosed by her GP and counselor with generalized anxiety disorder, social anxiety and clinical depression. She thinks she has had these mental illnesses for a very long time, but learned to hide it and act normal during her teenage years. Ciara is still taking medication and goes to therapy with her counselor regularly. She does not believe her mental illness is caused by anything.

"Honestly, I don't believe that anything "causes" mental illness. I believe that there are naturally going to be things that trigger you, and cause the illness to flare up," she shared. There were a lot of triggers that caused Ciara to become mentally ill. For instance, she was told that she wouldn't be able to have children. Additionally, her father became extremely ill by getting multiple episodes were his heart stopped, affecting his memory and motor skills.

Ciara was prescribed anti-depressants that at first, caused night terrors. Her counselor had to adjust her dosage. Gradually, she started to function better, and because of this, Ciara pushed her recovery way too quickly. She reduced her medication too soon and kept lying to herself that she did not need her anti-depressants. Eventually it caught up with her.

She kept telling herself, "Why am I being an idiot? If I had diabetes would I get upset about needing insulin?" After a while, she started to take her medication again, and only lowered her dosage if her healthcare professional advised it.

This affected Ciara's life; she felt awful. She would have panic attacks every day and wouldn't eat. In addition to this, she experienced terrible insomnia, and didn't want to get out of bed in the mornings. Ciara failed college, and was extremely lonely, as her friends were always away due to work and school. Although she felt lonely, she wouldn't open up to anyone including her boyfriend.

Ciara continually had paranoid thoughts, stating, "I thought people were looking at me. I thought that they were making fun of me, that they thought that they were better than me. I turned into this horrible, bitter person."

Sadly, Ciara has self-harmed and has considered suicide many times. This scared her because she would look at sharp objects as if they were old friends. Ciara also thought about hurting others, but she never did.

"I thought about crashing my bus to college, and how it'd shut up all the girls that are always in front of me, always laughing, always sneering. In hindsight I know that this perception I had of these people was incredibly twisted by my paranoia." Ciara ended up telling her counselor about her paranoid thoughts and that helped her tremendously. Moreover, she also spoke to her two closest friends and explained her illness to them.

The turning point for Ciara was her boyfriend of eight years, Vinny. He had supported her throughout her illness even though he doesn't understand it. He distracts her when she needs it, and if the medication gets her too sleepy, he helps her into bed. "I honestly don't think I'd still be around without him," she shared. Ciara keeps herself busy by exercising, spending time with friends, and using positive reinforcement (mantras).

This is the lesson Ciara has learned from this ordeal:

"I learned that stigma is a terrible thing. Mental illness is actually incredibly common in Ireland, but it's treated as if it's something dirty. Hell, I felt the same when I got sick first. It was one thing to see a counselor, and another to take medication. I think if I could give my younger self any advice, it would be to stop seeing meds as a weakness, and start seeing them as what they really are; medicine."

This has changed her outlook on life. It's hard for her to feel excited about things nowadays. Ciara feels cynical, constantly waiting for something bad to happen. This is her advice to others struggling with similar situations:

"You are not weak. Needing medication is just that. No-one cares if you need to leave early, or you have to take anything. It's just a pill. If it keeps you from falling into the abyss, then it's good for you."

STORY # 19

BORDERLINE PERSONALITY DISORDER, ATTENTION DEFICIT DISORDER, POST-TRAUMATIC STRESS DISORDER & EATING DISORDER NOT OTHERWISE SPECIFIED

Anonymous is from Atlanta, GA and she loves to play the piano and guitar. She aspires to become a veterinary technician. She has been diagnosed by a mental health professional with borderline personality disorder (BPD), attention deficit disorder (ADD), post-traumatic stress disorder (PTSD) and eating disorder not otherwise specified (EDNOS). All of her mental illnesses have been caused by an unstable and abusive household.

She has been to treatment and has received dialectical behavior therapy (DBT) and cognitive behavioral therapy (CBT). Anonymous has dealt with debilitating symptoms such as self-harming, panic attacks and loss of interests in activities. Sadly, she has self-harmed and was actively suicidal. Even her eating habits have changed drastically; she has binged and starved herself. She avoids certain places in order to evade triggering flashbacks. She constantly has intrusive memories that make her feel uneasy.

This has completely affected her daily life. Anonymous was not able to function at all. She slept a lot in order to avoid bad thoughts. "I thought I was a failure for dropping out of school twice. I also believed I was fat and ugly. I thought I didn't deserve anyone to love me, that I was damaged goods. I also was very afraid of men and would imagine them hurting me as I'd pass by someone on the street," she shared.

This affected her relationship with others. Anonymous lost all of her friends. No one wanted to be around her, making her feel hopeless.

"I felt done with the world. I felt so horrible, as if my whole life was falling in around me. I kept telling myself I peaked in high school and the rest of my life will be a waste. I felt scared most of the time, of what I would do to myself when things went wrong."

Anonymous was forced into treatment, and that didn't help her much, though on September 21st, 2014, things started to turn around. That was when she realized she needed more help, so she admitted herself into a psychiatric hospital after telling her parents she needed to go back for treatment. She was put in an intensive unit for four months. She was taught how to be confident and accept what had happened to her. She now transforms her struggles into poetry as an outlet. Anonymous is still copping with her PTSD, but thankfully she has been able to control the other mental illnesses she suffers from.

Even though she has progressed a lot in her recovery, she still has a difficult time with intrusive thinking. Anonymous said, "Sometimes I'll get random painful thoughts such as, 'You shouldn't eat today' or 'You're the only reason your parents stayed together. You ruined their lives.', so that sucks. I continue to see a therapist once a week to do trauma cognitive behavioral therapy. It's hard work. It's kind of like a band-aid every week. You have to keep ripping it off until it doesn't stick as much to you. I have to keep telling my story in order for it not to harm me anymore."

The strategies she used to beat her illnesses were to stick with DBT and CBT therapy. She surrounded herself with helpful people. Anonymous had great resident advisors that taught her a lot. She learned that people can love her without wanting anything in return and that she is worthy of love and connection. After realizing she can do anything she sets her mind to, anonymous took baby steps and has now been able to become independent.

This experience has changed her outlook in life; she shared:

"It taught that there are horrible people in this world who will only hurt you and discriminate against you; but there are also so many wonderful people who just want to love you. I used to look at life and see all of the bad people and was so afraid and angry and now I see all the people who have helped me and they outnumber the people who have hurt me."

This is her advice for others struggling with similar situations:

"Get help immediately. Don't wait for it to get worse and your whole life crashes around you. I waited too late in the game and it really hurt me in the long run. If you feel depressed or if something traumatic has happened to you, go to therapy and go soon."

STORY # 20

ANXIETY DISORDER, POST-TRAUMATIC STRESS DISORDER & DEPRESSION

Keri is from Arizona and when she is not working or at school, she enjoys writing, reading, and drawing. When Keri wants to unwind she watches movies and plays video games. Her future goals are to finish her bachelor's degree and the book she is writing. Five years from now she hopes to be back in Colorado, or out of Arizona. Keri would also love a job where she can help others. She suffers from anxiety, post-traumatic stress disorder (PTSD), severe depression and has an addiction to self-harming.

Traumatic events caused her mental illnesses. Keri was raped as a child, and her mother had a 10-year battle with cancer before passing away. Moreover, a year later, Keri found her father dead. These events made her feel helpless.

"The helplessness of these events left me drowning until I was numb all the time. Cutting and hurting myself was the only way to break through the numbness."

Keri has never consulted a mental health professional. Her parents threatened to take her to one, if she didn't let go of the rape trauma. The diagnosis she gave herself is from the various psychology courses she has taken and from recommendations of people she is friends with in the psychology field. Keri dealt with terrible symptoms. She said:

> "I felt immense sadness, an inability to enjoy anything that I once did, anger at everyone else because I felt alone with my troubles, an inability to trust anyone since it had been someone close to me that had hurt me, sudden feelings of complete numbness that would come after a bombardment of anxiety and fear."

This affected her daily life; Keri stopped talking to her friends and family. They became hurt because she closed herself up. Her work life was affected and she constantly thought about ending the bad memories. She stole her brother's razors, breaking it to cut with the blade. Keri mentioned, "When I got older and was able to buy my own supplies, I kept a small box fully stocked with gauze, Neosporin, and blades. I spent a lot of money on keeping that box stocked." Thankfully Keri hasn't self-harmed in over 132 days, although she still craves for it.

When Keri's' parents found out about her predicament, they felt scared and upset that Keri didn't come to them for help. This experience shook her relationship with her parents. Keri has great friends, who stood by her and listened to her when she was ready to speak. There were moments that she felt alone, stating, "At first I was angry when they demanded to know what was going on, angry that they were acting like they cared when I had been doing this for so long. I mean if they had cared then shouldn't they have noticed sooner? Who were they to demand anything? I felt trapped when they wouldn't let me go, I felt like they had backed me into a corner. It took a long time for me to relax and finally start to open up."

The turning point for Keri to overcome her mental disorders was studying psychology. After learning about mental illnesses and the causes of them, she was able to better manage them. The moment Keri was able to accept her addiction was when she was sitting in her apartment's laundry room; a child came up to her and started tracing one of her scars. Keri freaked out, but the boy said:

Boy: "You've got sad lines just like my sissy."
Keri: "Sad lines?"
A girl comes rushing up to them, looking scared (little boy's sister)
Boy: "Yeah every time she gets sad she gets another one. Do you get sad a lot?"
Keri: "Sometimes"
Boy: "I try and help her, I give her a big hug every time I can, but she still gets them. She'll try and hide because a lot of people may not understand why she gets them. But you know what? One day she'll look back on them and she may not be so sad anymore, when she looks at them she may just remember her amazing little brother and his amazing hugs."

This was Keri's thought:

"To be honest I don't know where the words were coming from; I just remembered seeing the look of relief on the girl's face. From then on, I started looking at my scars as almost a gift, or sign of courage. These mean I'm still here, still fighting. And since I have first-hand knowledge maybe I could help someone else."

One of the strategies she used to beat her mental disorder was to remember the girls face from the event at the laundry room. Keri also uses writing as an outlet. For example, Keri writes what she is feeling by putting it into a scene with as much emotion as possible. Another technique she used was working out, which gave her a sense of control. She surrounded herself with friends which provided her with a safe place.

The lesson Keri learned was, "Basically what doesn't kill you does make you stronger, as tired as that expression may be. It showed me that I'm a survivor and no matter what gets thrown at me I can win." To prevent herself from falling into depression again, Keri is willing to see a mental health professional. She realized that there is no need to put herself through that anymore.

This is her advice for others struggling:

"Seek help. There is nothing shameful, nor is it a weakness to get outside help. Just like when you don't know the answer to a problem, you ask your teacher, you ask for help from a psychologist/psychiatrist to help make yourself better. Also ignore what mainstream media says about those suffering from mental illnesses such as rape victims, PTSD sufferers, and those with depression. You are human, you had a horrible experience, but you are no less worthy of love and a good life. You are not used up, you are not trash, you are an amazing person that may touch more lives than you can imagine. Just keep fighting."

Keri would like to share this:

"As a writer and reader, I love learning new words from different languages. One that I learned that I feel pertains to this is called "Kintsugi". It's when a cracked piece of pottery is fixed with gold, silver, or platinum, often making it more stunning than before it was cracked. I think this fits with anyone who feels broken. Your scars and trails and broken pieces do not make you ugly, they make you unique and beautiful."

STORY # 21

BIPOLAR TYPE II

Franco is from Colorado, but currently lives in North East, Florida. He is an avid reader, usually reading four books per month, depending on his schedule. Franco loves to read all kinds of books, but prefers the topics about leadership, real estate, and personal development. He also sings and plays the guitar. Franco's goals include first pursuing an additional bachelor degree in accounting, and later, completing a MBA from Capella University. He wants to obtain his broker's license and either move into a leadership position inside the company he works for or start his own company.

Franco was diagnosed with bipolar type II after he completed college. He also stopped taking his meds on May, 2014. Thankfully, he feels better both mentally and emotionally. Although he still struggles with his mental disorder, he has been able to control it despite the difficulties in life. Franco believes the cause of his disorder was genetics, stating, "I was adopted at seven months old. When life became difficult around 13 or 14, I knew that something was not right. None of the circumstances of my daily life would lead me to believe that it was because of my environment."

At the age of 22, this affected him greatly. At that time, he began a regimen of medication and therapy. Franco mostly suffered from depression, but thrived during manic episodes. He said, "I did benefit from some of the attributes of my illness. I was, and still am highly functioning and effective." During his teen and early twenties, Franco was always busy with sports and school, which didn't give him time to acknowledge his mental and emotional state. He said, "In hindsight, during my high school and college career I did exhibit typical manic symptoms such as promiscuity, fighting, and not sleeping. Conversely, I excelled in school and sports. I was always in student government, lettered in three sports for four years, and played football in college."

Franco attempted suicide three times in his life, and has been hospitalized. The last time was in 2012, but thankfully his life has been great ever since. He checked himself in the hospital because he knew that the way he related to himself needed to change, in order to live a happy life. Franco has destroyed valuable relationships. For example, he does not speak to four out of his five sisters. But he managed to develop and maintain great friendships. He said, "since I have been working on loving, knowing, and appreciating myself, my relationships have been great. A big part of this is that I moved away and started over. I eliminated all the toxic people from my life after I detoxified myself." Franco also mentioned, "I am married and my wife and I have an extraordinary relationship. I have a group of very close friends, but they live in different states so I don't spend much time with them."

For many years of his life Franco felt angry and helpless, but he realized that he was making himself the victim. The turning point for Franco was realizing that he wanted to get more out of life. He added, "I have always known that I was capable of amazing things. I had done amazing things in the past, and self-loathing no longer suited me or what I wanted in life. Educating myself is what keeps me in control. Being in tune with my body, mind, and soul." He decided to change his way of thinking by understanding his limits and how to push them. The strategies he used to beat his illness was to focus on reading, journaling, meditating, as well as being honest with himself regardless of the situation or circumstances.

Franco surrounded himself with supportive people, especially his wife. He learned that he is strong, intelligent and that life can be good. This also changed his outlook in life. stating, "It made me realize how much I could have lost had I given up. More importantly, I know that the only limits I have regarding my future are created or eliminated by me." He now stays alert and honest with himself in order not to fall back to where he was.

This is his advice for others struggling with similar situations:

"Truly get to know yourself. Attempt to understand your feelings, learn how to think critically and objectively. Learn to trust yourself and eliminate the people and situations from your life that are not healthy."

STORY # 22

POST-TRAUMATIC STRESS DISORDER & DEPRESSION

Miri is from Wisconsin, but she currently lives in Minnesota with her grandparents. She enjoys volunteering at a daycare center. Her other hobbies include fiction-writing, journal writing, listening to music, and photography. She loves to have intellectual conversations with her grandparents. Miri watches the news with them, and together they discuss it. She also enjoys films. Miri said, "I highly doubt I will ever tire of The Fellowship of the Ring, the 1977 Nutcracker film, Spirit: Stallion of the Cimmaron, James Cameron's Avatar, or the new Cinderella." Miri's favorite book is Daughter of the Nile.

Her future goal is to be successful and happy. Miri said, "getting my GED and driver's license, as well as continuing to heal and thrive to discover who I truly am are my main goals as of now." She also wants to be a published author, but she is scared, not knowing where life will take her. She says, "I know what I absolutely do not want to do, and I have some ideas of what I enjoy doing. But I don't know what would inspire me to get out of bed in the morning with a smile on my face for the rest of my life. That is something that I hope will become more tangible as I continue the recovery process."

Miri has post-traumatic stress disorder (PTSD) and her depression has faded with medication. The reason for her mental disorders is past trauma. Her depression gotten the best of her when her uncle passed away in a jet-ski accident. Miri's mother has mal-de-debarquement syndrome, which has also affected her tremendously. Miri mentioned, "I took over running the household, because my mother was bed-ridden at that point. I was only fifteen. I did everything—the chores, the meals, homeschooling my three younger siblings, homeschooling myself—along with being at my mother's every beck-and-call." Not only that, but her PTSD took ahold due to a car accident during her driver's training combined with the emotional abuse she received from her parents.

Miri is currently receiving intensive therapy and medication for her disorders. Although she has been able to control it, it has been an uphill battle for her. She said, "I struggled most with feeling worthless, unneeded—even though I was the only reason the family was functioning, and generally that my very existence made everyone else's lives miserable." She felt like an outsider because she was blamed for every single thing that went wrong within the household. Sadly, Miri considered suicide many times. She added, "I think deep down I knew I would never go through with it. I can pin-point maybe three times where I got pretty close to doing something dangerous, but the closest was definitely February of 2015. I'd barricaded myself in a bathroom and was sobbing and crying, and there was a large container of bleach under the sink, and equal parts of me were screaming "Drink it" and "Don't you dare". Thank God, I didn't." She also self-harmed by starving herself, sleeping very little and cutting her wrists. Miri's father found out and made her promise not to self-harm again.

This is how she felt:

"I experienced a whole range of emotions at any given time all at once, and none of them were positive. Having adrenaline rushing through my system 24/7 didn't help matters either. I had to pretend I wasn't livid with how I was treated. I hate lying, but I learned how to do it very well. I was forced to conceal my body language, and my mother could be screaming at me, and I would be silent. My screams were in my head. I felt like I was going insane, and I would spend all night crying silently, saying "Why? Why? I can't take this much longer."

The turning point for Miri was when she visited her therapist three days after a huge fight with her mother. She told her therapist that she wanted to live with her grandparents. During that session, her therapist called them and explained how helpful it would be for Miri to move in with them. Her grandparents agreed and six days later, Miri was on a flight on her way to Minnesota. Miri said, "It wasn't until my grandparents were driving me back to their house, having picked me up from the airport, and my iPod was playing Bryan Adam's "Here I Am" softly, that I broke down crying, as it really sunk in that I was free of my parents. I was free. I made it, and it was overwhelming."

The strategies Miri used to control her mental disorders included emotionally attaching herself to fictional characters with whom she identified. For example, she looked up to Eowyn, Frodo and Faramir from Lord of the Rings, Dean Winchester from Supernatural and Katniss from Hunger Games. She said, "I would pretend they were there in the dark, protecting me from the nightmares. I would imagine that Dean would say exactly what needed to be said to my parents before hugging me and telling me it was going to be okay. Fictional characters kept me from giving up, because they always kept fighting, and I wanted to be like them." Talking to her grandparents and therapist also helped her. In addition, Miri uses her faith in God to stay strong. She said, "Since moving in with my grandparents, I have attended their Lutheran church, and have been embraced with open arms. I was offered the opportunity to be the official VBS photographer in July, and I loved every second of it. I will become an official member of the church this fall, and I will also be joining the choir. A couple from church gave me their piano for my very own—I never thought that I would own a piano—and have practically adopted me as their granddaughter."

This experience has changed Miri in many ways. She mentioned:

"I became what I had to be to survive. I am not proud of any of it. I am not proud of feeling the need to cut off all contact with my parents, but it is for my own well-being. I am not proud when I am reduced to a full-blown panic attack by hearing rowdy male voices or certain words. I am not proud when I can hardly leave my room some days. I am not proud when I still wake up sobbing from nightmares. I am not proud that my mind analyzes every single person and situation as a potential threat. I am not proud that I cannot hear my given name "Miriam" without hearing it said in my parents' disappointed voices, so instead I ask everyone to call me Miri, a request which so far has been well-received and supported by more than just my grandparents. I am not proud that I left two younger brothers and my beloved sister behind; cutting contact with my parents affected our relationships. I am just grateful that I have, to this day, been strong enough."

This is Miri's advice for those struggling with similar situation and mental disorders:

"Be informed. Read everything you can about your disorder, including actual stories. Reading stories like yours will be painful, triggering even. But it is worth it, because knowing what you have, and all the details can aid you in better explaining what you are going through to other people, who can then come alongside you and help you. And just knowing that you aren't alone, that other people have gone through what you have gone through can be so incredibly powerful and validating. Recovery is within reach, but the journey is different for every individual, so do not enter this process with set expectations."

STORY # 23

BULIMIA NERVOSA, EATING DISORDER NOT OTHERWISE SPECIFIED, DEPRESSION / BORDERLINE PERSONALITY DISORDER, GENERALIZED ANXIETY DISORDER & SOCIAL ANXIETY DISORDER

Maegan is form Ontario, Canada and she enjoys music and going to concerts. Maegan works at a restaurant as a cook and attends school for psychology. She loves to play guitar and watches Netflix in her spare time. Her goal is to graduate from her university and to work at a job that she is excited about.

Maegan has bulimia and EDNOS (now OSFED), major depressive disorder, borderline personality disorder, generalized anxiety, and social anxiety. Maegan said, "I've always been very sensitive, so I believe I've had my personality and mood disorders since before I can remember." Her eating disorders developed due to bullying in middle school. Maegan was diagnosed while she was attending an outpatient group for bulimia. She said, "I went for weekly psychiatric appointments, weekly group meetings, and was put on a bunch of different anti-depressants to stabilize my mood. I was hospitalized in early 2013 for 6 weeks in a mood disorder unit after a very bad depressive episode."

Maegan dealt with terrible symptoms. She constantly felt extremely depressive and felt uncomfortable in social situations. Maegan said, "I feared that I was being made fun of/mocked behind my back." Sadly, she would binge and purge up to 6 times a day. She also restricted her calorie intake to as low as 100 calories a day. This made her weight fluctuate, causing a body dysmorphic disorder, where she couldn't perceive her weight, causing her behavior to continue. Maegan began to self-harm during anxiety or panic attacks when she was 12 years old and stopped at 21, although she still struggles with urges. Sadly, Maegan attempted suicide three times; one of which landed her in the ER and in a 6-week inpatient stay.

This has affected her daily life. Maegan added, "I have, and continue to, suffer from chronic insomnia due to my anxiety and not being able to stop worrying long enough to get a good sleep on many nights." She was constantly depressed and tried to keep secrets about her behavior. It caused her to lose a lot of friends. Maegan skipped classes in high school. She also had to quit her job and drop out of her first year of university. Maegan said, "I was self-medicating with drugs and alcohol for a long time, and ended up getting arrested with a DUI. I carry guilt and fear from that to this day, because I could have easily hurt someone. I made a lot of bad decisions that will affect me for the rest of my life because of my mental state."

This is how her life was affected:

"Being anxious all the time makes making friends, and keeping plans very difficult for me, and I feel as though I'm missing out on a lot of great people and connections because I'm too nervous to put myself out there. I distance myself from people important to me for no reason that I can understand, and of course this hinders my relationships."

This made her feel scared and stuck more than anything, but the turning point for Maegan was being hospitalized and arrested. It was a wakeup call. She said, "a healthy me wouldn't have driven after drinking, and it scared me so terribly that I stopped drinking and abusing drugs for quite a while until I could learn to control it with help from a group I attended." The strategies Maegan used to control her mental disorders include talking to people who support her about her thoughts and urges. She also continues to take her medications, especially Prozac, since it stabilizes her moods and helps her manage her binging and purging urges.

Maegan has learned that she is stronger and that she can learn from the bad experiences in life. She mentioned, "it's made me much more empathetic to other peoples' struggles, as well as understand issues affecting different groups of people. I try to fight and stand up for people who have trouble doing it themselves, and I try my hardest to keep positive despite feeling depressed."

This is her advice for others struggling through similar situations:

"Talk about it and get help as soon as you possibly can! It is so important to let those who care about you know that you are struggling and how to help you. It's not a battle you need to fight alone.

STORY # 24

DEPRESSION, ANXIETY DISORDER, BIPOLAR DISORDER & ATTENTION DEFICIT HYPERACTIVITY DISORDER

Jas is a 15 year old from Ontario, Canada and she enjoys reading about other people's lives and thoughts. Her goal is to become a police officer and have a family of her own. Jas was diagnosed by a mental health professional in Toronto, Ontario with depression, anxiety, and bipolar disorder with signs and symptoms of ADHD. To this day she still has them. The feelings of being abandoned and being alone from her own family, and thinking every day that she wasn't "good enough" are what caused her mental illnesses. Jas went to a hospital multiple times and was treated with different medications and activities to help her cope with her illnesses, such as counselling.

Jas has had to deal with bothersome symptoms. She said, "I feel the hardest thing to do in life is breathing and trying to push through it. One day I would want to cut my veins open or be really happy and energetic." This affected her daily life. "Having a mental illness affects you a lot, knowing you can't have the energy to wake up or go do the dishes. The thoughts of killing myself or hurting myself would haunt me daily," said Jas. Sadly, Jas has attempted suicide multiple times and she almost succeeded once. But she thought to herself, what would happen to her family. Jas has scars on her stomach and both of her wrists and thighs.

Her relationships with others has also been affected. Jas mentioned, "Every day I feel so irritated by everyone and anyone talking to me; I was rude and grumpy, and of course how I was feeling affected people who loved me so much." This made her feel like she was going to be angry and sad her whole life, but she realized that it was her choice to get back on her feet. Jas added, "It wasn't the doctors or my mother; it was me. Because I was the one who was feeling like this, not them."

The turning point for Jas to control her mental disorders was to push past them and focus on things that make her happy. Jas thought that she was helpless, stating, "I thought nobody could help me; I didn't want anyone to help me because I wanted to prove that I can help myself." The lesson Jas learned from this ordeal was that not everything is going to end well, but that this shouldn't be a reason to affect her. This experience has changed her in many ways. She said, "I lost people in my life that meant a lot and I couldn't help myself but push people away. Today, I try to help people, and talk to them about what's getting them upset." Jas continues to fight her mental disorders.

This is her advice for others struggling in similar situations:

"Anybody out there, somewhere, can message me in my tumblr box (username: youre-cocky), and I will be here, I promise. I can't stand the fact of other people hurting so much."

STORY # 25

OBSESSIVE-COMPULSIVE DISORDER, CHRONIC STRESS & DEPRESSION

Anonymous is from Petaluma, California, and due to depression, she hasn't enjoyed much these past years. But she likes reading The Little Prince, The Book Thief, and I'd Tell You I'd Love You but Then I'd Have to Kill You. Her favorite movie is Little Miss Sunshine with Sandra Bullock. Anonymous is fond of knitting and her favorite music has always been country, but lately she has been listening to metal, punk, and alternative. She remembers that tacos used to be her favorite food. Her goal is to graduate from college and marry the love of her life. Anonymous used to want to be a politician, but within the past week, that has changed to book editor. She said, "I have chronic stress and high anxiety levels, so I think I would be happier as an editor. Plus, reading for a freaking living would be awesome, but we'll see."

Anonymous has had obsessive-compulsive disorder (OCD) since she was four years old and within the past five years, she has developed chronic stress, and her major depression developed about three years ago. She has no idea what caused her OCD. Anonymous said, "I just started having random tics and became an extreme germaphobe." Her chronic stress was due to school, because she wanted to get good grades on every subject so her parents wouldn't be disappointed. She added, "I volunteered a bunch, had a job, and I took all the AP and honors classes, and all that work and pressure really got to me." Her depression sprung from the death of loved ones. Anonymous mentioned, "it all started in my sophomore year of high school when my French teacher suddenly passed away. I've had to deal with death before, but never like that. From seventh to ninth grade, I had lost my four great-grandparents; but they were sick for a while beforehand, so I had time to get it through my head that they would be gone soon." In the year of 2015, Anonymous had a major breakdown when her best friend of many years passed away. She stated, "[best friend] had been poisoned by her girlfriend with pentobarbital five days earlier. If I didn't have my boyfriend at the time, I would have gone off the deep end, and I don't know what I would have done to myself." The hardest thing Anonymous had to do was sit at the funeral and realize she would never be able to hug her best friend or hear her laugh ever again. Not only that, but she and her boyfriend decided to break up, making her plummet deep into depression.

A mental health professional suggested therapy for Anonymous, but she never went to it. She said, "I never went, because I knew it wouldn't help; I like to do things on my own and don't like talking about myself because it feels like a pity party." Anonymous took Prozac for about four months, but it made her feel crazier and worsened her symptoms, so she stopped taking it. She always felt tired, making her oversleep. She felt guilty and ashamed of herself. She mentioned, "my self-esteem was at an all-time low; I stopped doing all the things I loved doing before, I lost my humor and imagination, I either ate too little or too much and recently, food doesn't even taste good anymore, which is bizarre 'cause I lived for food a couple years ago."

This greatly affected her daily life. Anonymous said:

"It made daily life a real struggle. Getting out of bed in the morning was the hardest part of my day. I didn't want to face reality, but I eventually forced myself to get up, because my thoughts were too much to handle. Throughout the day, I would have to distract myself from my thoughts literally every second of the day, so I could be a functioning human being. When I wasn't doing something, my bad thoughts like I'm a failure, and not good enough, and I won't get anywhere with my life, and just feeling guilty, would pop up instantly. I would spend all day wanting to go to sleep so I would get a break from my thoughts and so I would have that slight moment of bliss in the morning when I'm not yet aware of the stuff I was trying to forget. But I dreaded nighttime and felt scared, because I would be alone with my thoughts and wouldn't have any distractions. It took me forever to fall asleep too, because my mind just kept racing, and I couldn't get it to shut down in the slightest."

Anonymous wanted to die. She would wonder how it would feel to get hit by a car. There were times when she felt scared to drive because she just didn't trust herself. When she felt overly stressed she wanted to take a bunch of pills and sleep forever. But thankfully Anonymous never tried anything because she sees suicide as a coward's way out. Her only mistake was making her happiness dependent on her boyfriend, so after the breakup it caused a mess in her life. Thankfully Anonymous received help from a close friend. She could talk to her friend whenever she needed and felt her friend understood her.

Anonymous felt angry all the time, stating, "Losing those loved ones made me even angrier at the world and always questioned why all this was happening to my family and friends and me. It just seemed incredibly unfair; I mean, an eighteen-year-old isn't supposed to be able to visit her friend's grave, that's f**ked up." She also said, "It felt like everything happened all at once, and I didn't have time to recover from the last thing before the next thing happened." The turning point for Anonymous to overcome her OCD was after the death of her teacher and best friend. It made her realize that it was unnecessary to count stuff and washing her hands exactly for a minute was waste of time. Although she is still struggling with her chronic stress and depression, she has been able to lower it by changing certain habits in her life. Anonymous said, "I try to eliminate stress-inducing factors, like leaving my house on time and not waiting until the last minute to do my homework and such, and I've been doing breathing techniques to calm myself when I do get stressed." She now congratulates herself on her achievements, not matter how small it is and she has learned never to take anyone for granted.

This is how her experience has changed her:

"I've become a completely different person. I'm much more open and adventurous and more optimistic and I look for the bright side of things instead of focusing only on the negative. I'm more loving and try to act more altruistically. I just want to be happy for no reason in particular (being happy for a reason is dangerous—your happiness can be taken away in a split second). My best friend is the biggest goofball I know and always does funny stuff, so my motto for my life is 'what would make my best friend laugh?' and I try to do something every day that she would find funny. I've also stopped seeing myself as very unlucky. I'm actually incredibly lucky; I'm incredibly lucky that I've had so many genuinely good people in my life that I've loved dearly and whose mere existences have changed me for the better."

This is her advice for other struggling through similar situations:

"Don't f**king give up on yourself. Only you can change your life, but you have to truly want the change. And I know it feels things won't ever get better and you think your future looks bleak and you don't feel like there's any point in living anymore. I've been there done that, and I can honestly tell you that it does get better in time. I know you've heard that many times already and truthfully I didn't believe it either, but it's actually true. Just gather the courage and strength and trust that you have in you to hold on for a little longer. Please."

Anonymous would also like to share this:

"Never ever hesitate to tell someone how much you love them or appreciate them or how much you just simply enjoy their existence and their involvement in your life. You don't realize how much guilt you will have when those people are no longer in your life and you wish with all your being that you could go back in time and just say 'I love you' one more time or give them a random hug. Don't take their existence for granted, and don't be fooled in thinking you have all the time in the world to do those things. Because you don't. And you never realize it until it's too late. Please stop worrying about other people's opinions of you and don't pay your insecurities any attention. Life is way too short to not be yourself. I used to be so freaking insecure, but now I'm just like 'f*ck it, I'm gonna say and do stupid stuff whenever I want and you can bet you're a*s I'm gonna be singing along to the song that's playing in the grocery store.' Trust me, life is way more enjoyable when you actually be yourself and have fun, no matter what age you are."

STORY # 26

MAJOR DEPRESSION DISORDER & ANXIETY

Aldo is from El Salvador, but has lived in Los Angeles, CA since the age of 6. His hobbies include listening to music, writing, reading, and playing X-box games. Aldo's favorite movies are The Fountain, The Matrix, Bicentennial Man, and Whatever Dreams May Come. He also enjoys dark comedy such as, Wristcutters: A Love Story, Happiness and Rules of Attraction because they lift his mood. Aldo's favorite poet is Edgar Allan Poe and his favorite bands are Nirvana, System of a Down, Nine Inch Nails and Tool. He is trying to get back into drawing and painting.

Aldo goals have recently been set because he was a direction-less youth and didn't expect to live beyond the age of 18. Aldo only had one role model, who passed away when he was 13 years old. Due to that he started to slip into solitude and timidity. Now, aged 33, he realized he isn't going to die any time soon. Aldo now wants to become a Paralegal at the law firm in which he is working as a File Clerk. Not only that, but he wants to earn a Master's degree in English at a University or College. Aldo is currently writing a novel and have a few short stories that haven't been published yet. He said, "After becoming a Paralegal, I will move to Washington State. I've never liked Los Angeles much and many painful memories exist here. It would be best for my mental health to move away. I also hope that I can one day be a published author and hopefully be on the New York Times' Bestseller list."

In the year 2000, Aldo was diagnosed with major depression and anxiety. Aldo thinks he won't outgrow his depression and is unsure whether his anxiety attributes to it. Aldo received therapy and was put on the medication Paxil, but unfortunately it caused him to be more depressed and suicidal. It's what lead him to his first suicide attempt, so he now only receives psychotherapy. His mental illnesses were caused by childhood traumas, but thanks to therapy he has learned about stressors and how to avoid them. He now also relies on a support system to control his disorders.

Aldo also had to deal with terrible symptoms. He said, "Many of the symptoms still plague me, such as insomnia, restlessness, irritability, over eating, and fatigue." Aldo also mentioned, "My depression during my youth would often result in bouts of uncontrollable sobbing, loss of appetite, feelings of worthlessness, depersonalization, suicidal thoughts (though I never tried until I was on medications), anger, and shame." This affected his daily life especially during high school. Aldo went from having a 3.4 GPA to barely graduating. He added, "It was in my senior year of high school that my depression truly took hold of my life. I was hospitalized when one of my more observant teachers saw the cuts on my arms and took me to the counseling office. Aside from cutting, I would also burn myself, the scars are still visible on my left arm." Once Aldo graduated, he tried to work, but could never maintain a job for too long because his depression and suicide attempts always had him calling off work.

Sadly, in the year 2003 Aldo slit his wrist with a box cutter blade nearly severing a tendon and almost losing use of his left hand. He was put on a 72 hour hold which was extended to two weeks. It took a total of 12 sutures to close the wound. Aldo said, "I did it out in front of my school, and walked around for 3 hours waiting for death to take me. Unbeknownst to me, smoking thickens your blood, and in the 3 hours that I had walked around I chain smoked a pack of cigarettes. Dizzy and disoriented I called my best friend for help. I called her house and she picked up sounding surprised, not to be hearing from me, but because her house's phone line had not been working for a few weeks. I was the first call to come through in that time."

It is hard for Aldo to maintain friendships or romantic relationships because of his negativity. Although he has had several long-term relationships, they end up affected by his wild mood swings. He stated, "I sometimes require a lot of reassuring and nurturing, but there are also times when I need alone time and to be away from everyone. My girlfriends in the past have not been too keen on letting me be alone because they feel that we need to spend every moment together." This has made him feel like a burden, angry and unwanted. He feels as if he is a broken thing that no one wants because it's too much to handle.

Aldo's last suicide attempts has left him stronger. He said:

"I took 50 sleeping pills and I sat in the back seat of my car awaiting death. I became drowsy and I slumped over. I remember the cold beginning to creep over me despite it being a warm April night. I remember slipping away, I knew it was death looming and I can recall that as everything started to fade there was just cold and what seemed to be the vast expanse of nothing. I survived but the experience rocked my core. I've considered myself to be an agnostic for a very long time but as I lay dying, I had hoped that there would be something. Alas, it is just us and our mortality. The experience left me scarred, but I have decided to make the best of it. I've come so far from that night and I never thought it would be possible but everything since then has been the best time in my life.

The turning point for Aldo was when he realized his actions had caused him to lose sight and control of what he was trying to build. Although he will never really be over it, he decided that enough was enough. He learned that knowing his limits is the key. Whenever he feels like spiraling downward, he turns to his support system and asks for help. This was a huge struggle for him because after staying at a psychiatric ward he had no idea what to do! After he was discharged they did not offer any help. His friends have helped him along the way. Aldo added, "For years, my friends have been the only support group that I have. In many ways, they are the family I had always deserved but did not have. They always listen attentively and offer their support not just emotionally,. but also a place to stay when I don't feel safe or I am tired. They offer the push and reassurance that I can achieve what I have set out to do."

The lesson Aldo learned is that it is better to be alone than in bad company and it is not worth giving up your happiness for anyone. This experience has changed Aldo. He now pursues the things that make him happy. He also wants to improve his life. This is his advice for others struggling with similar situations:

"It's never as hard as you think it will be. Ask for help from the right people who care about you. If you cannot find it or don't think you have, then take it upon yourself to get professional help. Call a suicide hotline, chat with someone. I've often chatted with strangers just to get it off my chest. They don't know me and so I feel no judgment, only release and it is very helpful. Also, listen to the clichés. They are clichés because they are right. Patience is a virtue, it's true. I learned over and over again. That's not to say that you should be complacent or wait for things to happen. Some things you have to actively seek out and work for them."

Aldo would also like to share this:

"I've learned a lot of over the years but most importantly I've learned that it doesn't matter what others think. Do right by you. If you feel like crying, then cry, you will feel so relieved afterwards and it's healthy and therapeutic. Cry until you can't cry anymore. In the same vein, don't worry about others' feelings. You might be worried about hurting someone's feelings, good or bad, and so you let yourself be in an uncomfortable situation because you would rather be nice. Don't. I learned that you can only control how YOU feel. I would rather be nice and avoid hurting someone's feelings even though they would make me feel uncomfortable but in the end how they feel is not of your concern. They either deal with it or don't. You might lose people because of it, but really it's their loss. Be honest. If you try therapy and you feel like it might not be working, ask yourself: Am I being honest and open with this person? Chances are that you are not. You have built a barrier to protect you from EVERYONE, but a therapist is only trying to help. So be open and truthful and results will follow. Ultimately, if you still don't feel like the person isn't helping then it's okay find someone else. What matters is that you get help."

STORY # 27

SCHIZOAFFECTIVE DISORDER & BIPOLAR TYPE II

Anonymous is from Coral Springs, Florida, but currently lives in Acworth, GA. She enjoys the Harry Potter Series so much that she has read it at least five times. She also loves Doctor Who and reads about string theory and parliamentary procedure during her free time. Although she has stopped putting time limits in her goals, she would like to either finish graduate school or work in a community mental health clinic.

Anonymous was diagnosed by a psychiatrist and still struggles with schizoaffective disorder and bipolar type II. Her first episode was caused after a stressful fight with her mother. Her psychiatrist prescribed her 400 mg of Seroquel. She suffered horrifying symptoms. Anonymous said:

"It started with paranoia – I became convinced cameras were recording me. Then I thought demons were watching me. I woke up in the middle of the night in complete terror, and couldn't go back to sleep. I started hearing noises and voices. I heard footsteps, doors opening and closing, alarms, and whispering. I saw "shadow people", bugs, and other weird things. I thought all of it was real. I became obsessed with demons and the supernatural (I held no believe in spirits previous). I believed a demon, named Jessop, was attacking me spiritually."

Not only that but Anonymous also had suicidal thoughts and self-harmed. But thankfully her fear of going to hell stopped her from committing suicide. The reason Anonymous wanted to kill herself was because she had intrusive thoughts about hurting others. Afraid, she thought dying was the best way to prevent herself from acting upon it.

This affected her daily life in many ways. Anonymous was in college and had a 4.0 GPA she could no longer keep. Anonymous couldn't think or focus in school anymore. She no longer understood anything that was happening in class and lost all motivation for life. Anonymous became socially withdrawn and didn't understand that something was wrong; she just felt weird. She withdrew herself from her friends. She stated, "I had been going to my best friend's house twice a week for dinner and a TV show, and I stopped completely. I turned off my phone so people couldn't reach me." Even though she was acting strange her friends stayed close to her and tried to give her support.

This made Anonymous feel terrible. She added, "I felt desperate, frustrated, and sad. I kept saying 'I'm different now' and was convinced people would no longer want to be friends with me." The turning point to control her mental disorders was her best friend, who knew what was happening. Anonymous' best friend took time off work to accompany Anonymous to see a psychiatrist, and explained what was happening with her friend. Thanks to this the psychiatrist prescribed anti-psychotics, making Anonymous feel like a whole new person a week later.

The strategies she used to control her mental disorders included going to psychosocial rehabilitation every two weeks. Anonymous also goes to support group meetings almost every night. When

Anonymous is not hallucinating and stable she writes to herself notes in a journal to remind herself that that Jessop is not real. She surrounded herself with friends that cared about her. She said, "My best friend called and checked on me every day, asking, "How are you feeling today?" I would tell her all the craziness, and she would say "Just hold on. Please. Just hold on. It'll get better." My other friends called regularly as well. One of them told me, "We are not going to let you lose yourself." They came to my house, the brought me food, they helped me with school, and kept an eye on me."

Anonymous learned that with the help of great friends you can overcome anything. This experience changed her outlook in life. She now appreciates the good moments in life and understands that bad days will pass. This is her advice for others struggling with similar situations:

> "Find a couple of people you trust that you can be open with. Find a psychiatrist. Take advantage of prescription patient assistance programs if you can't afford the medication. Educate yourself as much as you can. Don't give up. You WILL get better.

When life is good, say 'thank you' and celebrate. When life is bad, say 'thank you' and grow."

STORY # 28

DEPRESSION

Anonymous is from Denmark and he is in a long-distance relationship. He enjoys playing drums and computer games. He also loves to watch fantasy movies. His goal is to be with his family in the United States. Anonymous was diagnosed by a therapist with depression. An anxiety attack provoked his mental disorder. He is still working with the root of the problem with his therapist.

At first Anonymous felt anxiety. He said, "I overthought and over-analyzed things to an extreme that was uncontrollable. I couldn't feel myself, didn't understand why I was so sad and angry at the same time. I didn't have the energy to go to work or to even appreciate the things that I actually normally had fun doing. I wasn't sure of myself and my self-worth dropped completely. I lost my confidence slowly and I couldn't do my job properly."

This affected his daily life in many ways. Anonymous became lazy and stopped cleaning. He never left his room and began smoking in it. He also stopped spending time with his friends. He stated, "I didn't have the energy and didn't 'feel' like being social. It still persists today." Even though Anonymous did not want to continue living, he did not consider suicide as an escape. He added, "It was not that I wanted to take my own life or even thought about it that way, it was more a mindset of: why even live?"

This affected his relationship with others. Anonymous lost a friend he thought was close to him, and lost count of all the people he used to talk to. He said, "My friend had enough of me and my constant pouting; he yelled at me and honestly made me feel worse, but at the time, I sorta understood him." This made Anonymous feel worthless and he thought he wouldn't be able to improve.

The turning point for him was realizing that his emotions are valid and that it is okay to feel that way. Due to his mental breakdown, Anonymous is in the process of discovering himself again. Anonymous continues to go to cognitive behavioral therapy and talks to his therapist about deep underlying emotions of abandonment and commitment issues.

This is his advice for others struggling with similar situations:

"It all gets better, keep grinding, keep focused on yourself and your emotions. All of your feelings and emotions are telling you what's up. Telling you exactly what you need to be doing, sometimes it's just hard to hear over the noise of other people. Remember, there is only one person in your life and that is you. You are the only person who can change your life, ask for help if needed but it all starts with you"

He also wants to share this:

"Continue struggling; don't stop struggling. It is through your struggles you come through and develop. Everything will be better, I can promise you that, but all you have to do is to continue in the mess. There are many ways to overcome a depression and mental breakdown, but one of the greatest ways is to give yourself very few but easy tasks each and every day. Today I will drink 2 glasses of water, tomorrow

I will do the dishes – set small goals you can achieve easily and trust me, you'll feel better but the best advice I can give and the last thing I want to share: Speak to a therapist"

STORY # 29

MAJOR DEPRESSIVE DISORDER, BORDERLINE PERSONALITY DISORDER, PERSISTENT DEPRESSIVE DISORDER, ANOREXIA NERVOSA & BULIMIA NERVOSA

Janna is from California and singing is her passion. She enjoys acting and watching indie movies. She is also fond of music. Even though her playlist has various music genres, she mostly listens to punk, rock, and grunge. Jana is a Virgo and she considers herself to possess many of the typical Virgo qualities such as being rational, cold hearted, intelligent, and analytical. Her goal is to become a famous singer and actress. Janna said, "It is the only thing I want in life and I'd die for it. In five years, I hope to be debuting an album and acting in movies and TV shows. Without this dream, I would have been long since died."

She has been diagnosed by many psychiatrists with major depressive disorder, borderline personality disorder, dysthymia, anorexia, and bulimia. Janna does not know what caused her mental illnesses. She has been in an inpatient treatment in a mental hospital six times and has been in an outpatient treatment twice. Janna has also been to different group and individual therapies. She is currently on medication as well.

The symptoms Janna felt took a toll on her life. She stated, "I feel heavy. Like this stuck in molasses feeling. Or like weights are tied to my arms and legs making it hard to move and get out of bed. My chest feels heavy sometimes like it is decaying into itself. I can sleep for 17 hours and still need more rest or I can sleep for none and be just fine." Janna did not perform well in school. She added, "It was seemingly impossible to pick up a pencil and do homework. I mean why I would care about my grades if I didn't care about my life." Janna stopped talking to everyone and ignored anyone who tried to talk to her. Her room smelled stale and was covered in dirty clothes because she had no energy to clean anything. Janna said, "I didn't go out, I just stayed in my room for weeks on my phone or staring at a wall."

Sadly, Janna attempted suicide a few times. She said, "The first time I took 35 of my antidepressants. The second time I took 17 aspirins and 23 Tylenols. After that didn't work I tried to slit my wrists and then hang myself." Janna also said, "Just imagine going to bed every night terrified you would wake up in the morning. Praying to god to take you in the night. I can't even begin to accurately describe the pain of wanting to kill myself every single day." Not only that, but Janna would cut nearly every day for months and would also throw up every meal for weeks.

Janna did not have any relationship with others. She said, "I cut everyone out and ceased communication with the world outside my house." This made her feel angry and trapped. She added, "I was raised as a solitary independent person. My mother had cancer so she wasn't available. My father was busy trying to keep my two sisters, who were 9 and 11 years older than I was, involved in their soccer and basketball games. My life was spent alone or in the backseat of a car having no one to talk to but myself." The turning point for Janna to gain control over her illness was her desire to become a famous actress. She also keeps herself busy with school and work.

Janna feels like she hasn't learned a lesson. She said, "I don't believe people are supposed to learn lessons. I mean it's a disorder and it hurts. You just start to put pain and things in perspective. If anything, it has drained me and made me empty. I don't see a lesson in that." Her illness has changed her outlook in life. Janna stated, "Since my early years I have always been sad. I can't imagine what my life would be like if I was happy. I look at life as meaningless and insignificant. Nothing we do matters."

This is her advice for others struggling through similar situations:

"Three simple rules in life:

1. If you do not go after what you want, you'll never have it.
2. If you do not ask, the answer will always be no.
3. If you do not step forward, you will always be in the same place."

STORY # 30

PANIC DISORDER, DEPRESSION &
BIPOLAR DISORDER

Bethany is from Montgomery, NY, and she loves photography and exploring abandoned buildings. Her goals include having a stable job and a home. She'd like to be married and live comfortably. A mental health professional diagnosed Bethany with panic disorder, depression and bipolar disorder. Although the reason for her daily attacks are unknown, her mental disorders stems from not being able to deal with death. Bethany receives medication and therapy.

She had to deal with terrible symptoms such as, not being able to leave her house, being unable to drive, and having blurred vision. She felt like she couldn't breathe. Bethany said, "The walls felt like they were coming down on me." She's also suffered from insomnia, weight loss, and felt completely numb during the whole experience. This affected her life, and she became suicidal and lost her job. Bethany had to be put on disability and lost complete independence.

This affected her relationship with others. Bethany's fiancé didn't know how to handle it at first, and she became extremely dependent of her mother until her mom began suffering from health issues. This made her feel horrible. Bethany said, "I didn't feel like a 'normal' 20-year-old should." Although Bethany is still struggling, the turning point was realizing that life is too short to be sad and panicking all the time. She stated, "You have to live each day as if it were the last."

The strategies Bethany used to control her mental disorders was going to talk therapy, and doing art and photography. Bethany's fiancé also went to therapy and treatment, so he could help her during a moment of crisis. The lesson she learned from this ordeal is that "You are your own enemy!" Bethany is still learning to love the good and bad parts of herself. She is now enjoying life through a new perspective.

I am glad Bethany, little by little, is gaining back control of her life. It is not easy, but with determination and the help of loved ones, she will be able to make it through.

STORY # 31

DEPRESSION

Anonymous is from Southeast, US, and she enjoys cooking, baking, writing, drawing, and playing the guitar. Although she still struggles with depression, her goal is to be happy. Anonymous had a therapist she briefly saw, but she stopped going because she felt uncomfortable. She believes the root of her mental disorder is due to genetics.

Anonymous dealt with debilitating symptoms, she said, "I felt nauseous and dizzy frequently. I'd also experience headaches a lot." This affected her daily life tremendously. She constantly had negative thoughts about herself and her appearances. Anonymous shared, "I would often talk to myself by creating two personalities (a good side and a bad side) and having them discuss who I was and who I felt I should be." Because of her struggles she attempted suicide twice and self-harmed.

Her relationship with others was affected because Anonymous was extremely temperamental, lashing out on others. This made her feel trapped, she added, "I felt angry, like my angst and sadness was bottled up inside me. Whenever I tried to talk to someone about my problems, I would feel extremely guilty because I would whine about my mental condition while thousands of people had it so much worse than I did." The turning point for Anonymous to control her mental disorder, was when she began exercising, going outside, and making new friends. Her friends gave her the support she needed.

The lesson she learned from this ordeal is that life is valuable, and battling a mental illness alone is no way to spend the only life you've got. Not only that but her outlook in life changed, anonymous admitted, "I am encouraged every day to be a better, brighter, and happier person." She now encourages herself by reminding herself all the amazing things she has in my life, and all the things she has yet to experience. This is her advice for others struggling with similar situations:

"You don't have to be alone. If it feels like there is no one out there for you, someone always is. You can always reach out and establish a new friendship with someone, as well. There is always help."

STORY # 32

SCHIZOPHRENIC DEPRESSION

Kris is from the East Coast of the U.S. and she enjoys all types of music. She said, "I like to think music is a part of me, and a way to escape reality when I need it." Her hobbies include drawing (doodling), writing, and roleplaying, which is strictly just writing. Her goal is to attend James Madison College as a social psychology major. Kris also wants to move out of her parents' apartment, and live with her boyfriend in a townhouse.

Kris was diagnosed by a psychiatrist at a mental hospital with schizophrenic depression, meaning when one acts up, the other acts up. Not only that, but she also has sleeping issues, OCD symptoms, social anxiety, and permanent paranoia. She believes that her mental illnesses may have been caused by not consciously realizing she is transgendered while growing up. Another factor may have been the fights and financial problems her parents had. Her psychiatrist prescribed her various medicines and combined it with group therapy, in-hospital therapy, and out-hospital therapy.

Kris had to deal with debilitating symptoms. When it came to the depression she felt anxiety, her sleeping cycle changed, leaving her constantly exhausted. Kris also felt helpless and isolated. The schizophrenia makes her feel paranoid with delusions and hallucinations. She also battled with cognitive impairment, lack of motivation, social withdrawal, and sometimes felt emotionless.

Sadly, Kris attempted suicide twice and has self-harmed. She's had thoughts of hurting others, but never attempted anything. Additionally, her relationship with others became affected. Kris lost many friends and an ex-boyfriend. Her current boyfriend has a hard time understanding her, she disclosed, "The boyfriend who I have now has difficulty with my depression sometimes, but he has depression as well, so it helps. He hasn't experienced my schizophrenia full on, meaning hallucinations, but he's seen me get more paranoid recently. He says he's worried for me."

The turning point for Kris to control her mental disorders was getting out of high school, she graduated with the GED program 2 years earlier. After starting college and flunking out the first semester due to depression, she took time for herself and got help from her 2 friends and boyfriend. They helped her get back on her feet. Kris shared, "They gave me time when I needed, respected my negative thoughts, and stayed with me unlike everyone else. They would stay on the phone with me if I was having a panic attack, my boyfriend would let me come over just to sit down next to him, and they made me remember what it felt like to smile without a mask again." The strategies Kris used to maintain control was listening to music, writing poetry, and swimming.

This experience changed her outlook in life, she said, "I matured much faster than a lot of people in my grade or 'generation', and it has given me a lot of life experiences. There's still a lot I have to go since I'm only 18, but I have been through more than the average young adult I believe." This is Kris advice for others struggling through similar situations:

"No matter where you are in life, there is always a different perspective."

STORY # 33

DEPRESSION

Sofía is from México and moved to the U.S when she was 12 years old with her family. Her greatest passion is photography, especially lomography. She also loves to read. Her favorite books are from the author Anne Rice. Other great books Sofía has enjoyed reading are: I Am the Messenger by Markus Zusak, To Kill a Mocking Bird by Harper Lee, Frankenstein by Mary Shelly, and The Great Gatsby among much others. She is fond of playing the violin, is vegan, and watches as much movies as she possibly can during her free time.

Sofía's goal is to graduate and become the best programmer. In 5 years, she hopes to be in either Canada or New Zealand. She wants to also travel the world with her boyfriend. Sofía would love to rescue and adopt many animals. She was diagnosed by a psychiatrist with chronic depression, but thankfully she has recovered. Sofía's had depression since she was young. She said, "Ever since in the second grade I felt lost and sad most of the time, and when I was 9 years old, my parents got divorced. It went downhill from there." Sofía's psychiatrist prescribed her citalopram, bupropion, and sleeping medication, along with psychotherapy.

She dealt with terrible symptoms, Sofía always felt exhausted. She shared, "I lost so much weight: I got to weigh 78 pounds. I slept all day and stayed awake at night. I couldn't focus on anything, really, but I was always overthinking every single thing that I did or said or how others treated me." She tried to kill herself on different occasions and the medications she was prescribed with affected her. Citalopram made her nauseous and sleepy. Bupropion was worse for her, she added, "Besides the nausea, my hands were shaking all the time, which made everything more awful because I was in art school then. It made it impossible to draw. My vision got blurry at times, and when I told my psychiatrist he said that it was normal, and that I should not stop taking my medication."

This affected every aspect of her daily life. Sofía was alone most of the time and didn't talk to anyone. She explained, "I couldn't make any friends, and when I did I couldn't find a way to keep that friendship." This led her read many books such as, Hold Still, Go Ask Alice and Willow among other books. Sofía was also bullied. She confessed, "It was hell going to some family gatherings because always someone had some negative comment about how I looked, how I seemed. It drove me away from my mom and my brothers amongst other people. I hurt myself. I tried so many times to run away, but thankfully there always was a friend that found me. I cannot tell you how many times or how many hours a day I spent planning my death. I felt worthless. I felt like no one would care if I died, I thought about who would be at my funeral, who would cry and who wouldn't."

Sofía became addicted to cutting, she said:

"When I was 13 I started cutting myself, but it wasn't until I turned 14 that I attempted suicide for the first time; I grabbed as many pills as I could and swallowed them. I locked myself in my room and waited to die, but I didn't. By then, I was addicted to cutting. I could barely stand a day without it. I carried razors around with me. I did it every chance I had. It got so bad I could do nearly two hundred cuts in one sitting. I think overcoming this addiction is one of the hardest things I've done."

After leaving a terrible relationship, Sofía became obsessed over him. She became sick and lost too much weight. Her eyes looked yellow and dry. She stopped eating and drinking water. She seemed lifeless. The turning point for Sofía was during the summer of 2013, when she decided that she needed to get help. After going to see a doctor, he recommended Sofía to see a psychiatrist and told her mother she wanted to kill herself. This made her mother cry, Sofía mentioned, "I had never seen her so devastated and determined. When we got to the car after the doctor's appointment, she turned to me and cried for so long. She told me that the thought of losing me was more than she could handle. She told me she loved me, and that she'd do anything and everything to keep me alive."

The strategy she used to overcome her mental disorder was taking it one day at a time. She kept fighting for her family, but her boyfriend, Luis helped her the most. She explained, "He met me when I started going to the psychiatrist. He literally has seen me at my worst, he walked next to me on my road to recovery, and also has stayed now that I'm healthy. I remember one time I ran out of medicine, and it all got so terrible, but he didn't back out. He met me at the park with his guitar and sang me some beautiful songs about having to keep fighting and he also bought me my medicine. I truly believe that it's love that helps the most."

The lesson Sofía learned from this ordeal is that life is rough, that she needs to keep going, to enjoy herself and nature. This experience changed her outlook in life, she said, "I believe in love. I believe in honesty, and that we shouldn't lock ourselves away. I am now a more open person, I accept and understand others more easily." She now speaks up whenever she starts feeling down. She realized how great it can be to open up.

This is her advice for others struggling with similar situations:

"Please don't give up. Talk to someone you trust. Remember that you're not alone, and that all you have to do is ask for help."

STORY # 34

DEPRESSION & GENERALIZED ANXIETY DISORDER

Anonymous is from New Zealand and she enjoys math, musicals, and Marvel movies. Her goal is to work in the States for Google. She was diagnosed by her doctor and counselor with generalized anxiety disorder (GAD) and depression. Thankfully her depression is gone, and still struggles, but better manages her GAD. Anonymous was medicated with Citalopram and took Cognitive Behavioral Therapy (CBT).

Various situations caused her mental disorders. Anonymous said, "Ignoring early symptoms, [poor] emotional management, and pouring too much of myself into other people." This made her feel constantly scared and apathetic. She also shared, "I got massively overwhelmed by everything. I constantly felt numb and overly sensitive." This affected her daily life in many ways. Anonymous failed university papers because she stayed in her room and did not do anything. She stopped talking to her friends and believed nobody cared about her. She added, "I didn't think I was important. I hid behind my computer or phone screen when I spent time with people."

Thankfully, anonymous never considered suicide. Although she would pinch the inside of her upper arms until she bruised just to feel something. Her mental illnesses affected her relationship with others, she explained, "I lost touch with a large group of friends because I disappeared off the map. I broke up with my boyfriend also, though that might have happened anyway."

The turning point to better manage her mental illnesses was to learn that she was important and that her feelings were valid. But the biggest turning point for anonymous was when she learned how to separate the feelings of anxiety from herself. She disclosed, "I learned how to stop it from overwhelming me and learned to put them aside, so I could still do things that I needed to do." The strategies she used was to personify her emotions by turning them into little characters. For example, when anonymous felt anxious for no reason, she would tell herself, "Its ok, it's just Bruce". With this technique, she was able to separate her feelings and comfort herself.

To diminish her anxiety attacks, anonymous would ask friends to go out for coffee. She said, "Coffee would often turn into running errands or something and that massively reduced the time I spent alone which meant my brain didn't have as much time to go in spirals." The lesson she learned from this ordeal was that she needs to fight hard for the things she really wants in life. Although she admits being less sympathetic, she added, "Unfortunately, it's made me a little less sympathetic sometimes to other people with depression because I fought so hard to drag myself out of it. It's really hard to watch my friends making the same mistakes I made and not doing anything about it."

This is her advice for anyone struggling:

"You're going to have to work really, really hard if you want to get better. It doesn't magically happen and nobody else can do it for you. However, you don't have to get better all at once. Every little moment is a chance to take a step in the direction you want. Right now, you have the choice to fight and get up even though your brain is screaming to stay safe and alone. You've got to stop listening to the unhealthy things your brain is saying and fight for the future you want. It's not going to be easy, but if you do it one step at a time, you'll be fine."

Anonymous would also like to share:

"We have an instant gratification culture. I know a lot of people waiting around for that one thing that will make them better instantly. It doesn't exist. You've got to make your own future. One step at a time."

STORY # 35

BIPOLAR DISORDER

Kira is from Quebec, Canada and she enjoys writing and playing video games on her free time. Her goal is to graduate from university with an undergraduate degree and from there work her way into grad school. She would like to focus on clinical psychology and is open to getting a degree in social work. Kira would like to use her knowledge of Mindfulness to research and practice in the future.

She has seen different psychiatrist and they have leaned towards depression, generalized anxiety disorder (GAD) and borderline personality disorder (BPD), but she has been officially diagnosed with bipolar disorder. Kira does not know what caused her mental illnesses, but there has always been mental health problems within her family and when she was young her teacher recommended her to see a professional. She suspects that her diagnosis with depression contributed to her illness because she was prescribed with SSRI and that did not help her manic episodes.

After being hospitalized in 2010, Kira now sees a therapist and attends to weekly mindfulness groups. She currently is taking Quetiapine, Lithium, Topiramate, Lamotrigine and Asinepine medications. She is planning to attend a BP peer group later this month, which she is excited and nervous about. It has been difficult for Kira to deal with certain symptoms. She shared, "I recently have been experiencing psychotic symptoms again. Every little sensation input gets misinterpreted and fits into my paranoid delusion: that a shadow becomes a man that's trying to kill me." Kira also said, "There's a white figure living in my room, a demon [whom] is communicating with me through subway ads telling me that I have bladder cancer. It feels like you're constantly being lied to and the liar and victim is both yourself, which is quite the predicament you put yourself in." Every winter Kira experiences hypomania, and starts to drink and smoke excessively. She becomes energetic and starts projects that she never finishes, becoming emotional. During the summer she crashes and disconnects from others, constantly telling herself negative speeches.

This has affected her daily life, Kira explained, "It's like your life is running off the tracks and you are trying to steer it back on course constantly. I feel like I'm always a step behind everyone else. All of my friends who are my age (or even younger) have already accomplished what I wanted to accomplish. It's very isolating. It's even more isolating because you feel like you're making an excuse for yourself by saying that you're chronic illness is just making you take things a bit slower." In 2010 Kira began stockpiling her antidepressants and planned to commit suicide. Thankfully a nurse at her school noticed her odd behavior and convinced Kira to seek out help.

This also affected her relationship with others, Kira mentioned, "When I was left by my ex, I definitely felt abandoned, I still do. I felt like I could trust her. I felt like I gave a part of myself and when it came to someone supporting me through a really challenging period of my life, I was left to the wayside. I have a difficult time trusting people with my story, but because my illness is a part of me and my identity, it's really difficult to interact with anyone."

Thankfully, Kira is now happily married and her partner supports her through the difficult times.

Kira still struggles with her disorder every day, but she has realized that the difficult moments don't last very long. Her symptoms although persistent, don't last for every second or every day and she is able to look forward to a bright future. Kira surrounded herself with friends and family that support her even though at times they may not understand. She is still a little timid, but has realized that she is strong. This is her advice for others struggling with similar situations:

> "I suggest trying mindfulness. I've learn so many things from its teachings. My advice is not gauge yourself against others, it won't work for you. It's like comparing apples and oranges."

STORY # 36

SCHIZOAFFECTIVE DISORDER

Anonymous is from Kentucky, USA and she enjoys reading James Patterson books and all kinds of music except for country. She also loves writing poetry and stories. Her goal is to attend college during the spring. She said, "I'm still not sure what I'm going to major in, but I just want to get my basics over with first. I still have time to decide what I'm going to do with my life, so I'm trying not to rush it and feel pressured about it." Anonymous hopes to go far in life and have a successful career.

In 2011, she was diagnosed by a psychiatrist with Schizoaffective Disorder, which is schizophrenia with bipolar disorder. Her mental illness is due to genetics, she stated, "My mother and her mother have bipolar disorder; my dad and his mom have depression and anxiety; and my father's dad had schizophrenia." Anonymous also believes that an abusive childhood may have also contributed to her mental disorders. Currently, she receives therapy once a week and is on medication.

She has dealt with terrible symptoms. Anonymous said, "[depression] It was a wave that crashed over me and kept me under." She had mood swings most of the time. During manic episodes, her thoughts would race so fast that she would have difficulty grasping a single thought and her words would come out too fast be understood. Anonymous began seeing shadows that weren't there. Then she would hear the shadows whisper her name, making her extremely paranoid that the shadows were out to hurt her. She mentioned, "I was afraid of any shadow I saw after that, real or not. And I started hearing the whispers more often, whether I was with a group of people or by myself. They had me convinced that everyone was out to hurt me, so I shut myself away from my friends and family."

This affected her daily life, Anonymous lost interest in everything she enjoyed doing. She added, "I didn't like to read anymore since it was too quiet. Any time I was alone, I'd listen to music on full volume to shut the voices out. It was very hard to concentrate in school and at home. My parents got worried after they noticed my depression, but I guess at first they just thought it was a phase." Sadly, Anonymous has cut herself and attempted suicide once, but thankfully failed in the attempt. She said, "The way my sisters cried and begged me to live when they found out I had tried to kill myself, I don't care how much pain I'm going through, I'm never going to attempt suicide again. I can't stand the thought of one of my sisters finding my dead body." After finding out, her family made an appointment for Anonymous to see a therapist, but she only went once. No one brought up the subject again because they wanted to forget.

This made her feel happy and sad, she said, "I was happy they were leaving me alone, but I was sad because deep down, I really did want help. I just wasn't ready to admit it to myself at first. I felt trapped, desperate, paranoid, and lonely. I kept pushing people away because that's what I thought would be easier for everyone." The turning point for Anonymous was when she finally told her parents what was going on in her head. It took time, lots of therapy and medication, but Anonymous was able to improve her mental health. She stated, "But I would have times where I thought I was better, stopped taking my meds, and had to repeat the cycle. I had to go to a crisis center once before high school. After starting high school, everything I had worked for, crashed. The huge amount of people at school caused me to have panic attacks, the classes and teachers stressed me out so much, I ended up having to go back to the crisis center two months into my freshman year, and then they sent me to a psychiatric hospital after the doctor determined that the five days at the crisis center wasn't enough. After speaking to my therapist and doctor, my parents pulled me out of public school and I was homeschooled for the rest of my high school years. If they hadn't taken me out of public school when they did, I'm not sure if I'd still be here right now."

The strategies she used to control her mental disorder were to take her medication and go to therapy. She started to read, write and listen to music again. Her loved ones helped her by giving her space and listening to her when she needed to talk. The lesson she learned from this ordeal is that suicide is a permanent solution to a temporary problem. This is her advice for others struggling with similar situations:

"To anyone out there going through things like I did, you're not alone. Whether you know it or not, there are people that love you and want you to recover from what you're going through. It'll take time, a lot of patience, and some support, but you'll come out a happier, stronger person. You can get through this, I promise."

STORY # 37

DEPRESSION & EATING DISORDER NOT OTHERWISE SPECIFIED

Anonymous loves to dance; she has been dancing for 12 years now. She enjoys spending time with children and eating cookie dough. Her goal is to open a dance studio or become an actress. Anonymous still struggles with depression and EDNOS (Eating Disorder Not Otherwise Specified). Depression runs in her family, and she believes her eating disorder and depression might have been triggered by the negative image she has of herself.

Anonymous was diagnosed with depression, but her EDNOS was self-diagnosed and she currently takes anti-depressants. She has struggled with debilitating symptoms, Anonymous said, "Honestly, I didn't feel much of anything. When I didn't have to do anything, I would just lay in my bed a lot because I didn't have the motivation to do anything else. If I had to do something, I'd put it off as much as possible. I felt like a zombie most of the time, but I never really showed to others." Also, at times she would feel extreme anger and rage, for no apparent reason.

This affected her daily life because she stayed in her room all day, avoiding any interaction with people. It took a lot of energy for her to smile because she wanted to hide her feelings. Her lack of sleep at night made her want to sleep all day. She used to self-harm, which caused her depression to worsen. She stated, "I would cut myself to feel something, or to release the anger I felt." Her relationships with others weren't affected that much because she hid her depression well. This made her feel trapped, she said, "I didn't feel like I could confide in anyone about what I was dealing with, but I couldn't deal with it by myself."

Anonymous didn't realize that what she was feeling wasn't normal, which downplayed her problems, but she slowly figured it out. One evening she talked to a close family member about it and got help. The strategies she uses to control her mental disorder is to take her medication. She also tossed out all of her blades, so she couldn't self-harm anymore. The lesson Anonymous learned from this ordeal is that she is strong, she said, "It's a lesson I've learned more than once." This experience helped her notice that the world isn't so bad when you know where to look. She doesn't know if she can prevent herself from falling again, but she now cuts herself some slack sometimes, which is something she never used to do.

This is her advice for others struggling with similar situations:

"A lot of people say that you can't just smile away depression. They are right, but some of it is actually wanting to get better and DOING something to get better. Like taking your meds, talking to someone, and most importantly, taking care of yourself."

STORY # 38

ANXIETY DISORDER, DEPRESSION &
BORDERLINE PERSONALITY DISORDER

Anonymous is currently 20 years old and lives in Canada. She is a trumpet player and loves movie soundtracks. Her favorite food is pasta, and she also enjoys 18th century literature such as, Charles Dickens and Jane Austen. Anonymous pictures herself being successful one day, she said, "In 5 years I see myself in a serious relationship, finishing my degree and starting my career in marketing/management." She began to struggle with her mental health since she was 16, and it became serious at the age of 17 when she was about to graduate from high school.

A therapist diagnosed her anxiety and depression, but her borderline personality disorder (BPD) was never diagnosed because her mother was in the session and Anonymous felt embarrassed about her symptoms. She said, "I guess my thing was that I was ashamed about my BPD which caused me to keep it to myself." Thankfully she has fully recovered from depression and BPD, but still struggles with her old anxious tendencies. Anonymous figured out she had BPD during a psychology class she took in high school. She stated, "We were reading all of the symptoms and I realized that we were talking about me." She is not sure what caused her mental disorders, but it could have been triggered after her high school boyfriend cheated on her 6 months after they started dating. Anonymous added, "I can't really pinpoint the beginning, but it was aggravated by my then-boyfriend's flirtatious nature with other girls. My depression and anxiety started after we broke up and because we saw each other every day it made me more anxious and depressed."

This affected her daily life, Anonymous' attitude changed and her friends started to ignore her. She didn't have anyone to talk to. Her therapist set up appointments with her guidance counselor at school, so she could talk once a week during class time. It was a relief for Anonymous to have someone to talk to. She said, "It helped me to relieve some of the pressure from my depression. It also helped to release some of my anger and accept my situation." Her therapist gave her activities to do, making Anonymous anxious, because of this she would scratch her hand until it bled, but her therapist told her to find a quiet place to calm down. Her BPD cleared up on its own. What helped her was knowing the behaviors were related to the illness, this way she stopped herself from acting upon it.

She had had to deal with depressive symptoms like, not being able to get up and do anything. She mentioned, "I couldn't feel happy doing anything. I didn't smile. Nor could I laugh even watching things or doing things that I knew made me happy." Her anxiety made her constantly nervous and stressed. She said, "At first it was just around my ex, but it started to take over other parts of my life. That combined with the lethargy from my depression meant that my grades in school dropped. Eventually, the anxiety got to a point where it started causing my chest to tighten up when I felt stressed. At first I thought I was having a heart attack, but I lived. The chest pains were debilitating, I would be incapacitated for anywhere between 10 minutes to over an hour." Anonymous also said, "Sometimes my chest would tighten up while I slept and I would wake up gasping for air. At first we thought it was medical and I had so many tests performed on me, but when no results came back we linked it to my stress levels and anxiety." Her BPD made her think that her ex-boyfriend was going to leave her, which triggered her to have "pregnancy scares" every month in an attempt to keep him near. She said, "When we broke up I kept up a 'pregnancy scare' for a month in an attempt to make him come back to me, I told him that I was feeling nauseous and would often run off to fake vomit when I knew he would be watching." This affected her so much, she would stab herself with needles and pins, and she did this because she wanted to feel something other than emotional pain. Her happiness was short lived every time it came around.

Everything for Anonymous was a struggle, daily tasks were difficult and she couldn't sit in a class without crying. Anonymous considered suicide once, right before she asked for help. While all of this was going on, her friends abandoned her because they thought she was making a big deal out of a break up. Her parents didn't know what to do with her; they felt as though they had lost her. Those that cared for Anonymous tiptoed around her and those who didn't want to deal with her kept their distance until she recovered. Her teachers could see that she was struggling with something, gave her extensions and let her leave class if she felt overwhelmed.

The turning point for Anonymous was the night she thought about committing suicide. After asking her mother to take her to see a therapist, her mom stepped in and helped Anonymous recover. She started her on herbal medications to relieve stress. Anonymous still practices the exercises that her therapist gave her years ago. This ordeal taught her that mental issues are not a joke and that no one can understand how you are feeling except for yourself. Anonymous is now more cautious and reserved around her relationships. She added, "I try to make sure I don't exhibit any BPD behaviors and I also try to stay unattached. I suppose that doesn't make for very good relationship material on my part, but I don't want to have to go through what I went through again, and I don't want my partner to have to go through that either." She also learned that she shouldn't be ashamed of her feelings and mental illness.

Her advice for others struggling through similar situation is:

"My advice to anyone going through BPD would be to remove yourself from the people you find yourself exhibiting behaviors around and then go and get some help. You can't get past it alone. For anxiety and depression talk to someone who will take you seriously- a professional. Your friends will not help you here, they can try, but they won't be able to give you the support you need. And make sure you find support systems that work for you, everyone is different. Find friends who feel the same, don't bring down your friends who are mentally healthy, they'll just resent you. Find a counselor, therapist, psychologist or psychiatrist- anyone who knows what to do to help."

Anonymous would also like to share this:

"Looking back, it was a dark period in my life. Mental illness is not a joke, and there's a very fine line between BPD and having a fight with your boyfriend. If I could tell you two things they would be: watch yourself, know what's healthy and what's not, and if you think you need help, GET HELP! If you hurt yourself or you have thoughts of hurting yourself please go see someone. I was very lucky, I knew when it was time for me to get help, but not everyone does. And if you currently have a mental illness whether it is one that I suffered from or a different one, please just think that you want to get better, because if you don't want to, then you never will."

STORY # 39

BORDERLINE PERSONALITY DISORDER, POST-TRAUMATIC STRESS DISORDER, DEPRESSION, ANXIETY DISORDER & EATING PROBLEMS

Madeleine is from Brisbane, Australia and she loves to write, produce music, read and exercise. Five years from now, she sees herself still learning and growing as a person. Eventually, she wants to be completely off her medications and be an independent individual. She was diagnosed with borderline personality disorder (BPD) and post-traumatic stress disorder (PTSD), along with depression, anxiety and some eating problems. Her father died when she was four years old and her mother remarried two years later to a man who already had a daughter. She lost contact with her father's family and experienced identity issues at an early age. Madeleine believes these events may have triggered her mental disorders.

At the age of 14, Madeleine was diagnosed with depression and anxiety and at 16 years old she was admitted to a hospital for a month and put on antidepressants. She started seeing a psychiatrist every week. On October of 2016, she was admitted to the hospital again for two weeks and was prescribed Zoloft and diagnosed with BPD and PTSD. After being discharged she started seeing a different psychologist and attended group therapy every week, focusing on mindfulness.

Madeleine dealt with self-destructive symptoms. She mentioned, "I would set myself up to fail. At my worst, I couldn't leave the house without spurring thoughts and ideation of suicide. My impulsive behavior led to negative consequences leading to my friends and family distancing themselves from me, I felt like I was getting what I deserved." This affected her life tremendously, Madeleine struggles with school and in the last 5 years she has been to 5 different schools. Sadly, she attempted suicide four times.

Not only that, but her BPD made it difficult for her to have healthy romantic relationships. Madeleine said, "I found myself becoming manipulative and cruel. Because of my reckless behavior, people distanced themselves from me which was quite hard, however, a bit of a wakeup call." They made her feel trapped, she stated, "I felt guilty considering and attempting suicide, but when my actions hurt and offended people I felt even guiltier."

The turning point for Madeleine was when she realized that people are not medicine. She said, "There is nothing wrong with me. I have accepted that this may be a lifelong thing that I can never get rid of. I have dealt with the sadness and now I'm focusing on the management of my mental health and ensuring it's my first priority." Madeleine wants to be the best person she can be. She is not going to let her mental illnesses define her. The current strategies she uses to control her disorder is to practice mindfulness, eat healthy, exercise, and erase negative people from her life.

This experience changed her outlook in life, Madeleine said, "Although mental illness sucks, it's made me appreciate life. I'm a lot less materialistic and find joy in little things like the feeling of the sun on my skin and hearing people I love laugh. I learned to take nothing for granted and that it's okay to not always be happy." Madeleine realized that people are not out to get her. To prevent herself from falling again, she has become aware of warning signs and her bad habits like impulsivity. She tries to make sure she is moving closer to her goals.

This is her advice for others battling through similar situations:

"PUSH THROUGH! Everything gets better in the end and if it's not better yet, it's not the end. Find help. No problem is too big or too small, you are worthy of help and if you don't receive sufficient support the first time, don't give up, keep on fighting. Focus on yourself. Love is a great feeling when it's good, but when it's bad it can tear your heart out. Remember that people are not medicine. You are the only permanent thing in your life."

She would also like to share this:

"They are allowed to be sad, they are allowed to cry. Their feelings are legitimate. When I was younger my family found it hard to believe that I had a real reason to feel the way I did. Mental illnesses are not always dependent on life factors and there needs to be more awareness of that."

STORY # 40

DEPRESSION, ANXIETY DISORDER & ATTENTION DEFECT DISORDER

Paul is a writer from Pennsylvania and he enjoys watching reality television, especially the ones that make him laugh. Paul said, "I Love Kellie Pickler, Chrisley Knows Best and Keeping Up With The Kardashians." He is fond of music and likes spending time with his family. Paul state, "I really love my Grandma and Mom; they're my heroes." He also enjoys spending every second with his boyfriend, Jon. Paul has recently read and fell in love with, Holly Madison: Down The Rabbit Hole and Marilyn: Her Life In Her Own Words. Paul's favorite series ever is from his spiritual advisor, Rhonda Byrne, he said, "Her books and words help me every day in life. She is the author of The Secret." His main goal is to be the happiest he can be. He added, "I know a few books from my novel series will be out by then, and I will be fully sharing my talents with the world, which is everything I have ever wanted."

Paul suffers from depression, anxiety and attention deficit disorder. He doesn't like to blame others and has forgiven them. Paul embraces and uses each moment to help himself instead of letting it go against him. Paul has been singled out by children and adults since pre-k through high school, he was sexually assaulted by a teenage boy when he was nine years old and has almost being kidnapped. Not only that, but in the 5th grade a teacher told Paul that he was special-ed. Thankfully, he has come to terms with his past traumas. He said, "I took back the light people tried to steal from me, and with each negative encounter I grew stronger. There are parts of me I won't ever get back, I grew up fast because I needed too, but I took back my life from those people who would never say sorry or take the blame."

Paul currently seeks treatment from a family doctor. He added, "You need to stay on top of it, because like it or not, it's part of you who are. Once you embrace it you'll realize the power you have." His mental illnesses affected his daily life in many ways. At times, Paul felt scared of the day ahead, because he never knew when a panic attack would come, but he has gained a lot of control. He has moments when he feels like his boyfriend will leave him; because of all the times he was told by guys that he could never be loved. But he knows none of it is real, because it's all in his mind. Paul has little secret signs that he asked the universe to show him throughout the day, and when he sees them, it reminds him that he is loved and everything will be okay. He said, "The universe is a powerful loving force. Everyone needs to connect with her."

Paul always carries himself with glamour. He relates to Marilyn Monroe in his own way. When it came to dating he used to tease men a lot. Paul said, "I loved powerful men, but never liked to lose power. Looking back it was to get revenge on the boy that hurt me when I was younger, because they always wanted me for my body, and not my heart." He used to party underage and used a fake I.D. He would also skip town with a few of his acting friends to New York City and did a lot of things behind his friends, and parent's backs. He wrote about a lot of it in his poetry book, Who I Am: Poetry.

Paul never thought about hurting others, because he knows pain. Sadly, he did attempt to end his life at 17 because all the lies he told finally caught up to him. He mentioned, "Once I placed the call they raced to my rescue. I'm grateful I was saved, because the joy I feel in my heart now." That was a defining moment for Paul, something needed to be done. Paul's friendships weren't affected much, but he did suffer a lot when it came to dating. He added, "I wear my heart on my sleeve, I have great friends that I've known for a long time, but when it came to dating I really suffered. I was one of the crazy people!"

Paul always felt trapped, but would never stop fighting to break free. His turning point was when he was introduced to The Secret Series about 4 years ago. Ever since then his life has been filled with so much love, and blessings. He is so happy and grateful for it. Paul said, "Even on the days I struggle, I know I am blessed, which is the truth of how I overcame it." He has many ways to maintain control; by giving gratitude before even stepping out of bed and giving thanks for his day ahead. He also has a journal where he writes 10 things every day that he is grateful for. Paul's fans help him every day with all their beautiful words and support. Not only that, but his family, friends and boyfriend are always there for him, including God, for always listening to him.

This experience has taught Paul to love everything about life and himself. He doesn't ever want to relive his past, but wouldn't want change anything because it made him who is today and he is happy. This is his advice for others struggling through similar situations:

"Never give up on yourself. Read some self-help, or uplifting stories. Also, here is my own quote I wrote for my poetry book, and I have it placed on the front page of my website: 'Remember to love yourself in every way, to be who you are, to become all you have ever dreamed of, no matter what stands, or stood in your way, to look in the mirror and say: this is who I am.'" ~Paul Travis

Paul would also love to share this:

"I want to send all my blessings and love to each one of you struggling. From the bottom of my heart, thank you, for joining me on my journey. Remember, we are not victims of emotional conflicts...we are human! Now, go walk that runway and show the world the beautiful star you are!"

You can continue to follow Paul on his journey by following him on twitter @paultravis_ or by checking out his website www.paultravis. net. It makes me happy to share this story of recovery with all of you. Paul is a strong and determined young man and with his ambition he can make it anywhere he wants.

STORY # 41

DEPRESSION & ANXIETY DISORDER

Alexandria was born in Toronto, Ontario, Canada and raised in Brampton, Ontario, Canada. She is originally Guyanese, from a small country in South America, located above Brazil and in-between Venezuela and Surinam. She enjoys writing, mostly poetry and short tragedies. She plays the flute, bass, violin, and harmonium. Alexandria is a fan of science fiction novels and prefers books from a male perspective. She is currently enjoying the Dragon Age video games and its fantasy world. Her favorite artists are Billy Talent and Lana Del Ray. Alexandria loves to cosplay; she designs and hand makes the costumes she wears to conventions from scratch. She danced for most of her childhood and is fond of archery and coaching it. Although she would like to be a youtuber with a respectable following, a model, or photographer, she understands that she will most likely be in school working towards her bachelor's or master's degree.

She does not see herself in a way five years from now. Alexandria's concept of time has changed throughout the years. She shares, "I lost any and all understanding I had about the concept of time for a period. There was no tomorrow or yesterday, in a second or a second ago, for a couple months."

Alexandria was clinically diagnosed with depression in 2012, and has been suffering since she was 15. Although undiagnosed, she also suffers from anxiety. She is unsure of what may have caused her mental disorders, but she thinks it may have been due to a buildup of various events. She said, "I went through a lot of things that a kid shouldn't really have to deal with. For example, I lost 5 family members including my grandfather whom I was very close too. A fight between friends, a love triangle, and school stress." Alexandria was prescribed medication for her depression by her doctor. She is a small girl, and her doctor made a mistake in increasing her meds in smaller intervals. She ended up feeling a terrible numb pain that landed her in the hospital. Ever since then she has stopped using her medication.

She had to deal with difficult symptoms, Alexandria added, "Well, I get very tired, I just want to sleep, with sleeping comes the nightmares in there too. I feel a loss of appetite, loss of interest in anything, lack of motivation, inability to pay attention to anything and the worst one, loss of memory." She felt emotionally numb with pain and lost her ability to take in her surroundings. She said, "I lost my ability to feel any spiritual presence or the comfort of moonlight. It was all taken from me." This affected her daily life in many ways. She became asocial, distancing herself from a lot of people. Not only that, but it took her a longer time to learn things. During university, Alexandria became lonely and during her second semester, her depression took over. She said, "I was unable to leave my room and if I did, it was for food (rarely) or to see my counselor (weekly), and I made sure my floor mates didn't see me. My entire semester went to hell, I couldn't pay attention in class and I couldn't stay engaged enough to do homework or assignments, when my anxiety kicked in I couldn't even go to class."

Alexandria had friend that lived on her floor who struggled with anxiety as well. Due to her anxiety, her friend would cut her forearm, leaving scars. Alexandria thought they were beautiful;

she saw it as her friend fighting a battle. So, to prove her own battle, Alexandria lightly scratched herself with a knife blade, never leaving a scar. Sadly, Alexandria tried to attempt suicide once, but thankfully failed. She took a 30 min bus ride to the city on a cold day, -30C. She tried to jump in front of a car, but her best friend's promise stopped her. Ever since then she hasn't actively looked for death, but she does still ask, "Can I die now?" or "Am I done yet?" Alexandria believes that what she feels isn't real.

This experience fortified some of her friendships, but she did cut off all of her friends from university. She mentioned, "I just became a burden I guess. I was a handful before depression, being loud and obnoxious earned me enemies. I'd become angry in the blink of an eye. I don't blame them though, if I had the option of leaving me, I'd do it too." This made her feel trapped, she said, "At a point I actually felt like I didn't want to get better because I lost so much of my personality and I felt it was all I had left. I felt like I shouldn't be happy, that I didn't deserve to be happy. It feels like your brain is turning black and you can't stop it. I can almost feel it behind my eyes. I was angry with God, if there is one, for forsaking me, mad at the devil for not easing the pain, overwhelmed by everything and yet, I didn't want help."

The turning point for Alexandria was one day during class, when she felt like she was about to break. She ran out and hid in the closest student office, asking for a safe place, one of the advisers called security and took her to the clinic. The clinic staff thought her university had enough resources so they did not treat her. After speaking to a woman who helped Alexandria look up the side effects of her medicine, they decided it was best to stop taking it. Thankfully, this decision helped Alexandria feel better. The strategies she used to control her mental disorder was to become active and busy. She started to eat healthy and tried to correct her sleep cycle. Alexandria talked to her school's counselor and got a dog to keep her company and grounded. But what helped

Alexandria the most was dropping out of school and going back home to coach archery at her high school. Helping out high school students in archery and giving them advice gave her a sense of belonging. She also surrounded herself with a great support team.

Alexandria feels like she did not learn any lesson from this ordeal, but she did realize that keeping in contact with close friends is important. Alexandria now knows she can help others with their struggles. This experience made her lose faith and the ability to feel the presence of God. This made Alexandria's childhood fantasies go away, she grew up and became very philosophical. She doesn't know what to do to keep herself from falling again, but she will try to continue to coach younger teens.

This is Alexandria's advice for others struggling through similar situations:

"To any one suffering from depression or anxiety, there probably isn't anything I can tell you that you haven't already heard. Talk to people, there are other people suffering too, pet a dog and if necessary, evaluate your friend group. When times get bad, get help. See a counselor or a psychologist or doctor. You don't have to go through it alone. Also keep a journal; it helps to see how far you've come. Don't feel discouraged if the first thing you try doesn't work. And please don't give up. There is someone who cares."

STORY # 42

DEPRESSION

Anonymous is from a small conservative town east of Los Angeles, California. Reading has always been a pleasure of hers. She is fond of The Bell Jar and Lolita. Anonymous listens to pretty much any type of music. Most of her favorite movies are cult classics. About three years ago she took up wing and blues dancing. For the majority of her life she has planned on attending veterinary school, however lately she has been reconsidering.

Anonymous was diagnosed in April 2014 with depression after being hospitalized for psychiatric reasons. She has been in and out of outpatient therapy since early 2013. She had to deal with horrible symptoms, anonymous said, "My depression mainly manifests as a lack of energy and motivation. When it worsens, it affects my concentration, focus, and causes me to be isolated." This has affected her life in various ways. She added, "It makes it difficult for me to maintain responsibilities such as school or work. I often stay in bed, sleep for ten or more hours, and skip meals. I am a victim to most cognitive distortions, most notably perfectionism, all-or-nothing thinking, future-tripping, and constantly comparing myself to others."

She has been suicidal since she was 14 years old and attempted it in September 2014 by overdose. Thankfully she has never struggled with self-harm. Not only that, but this has affected her relationships with others because anonymous feels ashamed socializing for isolating herself. This makes her feel utterly trapped. She stated, "My depression has greatly interfered with my college coursework three times in the past two years and I have virtually no idea how or when I am going to graduate. In addition, I do not foresee myself ever fully recovering from my illness, which gives me a bleak outlook on the rest of my life."

The turning point for anonymous to help control her mental disorder was to use cognitive behavioral therapy (CBT), Dialectical behavior therapy (DBT), journaling, mindfulness, and keeping track of her mood. She said, "I theoretically know exactly how to be mentally healthy, but it can be very difficult to implement the techniques into my life." Anonymous has surrounded herself with supportive people: her psychiatrist, mother, boyfriend, and good friends.

The lesson she has learned from this ordeal is that she spends too much time thinking about the past and the future. Her outlook on life has changed, anonymous shared, "When I was younger I assumed that as long as I did everything I was told to, graduate from college and get good grades, go to vet school, get a satisfying job, that life would be fine. Now I am much less focused on completing the young adult checklist."

This is her advice for others struggling with similar situations:

"I'd just like to say that it's okay to still be struggling. Other people may experience some of the things you do but everyone's struggle is different, and no one can know yours except you. Whether it takes five months or five years, I remind myself every day that it is worth it to keep trying."

Anonymous would also like to share:

"There are so many things I want to share about mental illness, but for brevity I will just mention two:

1) Love, protect, and do not ever judge survivors of suicide attempts. When the brain goes to that dark place it isn't functioning in a way you can predict. My mom is fully committed to helping and supporting me, but even she sometimes uses language that makes me uncomfortable, whether we're discussing me or others who struggle similarly.

2) Educate yourself and others about bipolar disorder. I love how much awareness is spreading about major depression, but I find that bipolar disorder is still grossly misunderstood, and those who suffer from it are among the most likely to commit suicide.

STORY # 43

DEPRESSION, ANXIETY DISORDER & EATING DISORDER

Anonymous loves music, especially punk-rock. She is fond of writing and composing music. Anonymous is learning to play guitar and piano, and is in choir at her school. She enjoys art and doodling a lot. Academics are also important to her. She loves science and is on the math team. Within five years she hopes to be in college studying physics. Anonymous suffers from depression, anxiety and EDNOS (caused by her emetophobia). She believes her depression could have been triggered by feeling left out.

She has been seeing a therapist occasionally after she started self-harming in 2014, but when things got bad she became suicidal, and ended up going to an intensive outpatient program at a hospital. Anonymous had to deal with terrible symptoms, she said, "I was extremely tired and depressed, and I didn't want to get out of bed. I was really fatigued and always short of breath. During anxiety attacks or uneasiness, I would feel flushed, shaky, and nauseous."

This affected her relationships with others because she didn't want to be around people. Anonymous stated, "Everyone got on my nerves, and I constantly fought with people- more specifically my mom and my boyfriend." This made her feel trapped and abnormal. She added, "I remember constantly thinking, I don't want to deal with this anymore." The turning point for her was when she started intensive therapy and taking medication. It made her feel like she was getting her disorders under control. Anonymous learned different things to control her anxiety, she learned coping skills. To focus on the present, she found ways to control her breathing. To cope with her depression, she became active and busy. To control her eating disorder, she'd remind herself to eat healthy.

Anonymous surrounded herself with supportive people, she said, "I had other people to give me the push I needed when I wanted to give up. My boyfriend helped me hang in there when the depression got rough and I wanted to kill myself, and my parents helped me overcome anxiety/EDNOS by helping me deal with my eating problems. My boyfriend also tells me he thinks I'm beautiful no matter what, so I'm not afraid of gaining weight." She has learned that she is in control of her emotions. This experience has changed her, she is now more herself and she has a better outlook on the future. To prevent this from happening again, she is attempting to change her lifestyle and simple routines that could be triggering her.

This is her advice for others struggling through similar situations:

"To anyone with emetophobia – you won't throw up if you eat food. Food is supposed to be in your body. Your body throws up to get rid of a harmful substance. You won't throw up by eating a healthy amount.

To anyone, remember you're in control of your emotions and your life and you'll feel better someday."

STORY # 44

BORDERLINE PERSONALITY DISORDER, POST-TRAUMATIC STRESS DISORDER, ANXIETY NOT OTHERWISE SPECIFIED, DEPERSONALIZATION & DEREALIZATION

Charlie is from Sacramento, CA and he is an artist and poet. His current goal is to recover as much as he possibly can from his mental illnesses and traumatic experiences. He said, "I hope in 5 years to be married to my beautiful, wonderful girlfriend." Charlie has been diagnosed with borderline personality disorder (BPD), post-traumatic stress disorder (PTSD), anxiety NOS, and depersonalization (DP) / derealisation (DR) disorder. His mental disorders have been caused by past traumas in his life. Charlie said, "My BPD and PTSD was caused by trauma from rape and repeated sexual assault. DP and DR disorder were caused by drug use and associated trauma during that time." He witnessed his brother get gunned down, jumped, and robbed by 5 other men. Not only that, but his house was robbed and he witnessed his brother OD.

The treatment Charlie received included cognitive behavioral therapy (CBT), dialectical behavior therapy (DBT), four months of rehab, and three months in a psychiatric treatment center. The

symptoms he dealt with were debilitating, he stated, "The symptoms I felt from BPD was black and white thinking, internal and
external rage, constant and ongoing emptiness, severe depression,
mood swings, severe self-injury, stormy, short relationships, and addiction with heroin and cocaine as my drugs of choice." His PTSD
gave him flashbacks and the anxiety made him scared to go out in
public. Charlie's DP and DR disorder consistently made him have
out of body experiences. He shared, "Feeling as if I am the only
person who is real in the world, my own voice not sounding like
mine, being unable to feel sensations (touch, sound, taste, etc.), in
a dream-like state, it feels like literal hell."

This affected his daily life because he could not function, it
was difficult for him to work every day. Charlie ended up skipping
school and failing all of his classes. He said, "I found myself lying
in bed for days on end doing nothing but drugs, drinking, and
self-injuring myself." Charlie hated himself and everything around
him. He felt that there was no hope and that he would be dead very
soon. By the age of 18 he attempted suicide twice. The first time
was when he was 15 years old, he tried overdosing on various pills
and alcohol. Charlie mentioned, "I started self-harming at the age
of 11, habitually and rituality continued for 7 years." Maintaining
his relationships with others was extremely difficult. His romantic relationships lasted 2 months at most, his friendships withered
away quickly and his family did not know how to handle him.

This made him feel alone, abandoned, hopeless, empty, desperate, and overall angry towards himself. Charlie said, "I thought I
was useless, that my existence on this earth did nothing, but upset
everything and everyone around me. I felt like a hurricane." The
turning point for Charlie was when he was 18 and he hit rock bottom. At this time he was a heavy drug user and self-harmed daily,
destroying his body. After his Charlie and his brother survived an
overdose on heroin and cocaine, he realized the life he was living
was not worth it. He said, "After the overdose, I took a very good

look at my life and did everything in my power to pick myself back up and start a new life for myself. I am still in the process of regaining everything I had lost through years and years of misery and mistakes." He realized before others could do anything, he had to help himself first.

The lesson he learned from this ordeal was to love himself. Charlie shared, "You really, really have to try. It's the most difficult thing I have ever done, but it will be worth it in the end." He sees the world very differently now. He added, "Reality hit me and there is no way I could un-see it. I've seen so much pain, misery, violence, and hurt to ever see the world through rose colored glasses." Charlie does not know what he can do to prevent himself from falling again, but he wishes he never picked up drugs when he was 14.

This is his advice for others struggling with similar situations:

"Please don't ever give up. No matter how hard it may be, no matter how empty, terrible, or destructive you may feel, please remember that you have so much more to offer to this world than you may think. Every day is a treacherous battle, and you must win. You must."

STORY # 45

BIPOLAR TYPE II, PANIC DISORDER & AGORAPHOBIA

Sarah is from Michigan, USA and loves to draw, paint, and write poetry; she is also very career driven. Sarah's said, "I would love to work at a design studio and be a full time graphic designer. A personal goal of mine would be to have one of my drawings or paintings hung in a gallery." She was diagnosed by a psychologist in 2012 with bipolar type II, panic disorder, and agoraphobia. Sarah still has bipolar disorder and will continue to have it for the rest of her life. She has been able to manage her panic disorder with proper medication. Even though she was diagnosed with agoraphobia, she doesn't believe she truly had it. Sarah stated, "I think with the combination of my severe depression episodes and panic attacks, they kept me from leaving my house and socializing." Sarah believes her mental disorders stem from genetics, because her birth mother was a bipolar schizophrenic. Sarah has different therapists, but has not been able to see them because she does not have the proper resources. Sarah also takes medication for her bipolar and panic disorder.

Sarah showed the symptoms way before she was diagnosed, according to her older brother. She said, "When I was younger I would lock myself away in my room. I didn't think much of it because I figured that's what most young teens do. When high school started I got 'sick' on the bus every morning. Sometimes I would even end up throwing up as soon as I got to school. I thought I was just sick and it wasn't until years later that I found out they were panic attacks." Sarah ended up skipping class and by junior year she barely went to school. She would sleep for 15 hours straight at times and didn't know she was depressed because it was never talked about in health class or with her family. She mentioned, "I became more educated by doing my own research. That's when I started to make sense of it and realized that I had a problem. I was embarrassed so I didn't talk to anyone about it. When mental illness was talked about among my family, they thought these people were faking it or it was an excuse to act out or these people were just plain crazy."

This affected her life. Her depressive episodes were basic, but her manic episodes made her irritable, angry, and she did not want anything to do with anyone. Sarah would come off as rude even though she didn't mean to be. Her family doesn't quite understand, so it causes some tension at times. This made her miss out on some important events. She said, "I remember one time my family and I went out to Big Boy's for dinner and I threw up right before we walked in the door from the anxiety. I sat in the bathroom the whole time my family was sitting there eating. I missed my niece's birthday party, trips up north with my grandparents, so many things and I don't think anyone really understands the toll it takes on your mind and self-worth."

At the age of 20 Sarah would scratch and pick her skin, it gradually progressed as this made her feel relief from bottled up guilt, anger, and frustration. She unscrewed the razor from a pencil sharpener and used that. Sarah ended up considering suicide and tried to overdose on pills. One time she cut deep in her hip to the point she saw fat, but a knock on the door from her mother made her stop. Thankfully she has been clean over a year from self-harming, but she still thinks of it during her depressive episodes. Sarah also stopped eating, to the point where she only weighed 104 pounds. When her family noticed, Sarah ate in front of them to cover up, but her mother had told her, "You're wasting away". That comment was a big wakeup call for Sarah. She is now at a healthy weight, but still feels guilty at times for eating.

This affected her relationship with others, her family thought she was just lazy and that the medication would fix her. This made Sarah feel angry. She added, "I remember once when I was doing the dishes and I was listening to music but I could still hear my grandmother and mother talking about me and my 'disorders'. My mom was standing up for me but my grandmother said that I wasn't even trying to be happy. That's when I lost it. I screamed that I try every day and just ran to my room and slammed the door." Her family understands her better now, but it is difficult to deal with the stigma. Sadly, Sarah's mother died in June 2013, this made her feel lost, but she has pushed herself to get better because she knows her mother would want her to be happy. In March 2014, Sarah stopped self-harming and went to Chicago to stay with her brother for two months. Sarah said, "That helped me more than any amount of therapy ever did. Having a change in environment and being around positive people just turned on a switch and I was actually happy."

The strategies she used to control her mental disorders were listening to music. Sarah mentioned, "I constantly had headphones in my ears. Listening mainly to Demi Lovato since we went through the same struggles and I relate to her music the most." She focused on schoolwork, painting, drawing, reading, and writing. Sarah used art to express herself and release any emotional buildup. She also found the right combination of medicine. Sarah's friends, Carlie and her mom, Jake, Kristina, and Kaitlin helped her by lending an ear in times of need.

This experience has changed Sarah, she said, "I am thankful for everything I've been through because I think it's made me stronger and more understanding. I put on a fake smile constantly and it made me realize that not every smile or laugh is genuine and you never know what that person is going through. So I make sure to smile and give compliments to strangers. It could brighten up their day."

This is her advice for others struggling with similar situations:

"Reach out. To your doctor, your parents, a friend, anyone. Talking helps and it could save your life. I know when it's bad, really at its worse, the last thing you want to do is talk. But I promise you, it's worth it."

STORY # 46

BIPOLAR DISORDER, ATTENTION DEFICIT HYPERACTIVITY DISORDER, MAJOR DEPRESSIVE DISORDER, GENERALIZED ANXIETY DISORDER, POST-TRAUMATIC STRESS DISORDER

Alyssa is from a small town in Alabama and she loves music! Alyssa enjoys yoga and dancing. She also tries to meditate as much as possible. Her goal is to finish a bachelor's degree in college. Alyssa said, "I plan on being a psychologist and opening up my own office." Currently Alyssa has Attention Deficit Hyperactivity Disorder (ADHD), major depressive disorder (MDD), generalized anxiety disorder (GAD), and post-traumatic stress disorder (PTSD). She used to also struggle with bipolar disorder.

Alyssa believes her disorders stem from her PTSD. She had a traumatic childhood where her father sexually abused her. Part of Alyssa's treatments was to receive medication that never addressed her underlying problem. It simply covered up her symptoms. She was also hospitalized before, but that did not help her because she was abused there as well. Alyssa also said, "I've had years and years of having a weekly counselor and it never seemed to help, but looking back I think it did or maybe it was just time that helped heal, I'm not sure."

She had to deal with terrible symptoms such as: losing her ability to focus due to her ADHD, her MDD made her feel empty, lonely, hopeless, and suicidal. Alyssa also lost her appetite and lacked sleep. Her anxiety attacks had her hyperventilating which led Alyssa to throw up sometimes. She stated, "My PTSD give me vivid, terrifying nightmares every night and extreme paranoia in any situation." When Alyssa had bipolar disorder the main symptom was instant mood switches, she could be crying out of sadness one second then crying out of laughter the next.

The combination of all of these disorders affect her greatly. She ran to drug abuse and self-injury for outlets. There were days she couldn't get out of bed. It's hard for Alyssa to keep up with her hygiene and she pushes everyone she loves away. She adde, "I would always tell myself no one would care if I were to die, which I now know from experience that to be untrue." To add onto that, Alyssa also said, "I attempted suicide twice. Once when I was 12 and again at 16. When I was 12 it was with alcohol and at 16 was with aspirin. I barely made it out alive both times."

Not only has this affected her daily life, but it has also affected her relationships with others. Alyssa does not trust men, no matter how nice they are or how long she has known them. She shared, "I have this overprotective feeling towards children now because I've learned how easy it is for people to take advantage of them. I'm sex repulsed at the moment, but I used to be almost a sex addict when I was younger. I used to do anything for attention from men because I was subconsciously trying to fill the void for a normal father figure in my life." Not only that, but it was hard for Alyssa to maintain friendships because people did not understand the reasoning behind her behavior. This made her feel very lonely.

The turning point for Alyssa was when she realized her dreams weren't really dreams, but in fact scenes from her childhood that her brain released during sleep. This helped her answer a lot of questions about what exactly her father did to her. She said, "Once I figured that out, I came to peace with it and then it made me stronger." Alyssa also said, "I am now hopeful and have a much more positive outlook on everything which I believe will get me far in life despite my current disorders." Alyssa has found methods that work to calm her down in times of stress and when symptoms from her disorders come about. For her anxiety, she uses simple breathing techniques and for her depression she reaches out to someone who will help. When she has terrible dreams, she reminds herself the past is the past. She controls her ADHD with medication and to manage her disorders she takes hot baths, meditates, volunteers, and does yoga.

Thankfully Alyssa received helped from her mother, she said, "She didn't always know the right things to say, but she did always show that she cared by asking if I wanted something to eat or even a hug at times." The lesson she learned from this ordeal is that you can chose to not let a bad situation define you. Alyssa shared, "It changed me for sure, but in the best kind of way. As corny as it sounds I'm a lot more proactive in traumatic situations, I'm emotionally stronger, and most of all I have undying empathy for those who have gone through any of what I've had to."

This is her advice for others struggling through similar situations:

"Reach out and DO NOT give up. It's beyond hard I know, but NOTHING would be the same if you didn't exist. I remember one time I was put on hold for 2 hours on a suicide hotline until I finally hung up and that's going to happen sometimes. When your best friend isn't going to answer the phone that's when you have to physically get up and go walk around the world until you find someone and they might not care even then, but reaching out like that makes you realize more than you'd think. It really calms the emotions and sometimes forces you to think logically which is what we all need in a crisis. Anyway, just remember you are here for a damn reason and you got to figure that reason out before you leave.

Pets are very helpful too. I highly suggest for anyone with a disorder to get a pet because remember they don't judge or discriminate."

STORY # 47

MAJOR DEPRESSIVE DISORDER & EATING DISORDER

Anonymous is from Germany and she loves to read Stephen King books. She used to enjoy horseback riding, Taekwondo, Gymnastics, and Volleyball. Her goal in life is to become stronger. Anonymous said, "I learned that taking it a day at a time is personally less stressful. But in 5 years I would love to be emotionally and financially stable and independent." She has been struggling with clinical depression for eight years now and an eating disorder (ED) for four years. She doesn't know what caused her depression, but she shares, "My ED was caused due to the depression; I felt if I changed the way I ate I had some form of control over my life, I was of course very wrong."

Anonymous received treatment in 2011, she added, "Since then I have seen around 10 to 12 psychiatrists, therapists, psychoanalysts, counselors, taken a lot of medications, and had two hospital admissions." At the beginning she felt sadness, nothing made her happy anymore, and she became isolated and miserable for no apparent reason. Anonymous began to cut in order to ease the emotional pain and it was difficult for her to stay motivated, she mentioned, "There were days where I was unable to get out of bed because it just seemed impossible, I saw no point in doing anything because I was worth nothing." So, she began to starve herself in 2011, anonymous said, "I felt like if I lost weight everything would get better even though I knew it wouldn't really, it was just another form of self-harm, another way to kill oneself, after restricting for 4 months I started purging, eating away the pain and getting rid of it afterwards. It was a vicious cycle I saw no end to."

This mainly affected her relationship with her parents because they suffered too. Her parents were in constant tears and there were fights all the time. Anonymous had to drop out of school for a semester and lost friends. She shared, "I started cutting more, causing permanent scars. I lost more weight, my hair started falling out, I was cold all the time, and I fainted several times a day. My body was failing and so was my mind." She considered attempting suicide more times than she could count.

Anonymous now takes one day at a time. She realized a bad day is unavoidable; but a bad life is. She is no longer on medication and has learned that whatever she is feeling will pass. Anonymous said, "I learned that talking about it helps ease the pain a bit and that hurting myself only makes it worse." She doesn't take things for granted anymore and is more compassionate towards others.

This is anonymous' advice for others struggling with similar situations:

"Talk to others, seek help, this is not the end, having self-worth doesn't make you a bad person, feeling depressed or suicidal doesn't make you less of a person. Everyone has their own demons to deal with. Depression can feel like a safe haven that slowly turns into a prison cell. But you're strong and you can overcome this if you choose to. It's a choice only you can make. In the end it's a war where anyone can prove to be a hero."

STORY # 48

POST-TRAUMATIC STRESS DISORDER, TRICHOTILLOMANIA & ANXIETY DISORDER

Anonymous is from Minnesota and she enjoys artistic hobbies such as drawing, painting, sewing, embroidery, jewelry making, and knitting. She also loves reading most books, especially science fiction of the snarky British variety. Anonymous is a typical crazy cat lady and absolutely adores her two fur babies. She is fond of watching TV shows such as Star Trek, Doctor Who, and Warehouse 13. She is fascinated by things that are conventionally considered a little creepy or macabre and her favorite books are Dracula and Frankenstein. Anonymous is aiming to become successful, she said, "I hope to have my first home with my husband within the next year or so. I am also hoping to be back in school and studying to become a forensic pathology assistant." She would love to have enough money to cover her bills with a little left over.

Anonymous was recently diagnosed by her therapist with post-traumatic stress disorder (PTSD), trichotillomania, and generalized anxiety disorder (GAD); although she suspects she has had these mental disorders for most of her life. At the current moment she is receiving therapy and establishing coping techniques. It is hard for anonymous to pinpoint what caused her disorders, she shared, "I am genetically predisposed towards anxiety and depression. I have multiple family members to have attempted/considered suicide. I have also been through significant traumas in my life which include: deaths of loved ones and witnessing/being party to the suicide attempts of close friends and relatives. I also grew up in a verbally abusive household and my father was an alcoholic."

Anonymous has dealt with various symptoms. Her GAD makes her shaky and sweaty, with an increased heartbeat. She becomes confused and is unable to verbally articulate sentences. Her trichotillomania provokes anonymous to pull hairs from her pubic area with tweezers often causing scars or scabs. She said, "I do this to help myself relax and deal with my emotions from the day. I am also highly perfectionistic, so I literally worry about making the area look "perfect." I obsess over pulling out any irregular looking hairs or smoothing out any bumps/ blemishes." Her PTSD has affected her sleep, constantly giving her nightmares. She has become sensitive to noise and is startled very easily. Anonymous stated, "If I am not paying attention and someone gets physically close to me without me noticing I tend to become very startled and can lash out. I am very suspicious of people when I am in public. I always want to know where people are and what they are doing. Everyone is a possible threat to me." Because of this anonymous can become dissociated and extremely fatigued.

This has affected her daily life, she mentioned, "I am often tired and struggle to deal with the stress and demands of daily life. Because of this I can tend to over caffeinate, which in turn can induce greater anxiety. I often have feelings of shame and worthlessness. I often think that my efforts are not "good enough" or sufficient and tend to be very hard on myself." Not only that, but during her teen years anonymous became suicidal, thankfully she never devised a plan, but she did daydream a lot about it. She did not self-harm, but she did have some destructive tendencies, such as depriving herself of a meal or the warmth that her body needed.

Since then she has been able to let go of those tendencies and is no longer suicidal.

Her relationships with others became affected, she said, "I was very cold and numb to everyone." Thankfully she is close to her mother and husband. They both have been supportive to her by providing love and affection. The turning point for anonymous was realizing she wasn't alone with her struggles. She also shared, "Finding similarities with other people has been a huge deal, through art, through faith, through fandoms, I have founds some of the "others" like myself." Not only that, but her therapist has also been a great helper.

The strategies she uses to maintain control is work on her mental disorders and learn coping techniques. Anonymous said, "I am growing as a human every day. I am learning to better cope through these issues by learning better self-care, grounding techniques, and coping skills. Quiet time with my husband or fur babies is also a huge coping mechanism for me." She also receives help along the way and allows herself to take a break. The lesson she learned from this ordeal is that she needs to be kind to herself, she stated, "Others, no matter how good their intentions, will let me down. I have to get better for myself and not for anyone else." This experience has changed her outlook in life, she said, "Sometimes I feel my life has been shaped by the traumas I have experienced. Each time I have experienced something traumatic it has sent shockwaves through my life, changing me. I am content with my changes. I have evolved, adapted, grown in strength. By learning what an earthquake can destroy I have learnt to build stronger foundations."

This is her suggestions for others struggling through similar situations:

"Be kind to yourself, body, and mind. They are truly the only possessions you have in this world and they will carry you through it. They will break and they will scar, but feel the strength of your heart hammering inside your chest and know that it hasn't failed you yet."

STORY # 49

ATTENTION DEFICIT HYPERACTIVITY DISORDER, ANXIETY DISORDER & DEPRESSION

Sharon is from Singapore and she loves to cook, read, and cycle. After being diagnosed, Sharon realized she wants to help others, she said, "I met others like me through workshops and therapy, I realized I really wanted to become a psychotherapist and help others that can relate to my experiences." She hopes in 5 years when she's 21 to be in university studying psychology. Sharon has Attention Deficit Hyperactivity Disorder (ADHD), generalized anxiety disorder (GAD) and depression. She believes her ADHD is due to genetics and that her GAD and depression is due to her family. She said, "My parents are strict and scolded me whenever I did something wrong, even over small things. For example, if I accidently spilled water they would call me stupid in Mandarin or something. So, I grew up following this sort of "no mistake rule" thus everything and every situation made me nervous." Sharon became so depressed she became dependent, she shared, "I felt so worthless and helpless, I began clinging on to my best friend more and more, finally she felt that I was too annoying and clingy and she broke the friendship off."

Sharon was diagnosed by a psychiatrist and was referred to a therapist, she currently receives psychotherapy. Her psychiatrist tried to find the right medication for Sharon, but none of the medicines worked and to her surprise, she found out that medicines did not work for any of her family members that have ADHD. Not only that, but Sharon had to deal with numerous symptoms. The ADHD made her lack focus, she was easily distracted and fidgeted excessively. Her GAD provoked panic attacks because she was always anxious. Sharon also suffered from headaches, muscle aches and nausea. The depression made her feel worthlessness and hopelessness. She excessively slept or had terrible insomnia. Sharon felt fatigued and lost interest in everything.

This affected her daily life, she said:

> "It became tiring to do anything, everything felt like it took too much effort. I would come home from school and just sit on the floor for an hour just to try and gather energy to go take a shower. In the shower, I would just sit and let the warm water spray on me as I try to fight off this extreme feeling of loneliness and despair. After an hour in the shower, I would finally come out only to stare at my clothes and think what an awful lot of effort it takes to wear them. After putting on the clothes, I would just lay in bed like a ragdoll and think of why my friend left me."

She would constantly be asking when her misery will end and thinking about how she was going to survive the next day. School was torturous for Sharon. She stated, "I was scolded in every class because I didn't do any homework. I had to act all happy and energetic in front of my classmates, during recess I would try to take a half hour nap because I was so drained." This affected her daily life, Sharon ended up isolating herself because acting like she was fine took too much energy, but being alone was also difficult for her. Sharon considered suicide and planned scenarios in her head, but she worried how this would affect her family. She said, "Most of the time I would think of hanging myself in school because I don't want my family living in the same house where I died. Plus, I detested school and a hanging girl would be a very ghastly image which was what I wanted."

This affected her relationships with others because Sharon convinced herself that people did not care, when deep down all she wanted was to scream for help. This made her feel trapped and confused because she couldn't grasp how depression and anxiety worked. She mentioned, "I couldn't comprehend why I felt that way. How can I just lose interest and feel so numb and so empty even when doing the things I love?" Sharon's first step to recovery was attending a workshop where she met others struggling with similar illnesses. This taught her that she was not alone and motivated Sharon to get better.

The strategy she used to help control her mental disorders was to have a routine. She said, "I wanted to give up and crawl back into bed to hide, but I forced myself and as the days passed, doing daily activities became easier and more manageable. When I was taking these baby steps towards recovery, positive thinking and exercising gratitude also became easier. I loaded my cork-board with all sorts of positive affirmations although on bad days they were quite hard to believe."

The road to recovery was not easy because a lot of Sharon's peers were insensitive. Her desk mate is Catholic and told her that she was an ungrateful brat and she will go to hell if she committed suicide. Not only that, but her classmates made fun of her illnesses saying things like "Oh gosh I need to make my desk tidy, I'm so OCD" or "Did depression and therapy make you this way? Hahaha" Thankfully, Sharon's immediate family tried to be understanding and nicer. This ordeal taught her to accept and love herself. She now has a positive outlook in life and tries to squeeze out every bit of happiness in a situation.

This is her advice for others struggling through similar situations:

"Don't ever feel ashamed of your mental illness. Sometimes you can't control how you feel, but this doesn't mean you're worth any less than anyone else. You're allowed to feel sad and you're allowed to feel happy. You are worthy of love and a great life. Trust me there really is hope so don't give up on yourself even though the situation is bad. You will grow, you will find the right people, you will learn to love and accept yourself. One day things will start to fall into place, but right now, all you have is the present moment so enjoy it. Always practice self-care and don't be afraid to take the first step towards recovery or seek help."

STORY # 50

AUTISM, ATTENTION DEFICIT HYPERACTIVITY DISORDER & SOCIAL ANXIETY DISORDER

Marjolein van Deurzen is from the Netherlands and she is currently a neuropsychology student. She enjoys theatre, watching plays and musicals, and loves acting. Not only that, but she loves art, history, Disney films, and cooking. Her goal is to be in a stable relationship and to mean something to other people. Marjolein was born with autism and ADHD, but her social anxiety is result of the two. She said, "I always felt very 'different' and was teased a lot by other children. I felt very inferior and became obsessed with the possibility that I would 'embarrass' myself in some way." Marjolein received different types of therapies as a child, but they didn't work for her.

Life has been difficult for her, Marjolein shared, "I often describe it as feeling as if I live in a world that is way too fast and way too loud for me. My brain processes information in a less efficient way and therefore things often seem to be more overwhelming than it would feel for a neuro-typical person." She felt uncomfortable with surprises or unexpected situations. Her ADHD made her talk a lot and her social anxiety constantly made her afraid to annoy others. Marjolein stated, "Furthermore, I have difficulties structuring my life, while I do need a lot of structure. I tend to forget things, lose them, or leave them. I generally feel like life slips through my fingers all the time."

This affects her daily life in many ways. Marjolein can feel very tired and irritable after a normal day of work, because a lot of stimuli is exhausting for her. She balances this out by staying at home for a while to recover. Marjolein becomes angry if she loses things that have sentimental value to her and it feels beyond her control. She mentioned, "I come up with lots of strategies not to lose or forget things, but as soon as something unexpected happens I'm out of my routine and I lose things. For example, I forgot my suitcase on the train a couple of times, mostly on days when it was either very crowded or there was an unexpected delay or something that caused distraction."

Marjolein doesn't feel uncomfortable telling people she has ADHD, but with telling others she has autism is a different story. She said, "People with autism are always portrayed in the media as loners with very little social investment who have one specific interest that they prefer to spend all day doing. I have always been an extremely outgoing person and I feel like people will no longer approach me, because they think I prefer to be left alone."

Marjolein's social anxiety makes her uncomfortable during social interactions. She prefers others to make the first move that way she knows she isn't bothering people. She has never received support from others with autism because they don't understand her. Marjolein explains, "I was also always a little bit of a drama queen because of that. In media, people with autism always come across as a bit 'robotic', they don't seem to express many emotions or don't know how to express them. I always wanted to show emotions to others. Crying felt so much better when others could see it, because it was the ultimate proof to the world that I too have feelings. See, I'm normal, I have feelings!"

When things felt painful or hard, she escaped the situation by fantasizing about a possible future in which everything was perfect. Thankfully, Marjolein has supportive parents, they have always tried to understand her. However, Marjolein always felt like she was a big burden to them. She said, "I have two brothers who are both neuro-typical and I have always feared that my parents secretly loved my brothers more than me and that they would even wish that I were never born."

Marjolein has never been in a romantic relationship making her feel insecure. She shared, "I cannot help feeling that men simply don't want me because there are so many 'normal' women out there. Why would they want to date a failure like me if they have the option of having a normal girlfriend? I feel like nobody can love me by choice."

The turning point for Marjolein was when she went to college. She never had any friends before that and was always bullied at different schools. In college however, everything changed. Everybody was extremely open-minded and accepting towards Marjolein. She said, "I felt more 'normal' than ever, without having to change anything about myself. All I had to do was be myself and enjoying what I loved to do. I discovered I had talents; for example, stage acting. Before that I thought I was basically a failure at everything. I am still learning a lot, but I think that this has been a very crucial point that made me overcome most of my social anxiety issues. I find myself less obsessed with what others might be thinking about me and the fear of humiliating myself. It is still there, but it is not haunting me as much as it used to. Simply surrounding myself with more supportive friends and learning to accept my condition makes me feel a lot better."

Since autism and ADHD isn't something Marjolein can overcome, she is using her mental illnesses as an advantage by trying become a role model for other people with autism, especially young women. She said, "Self-esteem issues in people with autism are very much taken for granted, and that was the primary thing I struggled with." Another experience that motivated Marjolein was personal tutor she once had. Her tutor asked what she wanted to do after college. After learning that Marjolein wanted to become a psychologist specialized in autism, her tutor told her that she could not become one because autistic people lack empathy. Marjolein shared, "I always considered myself very empathetic but she just laughed at me and told me I was daydreaming too much. I wrote essays for medical sociology about this experience and about the dangers of this kind of stigmatization and generalization. Now, next to providing support for people who are in the same situation, I also want to do something about stigmatization of people with autism. Perhaps even improve diagnostics."

The strategies she used to control her mental disorders was to surround herself with people she felt comfortable with. Marjolein uses different methods to help her stay focused. For example, she uses alarms on her phone to remind her of things she might otherwise forget.

The lesson she has learned from friends is to be less judgemental and demanding towards herself. Marjolein also learned that there are other perspectives and solutions to a difficult situation that need to be taken into account. She is now more relaxed and comfortable in her own skin.

This is her advice for others struggling with similar mental conditions:

"Embrace your individuality and try not to focus too much on the disorder itself. Especially if you were diagnosed at a young age, and having seen many clinicians it may seem like the disorder is everything. But it does not define you! You are a person, an individual and whatever is in the books does not all have to apply to you. Try to figure out what you like and what you want from life, as you and not as the person with the disorder. Also, there is nothing wrong with you. There will always be people who accept you for who you are, even if you haven't met them yet. Just try to do what you love, and you'll meet the right people on the way."

Marjolein would also like to share this:

"Documentaries and lots of media around autism primarily focuses on the family of these children and never on the feelings of these children themselves. I think this mainly has to do with the fact that most people with autism aren't very strong verbally and thus it's very hard for them to express their feelings."

STORY # 51

POST-TRAUMATIC STRESS DISORDER & BODY DYSMORPHIA DISORDER

Nikuya is from the state of Kentucky. Her favorite pastime is listening to and enjoying music, though she also is fond of makeup and art. Nikuya's current goal is to graduate with a bachelor's degree from the university she attends. Nikuya is excited at the prospect of being a first-generation college graduate. Though she looks forward to putting her degree to good use after graduation, she would love to take a year to travel the world before settling down. Nikuya was diagnosed with, and suffers from, depression, general anxiety disorder (GAD), post-traumatic stress disorder (PTSD), and body dysmorphia disorder. She believes the roots of her mental illnesses are related to familial and societal issues.

Nikuya previously received psychotherapy to treat her mental illness, but her current treatment is two psychotropic medications. Nikuya has dealt with various symptoms, including, but not limited to: feeling intense fear, self-hatred, and extreme sadness. She describes the fear as "So debilitating I couldn't breathe" and says her "Entire body would shiver like I was cold. I could be under three covers and [still] feel like I'm freezing." The depression kept Nikuya locked in and isolated her from her family and peers. Nikuya concedes she was without motivation and only "Wanted to sleep all the time." She says this felt like "hell," and reports "The anxiety kept me going, with the fear of failure if I didn't." Nikuya had a difficult time remaining calm due to her PTSD, and she easily became agitated when an argument with family or close friends arose.

This affected Nikuya's daily life tremendously. She began to lose interest in high school, and her studies were the first to be affected. Soon Nikuya began to distance herself from her friends and had difficulty making new ones. She also remained in an abusive relationship because she felt like it provided her much needed structure. Nikuya says her abusive partner "was controlling," but that she allowed it to continue Bbecause my self-esteem was so low I didn't feel like getting out of it." Nikuya admits she has considered suicide before, but denies ever attempting it. She also admits to self-harm, but is proud to have now gone more than six months without harming herself.

Nikuya's mental illnesses and failing relationships made her feel trapped, sad, and desperate for someone to understand what she was experiencing, though she concedes that she was not willing to explain her situation to anyone at the time. Nikuya struggled to maintain control. Her breaking point arrived in her freshman year of high school when she began to research painless methods of suicide. She also searched for ways to ensure that she was alone and would not be found until the suicide was complete. Thankfully, Nikuya discovered that she could use grounding techniques to control her mental disorders. Nikuya says she continues to use YouTube "Because there's meditative videos [that] calm [me] down." Nikuya credits her mother and grandparents in her recovery because they placed her in therapy and were supportive of it. She also is thankful for her current boyfriend stating him as supportive, as well as her supportive brother and sister who "love me too much to see me hurt myself any more than I already have."

Nikuya learned to not let her mental illnesses control her actions and reactions. She realized she cannot let herself be defined by her mental illness. This has changed Nikuya's outlook on life. She says, "I can look at life differently than others, and I've been told I'm an "old soul". This experience aged me, mentally and some aspects physically, and it changed my outlook on life because I am now trying to be as positive as I can [be], instead of letting all the negativity control how I live my life."

This is her advice for other's struggling with similar situations:

"Don't believe what your anxiety tells you all the time because sometimes fear isn't real, it isn't relevant, and everything really is okay. There is a light at the end of the tunnel for everyone, and just because I found mine and still struggle doesn't mean I haven't won, because I have. You will win too, you will find your light, and can dance in the sun when you get there, and it isn't far away. You can do it and never, ever give in. You are loved and cared for.

STORY # 52

DEPRESSION & ANXIETY DISORDER

Johanna is a teenager from Charlottesville, Virginia. She is a self-proclaimed nerd and identifies as a pansexual. Johanna is a writer and is an INFJ on the Myers-Briggs Type Indicator personality test. If she were a character in the infamous Harry Potter series, she asserts she would be a member of the Ravenclaw house. Johanna's goals include writing books, going to college, and to completely recover from her mental illnesses. Johanna has been diagnosed with depression and anxiety, and is currently receiving psychotherapy. The root of her mental illnesses, Johanna contends, is an inner battle between her sexuality and Christian beliefs. She also reports a genetic link as both of her parents have depression, though not as severe as the depression Johanna experiences. Johanna has suffered debilitating symptoms, such as self-hatred, panic attacks, lack of motivation, and exhaustion.

Johanna's negative thoughts and behaviors have had a tremendous effect on her life. She admits she has had a lot of suicidal thoughts for about 2 years. Sadly, Johanna attempted suicide last February and has self-harmed since the 6th grade. She reports that her symptoms have "Gotten better, though I still have relapses every now and then." Johanna's relationships with others have also been affected by her mental illnesses. Being an introvert, as indicated by the N in INFJ, Johanna does not naturally spend much time with other people. She says that having depression and anxiety added to her introversion causing further isolation, though these disorders did bring her closer to a few individuals.

Johanna said "I felt alone, sad, and trapped" by her mental illnesses. Johanna reached a turning point when she began to open herself up toward others, especially in regards to her sexuality. She says, "The first person I came out to was completely supportive and really helped me through a lot of stuff." The strategies Johanna uses to control her mental disorders include journaling, talking about her issues, reading, and self-care. The lesson Johanna learned from this ordeal is that she is worthy of life and happiness. She says that religion, sexuality, gender, race, age, or other individual or cultural factors are irrelevant in regards to life and happiness. Johanna contests that she can now "get through anything because I am strong." She has a positive outlook on life, loves herself, and is finally comfortable in her own skin. Johanna gives herself alone time and keeps her friends close to keep her from falling back in to her previous negative thoughts and behaviors.

This is her advice for others struggling with similar mental disorders:

"Talk to people. I can't stress this enough. Have a way to express yourself: painting, poetry, social media, novels, music, a blog; anything. Put yourself out there. Take care of yourself. Don't do anything you'll regret later. Look in the mirror twice a day and say: 'I love you.' Pet cats. Watch funny YouTube videos. Go for long walks. Go out to eat at shitty restaurants. Do whatever the F you want to do to make yourself happy. Don't hurt other people; you'll regret it. It's okay to find refuge in a band, or a book, or a movie, or a TV show, or a celebrity; don't be ashamed if someone you've never met or someone fictional saved your life. I'm in the same boat, bro. And I love you <3."

STORY # 53

DEPRESSION, PANIC DISORDER & GENERALIZED ANXIETY DISORDER

Sarah is a Christian from a small town in Alaska where she enjoys many hobbies. She says, "I love reading, running, and photography. I ride horses and go running with my dog in the summer, and I go snow-machining in the winter. I like going hunting (for need, not for sport). I love coffee and tea, and one of my favorite things is to go to beach bonfires with friends." Sarah's current goal is to graduate from college with a wildlife biology degree, and to no longer relapse in to self-harm.

Sarah has been diagnosed with depression, panic disorder, and multiple anxiety disorders. She has also struggled with self-harm and eating disorders. Thankfully, Sarah has made much improvement. She has not had a panic attack in months, and her depressive episodes does not occur as often. Even though Sarah is still struggling with her social anxiety, she has the ability to do many things on her own that she was unable to do before. Sarah is also proud to have gone five months with no self-harm, and notes only four instances of self-harm in the past two years. She believes her disorders are genetically predisposed from both parents, as well as from the abuse of her two ex-boyfriends. Sarah reports she was "emotionally, psychologically, and physically abused by an ex-boy-friend and another guy which led into the anxiety. They both were manipulative and played mind games, making me do things I actually didn't want to do with them physically." Sarah's eating disorder, she reports, stems from being made fun of by people at school and family members making note of her weight, even though her weight was never far from normal for her age.

Prior to Sarah starting psychotherapy, her mother took her to a nurse when she was 15 years old to address her panic attacks, and she was prescribed Zoloft. At the age of 17, Sarah began attending therapy and decided to stop taking the medication. Sarah is proud to report that she recently stopped therapy due to major improvement and her therapist agreed to continue seeing her only on an 'as-needed' basis.

These are Sarah's description of the symptoms she felt:

Depression: "I felt extremely sad or numb. I didn't care about anything, and I felt unable to physically move. I would sit or lie on my bed and just stare at stuff for hours, or I'd sit and cry uncontrollably for absolutely no reason. I was convinced no one liked me or cared. I mostly was an insomniac, but every now and then I'd sleep for 12 or more hours."

Panic Attack: "Hot and cold flashes, really sweaty, felt like a huge weight was on my chest and I couldn't breathe, hyperventilating, light headed, intense need to escape and run, uncontrollable crying, my body would shake, and the room would spin. My thoughts would go at super-speed about everything going wrong and questioning everything-'Why did I do this or that? Why did I put myself into this situation? This is so stupid! Why am I overreacting? What if they notice? What if they make fun of you?'"

Anxiety disorders: "Constant worry that I would mess something up. I was extremely self-conscious of how I looked. I felt like I looked fat and gross all the time, and it made me very nervous whenever anyone acknowledged my presence. My thoughts would get uncontrollable and mock me."

Eating disorder: "I could never think of myself as skinny enough. Fortunately, I never went to the degree many do, but I still hated what I looked like. I would hide in large clothes and avoided mirrors because every time I saw one I couldn't help but think "I'm so fat, what's wrong with me?," but then I couldn't stop looking in mirrors and finding all my flaws."

All these symptoms affected Sarah's daily life to the extent that she self-harmed for five years and attempted suicide once, but, luckily, she made herself throw up before it was too late. In the moment Sarah thought, "I couldn't leave my dog and horses, or do that to my family because I didn't want them thinking that I killed myself because of them. I also was terrified of killing myself because I didn't know what would happen after."

Even though Sarah is an introvert, she became more distant from her friends. Some of her friends noticed her isolation and made sure she kept in touch. Sarah remains friends with those who helped her to this day. Sarah's relationship with her parents became affected because she kept crafting excuses not to leave the house. Eventually, Sarah told her parents about her social anxiety, but they were immediately dismissive of the idea. Her parent's refusal to see the underlying mental illness caused a rift to form in their relationship. This made Sarah feel sad and trapped. She shared, "I felt like I had no control over anything, and like everything I tried doing was just going to end up going wrong, and there wasn't any use in trying to do anything."

After cutting herself up to 75 times per day and not eating adequately, Sarah decided to see a therapist for not being able to give a speech in her communication class. Her therapist taught her coping techniques. Sarah kept a record of her triggers, learned to recognize them, and prepared herself. She would talk back to her thoughts as a way of controlling them, and instead of self-harming she would call her boyfriend, read the bible, pray, go running, or cuddle with her dog. Sarah and her therapist slowly expanded her comfort zone, and now Sarah can go to different places. Others helped Sarah by talking through a situation and encouraged her to continue with therapy.

The lesson Sarah learned is that God will bring her peace, and that opening yourself to others will help. Her outlook has also changed; Sarah is positive, self-confident and is careful how she treats others. This is Sarah's advice for anyone struggling with mental illness:

"WHAT YOU'RE GOING THROUGH IS VALID! Look for someone you know you can trust and tell them what's going on. Please, please, please don't look to self-harm as a way of relief. It only makes things worse. I know not everyone thinks therapists are any good- but please at least try them for three or four sessions before quitting on them. There's always ways to get help, and if you're going through a mental illness, it isn't something to brush off and hope it gets better, or self-diagnose. And even if you do get put on meds, it's always your choice about them, they do help if you let them, and usually you're not on them for life. It's to level you out so you can work on how to cope without them. They're like physical therapists- retraining your brain how it should work."

STORY # 54

DEPRESSION

Anonymous is from Italy and enjoys rowing and cooking. She is still figuring out what her goals are. Anonymous is thinking about possibly being a consultant or editor. She has depression, but thankfully it has improved. She went to her university's counselling services for a few months to receive treatment. She never took medications; all she needed was to talk about what happened and her feelings.

Anonymous had to deal with tiring symptoms. She said, "I was feeling incredibly blue all the time. I was afraid of people; even walking down the street was difficult. I couldn't bear the eyes of people." This affected her daily life because she could not go out of her room unless it was strictly necessary. She avoided confrontation, and hid away from life. Anonymous did consider suicide, but fortunately, she never attempted it. Her relationship with others also became affected. Anonymous said, "I felt like no-one was understanding me. It was quite hard to listen to everyone else's problems while nobody noticed that I was so sad." This made her feel miserable and lonely, and she eventually directed anger towards her family as a potential cause of her mental illness.

The turning point for anonymous to seek mental health services was after a long night in which she cried for hours on end. She then sought help with a therapist at her university. She explained, "I'm so grateful to the university for making this service free and easily accessible." Her therapist assisted by not judging her and asking insightful questions. She shared, "It was such a relief to finally let all that sadness out!" The lesson she learned from this ordeal is that she is enough. Anonymous' outlook on life also changed. She learned to love herself and allowed herself to be loved. Anonymous has since achieved academic success. She says, "Now I know I'm worth something and that I'm strong. I know things are not going to be perfect all the time – life is complicated – but I know how to face the problems, and when to seek help." She has stopped any behaviors that make her sad and tries to stay positive. When she feels hopeless, she watches the TED talk by Brene Brown on vulnerability to remind herself that she is worth something.

STORY # 55

MAJOR DEPRESSIVE DISORDER

Andie resides in the Lone Star State, also known as Texas. Her current goal is to progress in her academic studies and refrain from dropping out of classes, which she has done in the past. She reports, "This will be my second semester in school, so I'm hoping that I can complete my classes this time. I wasn't attending my classes last semester because I would feel uneasy and anxious while being there, so I ended up dropping out halfway through the semester." In five years, she sees herself receiving a Bachelor of Arts in Psychology degree. Andie wants to apply to graduate school and get a Master's in Clinical Psychology.

In January 2013, at the age of 14, Andie was diagnosed with major depressive disorder by a psychiatrist after a suicide attempt. Later that year, Andie was experiencing depression with psychotic features, but the psychotic features resolved by the end of the year. Andie still reports struggling with depression, but says that she is improving. She locates the roots of her depression within a breakup. Andie loved her boyfriend and considered him to be her best friend. That is until, Andie says, "He cheated on me, lied to me, and argued with me every day. When he cheated on me with a girl, I wanted to be her... I skipped meals, threw up my food, slit my wrists, dressed differently, etc. I tried everything to be good enough for him." Sadly, that girl demonized everyone against Andie to the point that she received anonymous messages on Tumblr telling her how pathetic she was for trying to get her ex-boyfriend back. Andie also received death threats.

Andie was sent to a mental hospital for 15 days, and has been in an inpatient treatment facility four times, as well as an outpatient treatment facility three times. She sees a therapist and psychiatrist regularly and is prescribed medication. Andie's life has been affected by her mental illness in many ways. Andie would purge, cut, cry every day, smoke marijuana, and could not keep up with her hygiene. Negative thoughts began to pervade Andie's mind. She shared, "I told myself that I was worthless, useless, hopeless, unattractive, overweight, pathetic, unwanted, and meant to die." Eventually, Andie began to understand that something else in her mind, her mental illness, was causing these negative thoughts. Andie's mental illness caused her next relationship to suffer and led to Andie distancing herself from her parents.

Although Andie has not fully recovered, she takes life one day at a time by making a to-do list and checking tasks off as they are completed. Andie's family is supportive and tries hard to understand her by taking her mental illness in to account. Andie is motivated to stay strong for her little sister, niece, and nephew. Andie now puts herself first. She says, "I learned that you can't find happiness through a boy. You [must] put yourself first, and no matter how much you love someone, sometimes you have to let go." This ordeal has given Andie a new purpose in life, which is to help others with mental disorders.

This is her advice for others struggling:

"Remember that the pain is only temporary and that there is a bigger purpose for your life. I'm certain you'll find it one day. Until that day comes, push through whatever it is you're struggling with right now and make it to the next day."

STORY # 56

BORDERLINE PERSONALITY DISORDER, DEPRESSIVE DISORDER NOT OTHERWISE SPECIFIED, GENERALIZED ANXIETY DISORDER & AUTISM SPECTRUM DISORDER

Anonymous is from South Carolina and enjoys studying astronomy, geology, and psychology. She loves pizza, tacos, and sushi. Anonymous' favorite bands include Fall Out Boy and Panic! At the Disco. She is also very fond of drawing. Anonymous' goal is to graduate from college, hopefully with a degree in Biology or Psychology. Anonymous has been diagnosed with Borderline Personality Disorder (BPD), Depressive Disorder NOS (DD-NOS), Generalized Anxiety Disorder (GAD) and has traits of Autism Spectrum Disorder (ASD). Anonymous believes her disorders are rooted in childhood experiences, she explains "The way I grew up, with constant bullying and being mistreated by others, and growing up with the feeling I never belonged."

Anonymous' therapist was hesitant to officially diagnose her with BPD because of the stigma surrounding the disorder. Cognitive

Behavioral Therapy (CBT) has not helped Anonymous' symptoms, but Dialectical Behavioral Therapy (DBT) has. Anonymous has dealt with numerous symptoms. She says that she has felt "Intense feelings and fears of abandonment, mood swings, frequently depressed and empty, impulsive, constantly worried and paranoid about others around me, irritable, prone to having meltdowns and shutdowns, lots of panic attacks, and dissociation."

Anonymous' daily life has been affected in many ways. It became difficult for her to make and maintain friendships and other relationships. Whenever Anonymous became upset, she would either shut down and stop communicating, or breakdown and scream. Anonymous shared, "I would think others were planning things behind my back to hurt me, and [I] was mistrustful. It also affected school as I had trouble paying attention and working with others." She has considered and attempted suicide a few times. Anonymous also admits to hitting, scratching, and biting herself, as well as hitting other people. This type of behavior made her constantly feel upset and "Confused as to why I felt that way and behaved the way I did."

The turning point for Anonymous was after she had a complete breakdown at a friend's residence that resulted in abandonment by that friend. She said, "It negatively impacted my life a lot, and put a strain on me and my boyfriend's relationship. That event that took place made me do more research about myself and helped me get into a DBT program, and it also got me on medication (Risperdal, an antipsychotic) to help control my rage and outbursts of emotions." DBT skills such as mindfulness, distress tolerance, and emotion regulation has helped Anonymous control her mental illnesses. Anonymous' boyfriend and family still lack understanding of what she is going through, but they do listen and try to help to the best of their ability.

Anonymous is now more focused on her behavior and this experience has changed her outlook on life. She says, "My outlook

is a bit more positive than it used to be, and I'm happy with that."
This is her advice for others struggling with similar situations:

> "Things may be hard right now, but with time and help, things will improve. Do some research on the disorders you have or may have; learn about yourself and you may find a solution that can help your situation. Talk to someone that you're close to, or look for a support group online that you can talk to. If you look for help, I'm sure you'll find it somewhere."

STORY # 57

ANXIETY DISORDER & SEASONAL AFFECTIVE DISORDER

Anonymous is from Canada and she is currently finishing a bachelor degree in psychology. She is active in theatre and dance, and she absolutely loves performing. Anonymous is also an avid reader and is working her way through the classics. She wants to create a life that she is in love with; one where she is surrounded by wonderful, supportive people. Her goal is to start her future career. Anonymous has different disorders, saying she "struggle[s] with anxiety, and Seasonal Affective Disorder (SAD)." Anonymous believes her mental illness stems from both a genetic predisposition, as well as a negative relationship that was "terrible for my sense of self-worth here."

Anonymous has dealt with various symptoms that have affected her daily life. She shared, "I was suffering from panic and anxiety attacks, spiraling negative thoughts, and was destructible. When late fall hits, it becomes hard to get out of bed in the morning (sleep disturbances), I'm easily irritated, my self-esteem goes way down, and I will cry for no good reason. That lasts until about early spring." Her anxiety attacks made it difficult to concentrate during class. She also found it hard to associate with people due

172

to constant negative thoughts. Anonymous stated, "I thought I was useless and I wouldn't amount to anything because my grades were lower than they had been in high school. I also constantly thought I wasn't trying hard enough in my relationship with my now-ex. He made me feel as though my efforts were never good enough. He would tell me that the way I acted was stupid, so I would think it was and [would] try to change it."

Anonymous never seriously considered suicide, but the idea did come up in her mind every now and then. Most people were oblivious to the struggles Anonymous went through because she rarely gave voice to her negativity. Due to her inability to communicate her feelings effectively, she would withdraw from people for fear of not being liked. This made Anonymous feel incredibly frustrated. She said, "I couldn't seem to just 'snap out of it.' I felt trapped in my relationship with my then-boyfriend, trapped in what seemed to be a never-ending cycle of anxiety and frustration, and frustrated that I felt so sad and frustrated when there are millions of people on earth who have it worse than me."

The turning point for Anonymous was when she started getting anxiety attacks in the classroom; that was when she decided to get help. Anonymous reports she has gained the ability to control her anxiety and SAD with the help of cognitive behavioral therapy (CBT) from a registered psychologist. She maintains control by catching her negative patterns on time, and finding things to do with the people she loves. Anonymous also exercises, forces herself to take a step back when needed, and asks for help. She now sees herself in a positive way by reminding herself that she is smart and worthy of being cared about just as she is.

Anonymous' parents made a huge difference by helping her pay for therapy, and would constantly ask of her emotional well-being. Her friends would lend a shoulder to cry on, and made sure she had something to look forward to. Anonymous' perspective on life has changed. She says, "The biggest lesson I would say I learned was about self-acceptance; understanding that there's some things about yourself that you can't change, and that's okay." Anonymous is now firm with who she is, and doesn't let the opinions of others rule her life. She has become integrated, accepting and overcoming both the high and low points of her life.

This is her advice for others struggling with similar situations:

"My suggestion is to seek help from a professional and create a loving and understanding support system that will push you to be the best that you can be and accepts you as you are.

She would also like to share this:

"While I'm in an infinitely better place than I was when I first sought help two years ago, I still have bad days. I don't know if the bad days will ever disappear completely, but I know that it's part of the process and it won't last forever."

STORY # 58

DEPRESSION & RAPE RECOVERY

Lyanne is from California where she loves to dance, play instruments, and draw. Her goal is to be financially stable and happy, but she has difficulties seeing her future. Lyanne says, "I don't really like answering this question because I never really know what life is going to be from here to then, and I don't like the idea of my life being set in stone." Lyanne has always been depressed, but it worsened after being raped in college. She just started going to therapy and has been spending much effort creating a safe space, accepting what happened, and addressing her emotions. She shared, "I haven't been prescribed any medication yet. I'm also involved with several groups to help reach out to people on substance, depression, and sexual abuse."

Lyanne struggled with different symptoms, which she describes in her own words:

"I felt detachment from the people around me. A severe loss of interest in things that I used to enjoy, and a sense of heaviness in even getting up for the day. I often thought about self-harming. When I was intimate with someone, I would have these flashes of memories in my head and it would take me back to that certain event. It caused me to panic and have this urgency to escape. My chest would tighten and I felt as if I couldn't breathe."

As each day passed, Lyanne's life became more affected as she pretended like nothing had happened. Lyanne said, "I went on as if I had imagined that kind of thing could [not have] happened to me. But as much as I refused to acknowledge what happened to me, I didn't notice how I had become a victim of my circumstances." She felt like she was being eaten alive, and was constantly tired. Lyanne hardly ate and slept very little. She kept reinforcing her negative behavior and wanted to end everything because she could not understand what was happening to her.

Lyanne soon attempted suicide. After drinking alcohol for an entire day, Lyanne's emotions took over and she consumed an entire bottle of prescription sleeping medication. Lyanne immediately regretted her decision, but because she was intoxicated and took sleeping medications, she fell on to her bed and was unable to call for help. Thankfully, Lyanne was quickly found by her roommate, though she was found foaming at the mouth and unresponsive. 911 was rapidly called, and the paramedics gave Lyanne activated charcoal to clean out her system.

Even after what had happened, Lyanne still did not acknowledge her mental illness. She continued her self-destructive tendencies and fell into toxic relationships, pushing away everyone away, even those trying to help, because she felt that no one understood the severity of her emotions. This made her feel isolated and "Crazy because no one could understand what I was feeling. It was a combination of angry, sad, and desperate. I had spiraled downward so badly that life just didn't seem important. I was desperate to not continue living with that pain I had been suppressing because of my inability to understand how to deal with it. I felt worthless, I felt that being raped dehumanized me, and I felt unworthy of love. That somehow I was tainted to be in a life of misery."

The turning point for Lyanne was meeting a man at a party. She thought it would be a meaningless fling, but it turned out to be more. She says of the man, "He helped me acknowledge what I was going through. He understood my pain, but he didn't attempt to 'fix' me, nor did he attempt to 'save' me. He helped me understand that my emotions were rational and that my way of living wasn't dealing with the pain, it was masking the pain. He didn't run away from me. He accepted me in what I was, in who I was, and he made me realize that I wasn't a victim of circumstance; I was a victim of my own mind." The strategies Lyanne used to gain control was reaching out for professional help and support groups that specialize in substance, self-harm, and sexual abuse. This gave Lyanne hope because she met people that had been through similar experiences and had similar emotions.

Lyanne learned that past experiences cannot be changed, but reactions to experiences and what is taken or learned from an experience can be altered. She says, "I was so focused on the pain and the severity of it led me down a bad path. When I CHOSE to WANT a better life, and actually strived to change it, is when things turned around." Lyanne became stronger after this experience. She described, "Being raped changes you. He took a part of me, a part of my life that I can't alter or take back. And by my suicide he almost took my life. I wanted my life back."

This is her advice for others struggling:

"Guys, there is NOTHING wrong with you. I know there are a lot of people out there that have this negative stigma of mental illnesses and disorders. There are people that think that you're crazy, but honestly, that doesn't mean you are. The only person whose opinions matter is yourself.

Self-care is the most important thing out there. There's nothing wrong with being selfish sometimes. YOU [must] be your top priority. Understand everything is a process and the best step is the first step even if you have to ask for help."

STORY # 59

OBSESSIVE COMPULSIVE DISORDER & SCHIZOPHRENIA

Allison is a native of New York. She was once a lacrosse goalie. She loves alternative music; her favorite bands include Twenty-One Pilots, Vampire Weekend, La Dispute, and Neutral Milk Hotel. Allison is addicted to coffee and chocolate, and on the weekends, she enjoys venturing into the city and visiting thrift shops to combat her agoraphobia. Allison has prestigious goals. She says, "My academic goal is to attend college. Professionally, I aim to become a psychiatrist and help people like me. In five years, hopefully I'd have graduated from college and moved on to medical school."

Allison has been diagnosed with obsessive compulsive disorder (OCD) and Schizophrenia. In addition to those disorders, Allison suffers from severe anxiety, asocial tendencies, and self-harming. Allison reports the symptoms of her mental illnesses worsen with stress. She denies knowing the root cause of her disorders. Allison is on several medications to not only to control her schizophrenia, but control the horrid side effects from the antipsychotics. She is still in therapy on a weekly basis, and has been hospitalized eight times in the past four years.

Allison has had to deal with terrible symptoms, which include: "hearing voices (three of them, who I call the Sirens, like in ancient mythology), paranoia, bouts of dissociation, agitation, anxiety, loss of hope, and disorganized thinking, etc." Allison's life has been severely affected by her disorders. She had difficulty completing daily tasks, and she would often hurt her friends and family. Allison had passive suicidal ideations; at one point in time she had picked out a method and typed a suicide note. Allison admits she has self-harmed, and to this day she continues to fantasize about harming herself. Allison's disorders also began to affect her relationships. She says, "My friends started to stay away from me because I was sad, angry, and frustrated. My family tried their best to help me in any way possible, but their efforts were of no use. I ruined every positive relationship I had when I was at my worst."

Allison felt like a cornered animal. She shared, "The Sirens were telling me 'they are coming for you,' and 'they will take you away.' I honest to god thought I was going to be committed and I would never lead a normal life. And in a way, I didn't want to live my life the way it was being lived – in fear, in hopelessness, in isolation." The turning point for Allison was to work with a new therapist. She mentioned, "I, unfortunately, will never overcome my schizophrenia. But I started working with a new therapist who has literally saved my life. I started rebuilding all my decimated relationships, and the thing that keeps me going is that I am finally graduating high school and I will never have to go to the god-awful school ever again."

Allison used the skills she learned in DBT therapy to gain control while she was hospitalized. She has also learned to be more open and honest with those who help her, although this is difficult due to her extreme paranoia. Allison's family helped by standing by her, and her friends were understanding once she started socializing again. Both her therapist and psychiatrist are working together to ensure Allison does not have to be hospitalized again.

Allison prevents herself from self-harming by getting rid of her stash of tools. She reports, "There is no way I can 100 percent prevent myself from falling into psychosis and dissociation and whatever else again. I'm bound to fall again, but next time, I know I'll have a support system in place." This is her advice for those struggling in similar situations:

"So, here's the thing – everyone on this planet who says, 'It gets better!' is a f**king liar. It doesn't get better, but you do. You learn how to be better, by using new skills and having a safety net in place. And although your disorder doesn't get better (mine will be with me for the rest of my life), you get better at handling everything. So, keep your head up, because you will learn to get better."

STORY # 60

BORDERLINE PERSONALITY DISORDER

Mandy is from Brazil and she loves to sing, draw, write songs, and author short poems. She listens to music, especially Rock 'n' Roll. She says, "I usually pick songs by what they mean." Mandy enjoys watching historical movies and her favorite books are Lolita, by Vladimir Nabokov, and The Praise of Folly, by Erasmus of Rotterdam. Mandy's goal is to be happy, to be far from her mother, and to live in a nice house with someone she loves with two or three cats and a dog. She also wants to keep her mental illness under control and gain the ability to finish her degree.

Mandy has been diagnosed with Borderline Personality Disorder (BPD). She shared, "It's kind of controlled now, but I had a lot of problems in the past. I still have some issues with it every day, but I consider myself mentally healthy at the moment." Mandy believes her mental disorder is caused by genetics and the environment. Mandy explained, "A lot of my relatives have or had mental illness, some weren't diagnosed, but you could understand something wasn't okay. My mom is very complicated, she forgets things she says or does when she is angry, and tends to be very violent in those moments." Mandy tries to avoid using medications because she does not want to become dependent, so she goes to therapy instead.

Mandy has dealt with many symptoms that affect her daily life, such as being fearful and constantly changing behaviors. Mandy says she can feel immense happiness with someone who is nice with her, but if the person is criticizing, even if it is the smallest thing, it can turn her life into a nightmare for days. Mandy says, "I am very impulsive and I never had compulsion for drugs or spending money, but I couldn't hold myself near men. I would just try to attract any men near me that I could have some interest without thinking about consequences, like hurting my boyfriend." Mandy reports that her lack of self-esteem began to take control in many situations. For instance, if a friend complimented an actress, Mandy would compare herself to the actress, remarking that she was too unattractive to ever be like the actress. Mandy would also cry whenever a friend experienced success or achievement because she felt she was unable or unworthy to achieve the same. Mandy moved to many different cities, and in each school she attended, Mandy was bullied for being "weird." Mandy often ended up in the library alone.

This made her feel terrible and she wanted to die or disappear. She says, "I thought that nothing could make me happy since I was broken. I even had weird feelings and fantasies, that I wasn't human or that I was dead and in hell. Sometimes I was very rude to people and deeply desired that everyone died." Since Mandy lacked the ability to control these emotion, she attempted suicide dozens of times, the first being at 11 years old. Thankfully, her attempts were unsuccessful. Mandy self-injured once, and never tried again, because she did not want to suffer, just die. Since the age of eight, Mandy wanted her mother to suffer and feel the way she felt, but now she feels pity for her mother and understands that she is also mentally ill.

People thought Mandy was being dramatic, always overreacting, and victimizing herself when all she truly wanted was someone to open up to about her emotions and experiences. The turning point for Mandy was meeting people who had similar emotions and mental illness. After hearing others speak of their disorders, Mandy now understands herself better. She says, "Time, friendship and the treatment made me feel more comfortable with myself; I don't even see my BPD as a bad thing now. I just think that is a thing that I have inside me that can be used for good and for bad."

The strategies Mandy used to gain control of her disorder was to be more open, have fun with friends, and laugh. She uses art to express herself by drawing, and writing songs and poetry. Mandy's friends helped her understand that just because she has BPD it does not mean she is broken. This is the lesson Mandy learned from her path to recovery: "Trusting people can be very hard, as finding real friends can be. But if you give yourself a chance, you can find people that are as "weird" as you are. You may not have dozens of friends, but maybe giving one or two people the chance of hearing you can change your life." Her outlook on life also changed; she has realized that even if the world in not perfect, she can still find happiness.

This is Mandy's advice for those with BPD:

"Learn about yourself, understand who you are and what you feel. Accept yourself, see what your strong points [are] and the things that you do well. Then, start to slowly open yourself to people. Try to explain how you feel to close people in your family or your friends. If, like me before, you don't have these things, talk anonymously to people in the internet, make a blog about it. Draw, write, sing... express how you feel through what you can do. Sometimes being "weird" give us the power of doing things that "normal" people can't. Don't hate yourself for being different, learn how can you use that to do good and great things. The only one that can stop you from doing anything is yourself."

STORY # 61

BORDERLINE PERSONALITY DISORDER, ANOREXIA NERVOSA, ANXIETY DISORDER & DEPRESSION

G DN is from Texas who lives and breathes theatre. She said, "I would be nothing without it." Five years from now, her goal is to prepare and be on Broadway. GDN is not old enough to be diagnosed with Borderline Personality Disorder (BPD) just yet, but it's been suggested. She struggles with anorexia, depression and anxiety. She has no idea what caused her disorders. GDN shared, "I had a great life and I don't know what caused me to struggle so much." She has been in therapy since she was 9 years old. For her well-being, GDN was forced to attend residential treatment and wilderness therapy programs. Her anxiety makes her feel physically sick. She mentioned, "I felt unable to control myself or my actions." Her symptoms took control of her life. GDN became angry, self-destructive and impulsive. She attempted to self-harm when she was 12, but she realized it wasn't for her so she stopped. Thankfully, her relationships with others were not affected. GDN explained, "At the time, my friends and I bonded over our mental illnesses." Her friends helped her realize that she is a great person and worthy of love.

Her road to recovery began when she was unwillingly sent to two different treatment facilities. She said, "They helped me become the real me again, the people there are so amazing." The lesson GDN learned from this ordeal is to love herself and that nothing is ever as bad as it seems. She says, "Everything will be okay in the end, and if it's not okay it's not the end yet." Now, GDN eats healthy and exercises; she is grateful and appreciative of everything.

Recovery is a never-ending battle for her, and she just keeps moving forward; one step at a time. This is her advice to anyone who suffers from a mental illness:

> "Get the help you know you need. It's hard and it sucks, but in the end you'll be so grateful you did. And above all, love yourself and put yourself before other people." and "For other anorexics–one day of bad eating is not gonna ruin your life. Trust your body. It knows what to do, it's smart."

She would also like to share:

> "Live by the phrase "keep going, keep growing" it gets me through every day. That and 2 Chronicles 20:15, but I know not everyone believes in God."

STORY # 62

PANIC DISORDER & DEPRESSION

Dereka is from LA and she has gotten into photography this last year, she said, "I mostly snap pictures of myself, but it's helped a great deal in my mission to achieve self-love, to see myself as a person, and to finally like what I see. It gave me an opportunity to see myself not just through my reflection in the mirror." Dereka has a blog on Tumblr (pennylanedarling), and she likes to make short videos for fun. She craves anything that allows her creative side to come out. She is fond of coming up with ideas, and following through with them. She added, "I love anything that gets my imagination going. I love music, I love food, and I've owned the book 'Girl, Interrupted' for about 3 years now, and I've finally cracked it open." She is also a big movie fanatic and has played The Sims for a long time.

Dereka doesn't have any goals; she just wants to make it from one day to the next. She shared, "I can see myself in a place where I feel like I belong, I can see myself smiling, laughing, and above all: living. I can see myself at home, wherever that may be." Dereka lives with anxiety, panic disorder, and depression. She doesn't know what may have caused her disorders, but she remembers feeling worried about things that hadn't happened yet and feeling profound sadness at a young age.

After being diagnosed by a therapist during her teen years, Dereka felt like no one was listening to her. It was difficult for her mother to grasp the idea of mental illness due to her lack of knowledge, so she just blamed Dereka's father for her troubles. Because of this, her therapist kept making references of her father during the treatment, so Dereka felt like it was pointless. She was on and off 'Lexapro', but this medication did not suit Dereka because it kept her from feeling. She said, "I could tell I wasn't myself on it, and being 14, I wanted to feel. I just wanted to be normal."

Her daily life consisted of different symptoms, such as feeling empty. Dereka explained, "I felt a hole in my chest, an emptiness that couldn't be filled, I was anxious and constantly worried. My mind was always running a mile a minute even when I was sleeping. At times, I felt everything and it barreled down on me, and other times I felt absolutely nothing, and I reveled in those moments." Dereka has to deal with rapid heartbeats, cold sweats, sweaty palms, dry mouth, light headedness, bouts of crying, and feeling tired. She couldn't socialize without feeling frenzied. Dereka had to constantly think and plan out her interactions, she said, "I almost felt like I needed to plan out everything, right down to my movements, and facial expressions."

She first attempted suicide in the 2nd grade; Dereka tied a belt around her neck, but got scared and landed on her bedroom floor crying, for what she was capable of doing. Her second attempt was around the 8th grade when she took a handful of 'Benadryl', but made herself throw it up before anything serious happened. Dereka mentioned, "I never had intentions of hurting other people. I was only a danger to myself. I knew that, and was afraid of what I was capable of." During high school, she began cutting herself, using kitchen knives, razor blades, even broken glass. Moments like these felt like a release for Dereka.

Her behavior affected her relationship with her mother. Dereka said, "My mother was scared and acted out in anger towards me. She didn't understand what was going on, or why I was like this, she didn't have the capacity to be that 'hands on help' that I was screaming out for. We had a really bad relationship at one point, we were constantly fighting, and we pushed each other away." Because of this Dereka felt like a freak and that she didn't belong. She told one friend the truth about what was going on, and she was kind and understood. Everyone else tried to push their ideals on Dereka, trying to give a solution to her problems. Due to this Deraka felt like an outsider, she added, "I didn't relate to many people. I felt alone in my deep dark hole, that I had been living in for most of my life." She would become angry for waking up, when all she wanted was to feel moments of peace.

Her road to recovery began when she turned 21, Dereka decided to not be defined by her illnesses. Her mental disorders prevented her from doing things she really wanted to do. Dereka began to fight it by exposing herself to situations that brought her anxiety. She said, "Through this I learned what I was truly made of. I saw my true character, and I saw for the first time that fighter, that everyone always said they saw in me." Dereka also said, "I refuse to let it hinder me. It's still there, believe me, but throughout the years I've learned to adapt and fight, and find the confidence and self-esteem that I needed to be able to hold my head high without second guessing or feeling like I shouldn't belong anywhere."

Her friend and family tried their best to understand her, and be empathic towards her. During moments of loneliness, Dereka reminds herself that she is loved and cared for. The biggest lesson she learned was self-love. She shared, "You can never achieve anything if you don't start with yourself first. I allowed myself to fall in love with myself, by getting to know the girl I avoided in the mirror for so many years. It's very important to have a healthy view of yourself because that view shapes how you view others and the world itself." She now values true friendships and the strong bond that is between a mother and daughter. Dereka does not look for the bad in every situation anymore and plans on using her medication until it's not needed anymore.

This is her advice for others struggling with similar situations:

"I would just say that you're not alone, there's absolutely nothing wrong with you. You are not causing this to yourself. So, try not be so hard on yourself. It's rather easy to beat yourself up, but take some time, sit in front of mirror and study yourself, learn yourself and start to see yourself as a person. You are real and whether you want to believe it or not, you are beautiful. We are our own worst enemies, but it doesn't have to be like that. We are so much more than our illnesses; we have so much more to offer. You weren't made for pain. You weren't made to suffer, remember that."

STORY # 63

PERSISTENT DEPRESSIVE DISORDER, SOCIAL PHOBIA, BORDERLINE PERSONALITY DISORDER, NARCISSISTIC PERSONALITY DISORDER, POST-TRAUMATIC STRESS DISORDER, GENDER DYSPHORIA & DISSOCIATIVE DISORDER NOT OTHERWISE SPECIFIED

Rhett is from Israel. He is an atheist, absurdist, vegetarian and artist. His entire life revolves around the many forms of creation, whether it's painting, writing, photographing/ filming, or just brainstorming for original ideas. Rhett said, "I draw inspiration from literally everything. With that being said, I keep most of my work to myself because of my own ridiculously high standards and perfectionism." He spends most of his time gaming, his current favorite games are Layers of Fear, League of Legends, and Mad Max. He listens to all kinds of music genres, but he prefers alternative rock. Movie wise, he'd rather watch the horror genre and as for books, he loves to read about the Second World War and the Nazis. Rhett's future goal is to lead a group of fugitives in a post-apocalyptic setting where Putin and ISIS brought civilization to its knees or to simply become a professional dog trainer and move to Australia.

After being hospitalized, Rhett was diagnosed for being a threat to himself and others. He shared, "I was being 100% honest when I told them that if they didn't take me in, I'll either take my own life or another person's." Rhett was diagnosed with various mental illnesses, which are: clinical depression, dysthymia, social phobia, borderline personality disorder, narcissistic personality disorder, posttraumatic stress disorder, gender dysphoria, and dissociative disorder not otherwise specified. Rhett believes the cause of his mental disorders is due to genetics, society and abuse from his family. He was prescribed 'Lustral', 'Depalept' and 'Etomine', and received talk therapy. But the most therapeutic part about his admission was actually just being there. Rhett added, "We had our own school and lots of after-school activities as well as a regulated schedule and daily group sessions — and I believe that is what really helped me feel human again, because all I used to do before reaching out for help was lay in bed all day and wait for a silent death."

His mental illnesses took a toll on his life, Rhett dropped out of school when he was about 16, he barely ate and hardly slept. He self-harmed, started smoking, drinking, and using drugs. He said, "Somewhere in-between all the crying and suicide attempts I managed to get raped, almost ran away from home, almost became a prostitute, and almost murdered my ex. Honestly, I felt like sh*t." Rhett also shared to himself, "Damn Rhett, who would even want a self-centered, megalomaniac, disordered f*ck who hears voices and pretends to be a guy? You should just off yourself and rid the world of your existence."

Sadly, Rhett attempted suicide many times, but thankfully never pulled through. He tried hanging himself, jumping in front of a vehicle and walked slowly in the middle of a busy road. Since Rhett wanted a quick death he resorted to beating, flogging, and strangling his now ex out of frustration and resentment. He explained,

"I remember abusing others besides him, too — a couple years back, when I was still in school and an easy target for bullies, I had this habit of taking my anger towards them." He is not proud of any of the things he did and is trying to control himself.

Rhett's social life was a disaster. He was so hostile and paranoid that he convinced himself that every single person in the world would either rape or kill him. He ended up lashing out at people and truly believed that by acting that way, he was protecting himself from any harm. Due to his behavior, he ended up with a criminal record. Rhett does not consider his family as his own anymore and doesn't have any friends to lean on.

Because of this he felt forsaken, Rhett mentioned, "I felt like an abandoned dog — angry, lost, confused, and tired. I felt like I was waiting for a savior that I knew would never come. And that, in turn, made me feel the most alone than I've ever felt in my entire f*cking life." Rhett's turning point was six months ago, when he finally decided to seek professional intervention. He said, "That is the only reason I am still alive today, typing all of this. I didn't overcome my illnesses and I don't believe I ever will; but I'm trying to live life despite having them. I try to remember that I am just a person with needs, and that I have the right to take breaks and live life as comfortably as I can. I don't need to torture myself in order to get by, I'll adapt. I'll make the best out of what I have today."

Rhett doesn't have any strategies, he mostly acts on impulse. He eats, sleeps, and smokes pot whenever he feels like it. He takes things one hour at a time, and because of this he doesn't mind the idea of becoming homeless. Rhett tries to be as self-reliant as possible, evading help in fear of others exploiting any signs of weakness. But thankfully he turned to the hospital for help. He said, "The staff there helped me a lot, each in their own unique way, whether it was by giving me meds, managing my day until I get used to living like a human again, or by talking to me when I felt down."

The lesson he learned from this ordeal was to not get attached to the wrong people and to not let others run your life for you. Life has changed Rhett in many ways; he is now an atheist and absurdist. He used be an avid follower of God and had a naïve outlook in life. He explained, "It made me wiser, more resilient, and taught me how to fend for myself (sort of). I won't lie, it also made me pretty bitter and stingy. But I don't think anybody would remain a precious cinnamon roll after going through literal Hell." Rhett doesn't know any healthy ways to prevent anything from happening again, he is on his way to becoming an alcoholic, but is willing to reach out for help.

This is his advice for others struggling with similar mental illnesses:

"If you need a person to lean on just to get through the day, you go and lean on them (with their consent and approval while also respecting them). Feeling low on energy to do things is valid. Your experience is valid. Your past might be behind you but your scars aren't and nobody has the right to sh*t on that, ever. Take things slow. Process things at your own pace. Find people who will understand you and accept you for who you are and look past your 'labels'. Get a pet. Sometimes taking care of another being who loves you unconditionally can help ease the pain. Use art for venting. Be smart about what you spend your money on. You do you. I believe in ya'll."

Rhett would also like to share this:

"One of my friends is a combat veteran. His name is Jerome. When he was released, he soon found himself homeless. He had no family at the time. He suffered from severe PTSD, depression, and NPD, among other things. So he turned to alcohol and drugs when he saw society didn't give two sh*ts about a lone exsoldier with nowhere to go. And after a long while of self-destruction he just got up and said 'f*ck it'. He got detoxed. He tried to care for himself as best as he could. He found a job. And met his now husband, who helped him open a hair salon specifically targeting the veteran demographic. He gives them haircuts for free and offers a hot meal to go along with it. Also, they adopted an orphaned girl named Chyna. I know your situation might be a 110% different but I just wanted you to know that things eventually do get better. But it's ok if you won't be able to pull yourself up by your bootstraps because everybody's different. All I'm asking of you is to have a little hope. Because hope is what keeps us alive when the world comes crashing down."

STORY # 64

SEASONAL AFFECTIVE DISORDER

K aris is from Texas. She enjoys songwriting and testing new recipes while she gorges herself on television shows. She loves reading books that won't release their grip on her long after finishing them. Karis is fond of listening music for hours on end, for a million different reasons, all at the same time. She has different goals, Karis said, "My dream is to evolve. In five years, I will smile and mean it. Hopefully, I will be on the writing staff for television shows that I love and creating stories that will long outlast me." She sees herself doing what she loves and loving herself in the process. Karis also shared, "My only goal is to live in the happiness that I create for myself because I finally believe that I deserve it."

In 2012, she was diagnosed and currently still suffers with Seasonal Affective Disorder (SAD), she hopes to one day be healthy and symptom free. Karis believes that there was a combination of life events that contributed to her diagnosis. She added, "I was the first in my family to go to college. I moved from where I grew up in Houston, Texas to unfamiliar terrain in Providence, Rhode Island to attend Johnson & Wales University, alone. The environment was drastically different than what I was accustomed to and winters were harsh, long and grueling." During her sophomore year what she thought was homesickness persisted throughout the school year and affected her entire college experience. She explained, "I began a terrifying descent into the darkness that mirrored New England's winter weather, squirreling myself away in my room to avoid another day with no sunlight. The days turned into two years. My levels of serotonin decreased with the absence of the sun and melatonin increased."

Her mental illness was diagnosed by the university's residential on campus counselor. Karis began with Person Centered Talk (PCT) therapy with a licensed therapist in spring of 2012. After many sessions she discovered the right treatment path, a holistic therapy plan of supplemental vitamins that includes Fish Oil, B-12, Vitamin D, and eating more fruits and dark leafy green vegetables along with a healthy sleep schedule that would help regulate her circadian cycle. Karis said, "This treatment coupled with talk therapy worked well until I graduated in summer 2015. I now use light therapy and vitamins along with sleeping regularly to help abate my SAD symptoms. Treatment is working beautifully and I am able to function with more ease."

Karis had to deal with debilitating symptoms, she stated, "I felt lethargic and lifeless most of the day, for days on end. I craved fattening foods like carbs and sugar. There was loneliness, both of my own making and at not being able to feel the sun on my skin." She would sleep for more than ten hours a night and still wake, tired and fatigued. Karis didn't enjoy television, food, music like she once did.

SAD affected her daily life in ways she never knew could happen. She would wake up hours before anyone in her dorm to use the showers alone in the morning. As a culinary student, Karis had ready access to all the foods she craved. She said, "I would pile plates high with pizza, toast, rolls, and cereals at lunch and snack on cookies, candies and cakes all day long. My weight ballooned, my skin rebelled and I didn't feel like myself, only the shell of a person." Karis decided to sleep during her free time instead of studying, so her grades suffered. She had no motivation to attend class and sometimes it was a physical struggle to roll out of bed and get dressed. She said, "I started this damaging cycle of internal messaging with myself that nothing mattered. Not my grades, not my friends, not my family and not even my dreams. It was the most destructive thing that I have ever done to myself and the worst part was that it went unnoticed by so many in my life."

In 2013, Karis had suicidal ideations that she was not strong enough to live and attempted to take her own life by taking a paring knife and sliced her wrists. It was the rush of intense pain accompanied by the rivulets of blood streaming down her arms that made her realize she did not want to kill myself. Karis shared, "I wanted to no longer be smothered by the blanket of darkness that covered me. So, I cleaned the bathroom until there were no traces of me anywhere, I applied triple antibiotic to my wounds and bandaged them completely."

Karis had a difficult time with relationships. Her friends and family tried to keep Karis engaged and part of their lives, but she often cancelled. Other times she did not cancel and just watched the phone ring. She explained, "There were people around me who loved me when I couldn't seem to love anything in life. I kept myself at arm's length participating just enough to avoid questions about how I was doing. I was scared to answer truthfully so I stopped answering at all. Eventually some of these people grew tired of trying, of reaching out and they stopped."

Karis felt nothing, she added, "The shortness of the days, lack of light, the weight of a busy schedule and a tired body, the heaviness of a cluttered mind. I was trapped. And I was sad. Sad because I wanted the sun to bring my smile back when it returned and because I knew I had to endure the wait. I was angry that I wasn't letting myself be happy and I didn't know why."

The turning point was when she took an elective introductory psychology course her junior year of college and was fascinated by the exploration of human experience. Karis said, I was finally given answers to questions about myself that I had been struggling to find for years. I began to make sense of myself through analysis of psychological research and theories. I devoured every bit of information I was fed and I wanted more. I was excited about life, my life again." By semester's end, she changed to counseling psychology major in hopes to one day help another discover their true self.

Karis hasn't beat SAD yet, but has taken the first steps to overcome it. She opened up about her illness, diets, exercise, interacts socially and uses light therapy. Karis shared, "There were people who loved me and stayed, there were some who loved me and left but each one of these people were in my life because they chose to be. For a time, they chose to help me through a difficult period, whether they were aware that they helped or not." The lesson she learned is that having SAD doesn't mean she will always be sad and it's merely a percentage of who she is.

This is how her experience can change your outlook in life:

"There is something to be said about living under the cover of darkness. Darkness has the power to distort the senses, mute sounds and stifle sensations. Darkness can be a feeling, a physical weight on the shoulders. It can hide in the bones and surviving it will make you lighter. I survived and after years of no light, I became the light. Life has opened up to me with each rising of the sun and each breath that I inhale because there was a time that I wanted to take my last. I have looked through clouded lenses long enough and with help I was able to determine that even on days where there are no clear skies, I can still smile and meant it."

This is Karis' advice for others who are struggling:

> "Anyone who is currently suffering from a mental illness deserves a listening ear. If you feel that you might be suffering from any condition at all, talk to someone. It could be a friend, a parent, a teacher, or even a stranger in the checkout line. Voice your concerns. Chances are you are not alone. You deserve to feel better than you feel at your worst. Let someone help you, let the light in."

She would also like to share this:

> "This is my life living with SAD and many others live with this diagnosis as well. You, reading this, have helped remove a percentage of the stigma attached to the conversation of mental illness. You've made me less of a number and more of a person. Thank you. I wish you love and light."

STORY # 65

OBSESSIVE-COMPULSIVE DISORDER, AGORAPHOBIA & ANXIETY DISORDER

T ammy is from South Florida and she loves different forms of art, from fashion to film. Tammy said, "I love creating and acquiring new skills. I'm very passionate on self-improvement and strive everyday to be a better person. I'm hands down stuck in the 90s! I still watch 'Hey Arnold' among other cartoons religiously. This might sound weird, but one of my favorite movies of all time is 'Coneheads'! I just love weird and silly things."

She is proud to say that five years from now, she sees herself finally settled in a job that she feels completely comfortable in and her ultimate goal in life is to be content and proud of herself. Tammy was diagnosed by a psychiatrist with panic disorder two years ago, and has experienced Obsessive Compulsive Disorder (OCD) tendencies and agoraphobia. She still deals with occasional panic attacks and General Anxiety Disorder (GAD) on a regular basis. She said, "It's been a long road to get to where I am today. Two years ago I never could have imagined having my life back again."

Tammy thinks change in her life is what caused her disorders. She had just finished her cosmetology program at the time and kind of felt like she was thrown in an abyss. She shared, "I felt that my entire youth I was invincible and never realized how fragile life really is. I never thought about my own death. I feel like uncertainty triggered it. I lost my dad when I was 8 and two years ago I lost a good friend in a car crash as well, and it hit me like a ton of bricks."

Tammy has visited countless doctors and has gotten every test she could possibly get and it all lead to anxiety. Antidepressants were her treatment of choice as well as psychological therapy. The symptoms she felt were strong and it interfered with her life. She didn't have prior symptoms before her first panic attack. It just fully developed and escalated quickly. She added, "I felt severe derealization and had out of control thoughts about every wrong possible scenario. I lacked appetite, and ultimately I ended up weighing 99 pounds." Tammy lost about 15 pounds or more and couldn't do anything. She lost control over her life. Not only that, but the physical symptoms were unbearable; she would hyperventilate and deal with migraines regularly.

Due to this Tammy had to quit her job and move away. She thought her life was over and that nothing could help her. Sadly, she considered suicide and had thoughts of it everyday, but thankfully she did not want to take that route. This disorder isolated her from friends and family. Tammy explained, "I feel like mental disorders are so misunderstood. Just because it can't be seen physically doesn't mean it's not there and I feel like I wasn't given the support I needed and lost so many friends because of this." Tammy still feels extremely betrayed, but she discovered she has herself and God. She said, "It's been a roller-coaster of emotions. I met so many amazing new friends whom have been the support I needed and I feel like the people who truly want to be a part of my life are there."

She still deals with anxiety and panic attacks, but she is officially off antidepressants and actually feels better without them.

Her good friend Anson from South Dakota took her in, from there she became independent and it was a life changing experience. Eventually, Tammy moved back to Florida, took matters into her own hands and decided to get a MRI, multiple EKGs and an x-ray done, but they all came out clear. From there she went to a Good Samaritan counselor and took therapy every week. It helped her tremendously. She mentioned, "The antidepressants stopped working for me and I experienced multiple setbacks. From there I decided it was time to get off the pill and started working out and drinking more water. Guided meditation helped as well. It definitely takes a lot of willpower and self-love to get better every day. I'm not 100% recovered, but I'm just thankful I'm not where I used to be."

Tammy cut off all forms of caffeine, eliminated alcohol and any extreme sugary or processed foods. She kept her mind occupied and began using her creativity. In all the chaos, she decided to indulge herself in creating a brand. It's still in the works, but it is her big project at the moment. Others helped her through prayer, but most importantly they would not take it personal when her anxiety got bad and she'd to ask them to leave. They would make sure to reach out and check that she was okay.

The biggest lesson she learned is self-love. Tammy shared, "I always placed others before myself and I compromised my whole life. It was an eye opener seeing how I had neglected myself and that this time I had to take care of me." She also said, "My perception of life changed 100%. I doubted my existence for the longest. I feel like this experience changed me for the better and now I'm incapable of judging others as I know internally we're all fighting a battle." She now stays true to herself to prevent this from happening again. Tammy has the utmost respect for others and will always value people's opinions, but she will no longer take negative comments personal.

This is Tammy's advice for others who are struggling:

"Stop searching for every symptom online! This was something I did every hour of the day for two years. It made me so sick. Please just don't do it. Believe the doctors and follow what they tell you. Work out and drink water. I know we're not perfect, but to work out at least twice a week for 30 minutes helps tremendously. Also quit trying to get people to understand you. Be your own hero. Like-minded people like you will come to your life at the right time. Have faith." and "It may seem like it won't ever get better but it does. Not immediately. It's all a process. Slowly but surely with positive thinking and a lot of willpower it does get better. Stay strong!"

STORY # 66

MAYOR DEPRESSIVE DISORDER, ANXIETY DISORDER, POST-TRAUMATIC STRESS DISORDER, PANIC DISORDER & SLEEPING DISORDERS

Anonymous is from Oakville and was raised in Mississauga, Canada. She loves music and the outdoors, especially wildlife and animals. Reading is one of her favorite things to do and she also loves to learn. Five years from now, she hopes to be in post-secondary studying either paramedicine or nursing. Anonymous was diagnosed with clinical depression, chronic anxiety disorder, post-traumatic stress disorder (PTSD), and panic disorder along with a few sleeping disorders. She said, "I still have all of them and will most likely have them for the rest of my life." She is currently receiving Cognitive Behavioral Therapy (CBT), Dialectical Behavior Therapy (DBT), talk therapy and frequently visits her doctors. She was also given coping strategies that help her immensely.

Anonymous added, "The PTSD was caused by abuse and assault, the rest are present because of genetics or unknown reasons." She has dealt with many symptoms that manifest physically. She shared, "I stress over nothing, feel hopelessness, grief over nothing, extreme despair, less than zero motivation for anything, the unwillingness to live anymore, flashbacks and nightmares from PTSD, hyper vigilance, shaking and sweating, pulse and breathing increases, abdominal issues and migraines, vomiting, inability to focus or concentrate, irritability and easy frustration, crying fits, panic attacks, random panicking over nothing or a trigger, fear, overwhelming sadness, and many more."

Her mental illnesses have made it difficult to live a normal life. She can only work part time and often cannot make it to her shifts. Anonymous explained, "I often can't take care of myself because hygiene and health go out the window, including cooking and eating." She has negative thoughts such as suicide and unhealthy behaviors. She often drives everyone away and doesn't leave her house for weeks. Not only that, but she had to drop out of high school for some time.

Her anxiety and depression put terrible thoughts into her head. Anonymous said:

"Sometimes I told myself: no one actually loves or cares for you, you should leave your boyfriend because you'll never be good enough, he will see who you are and regret being with you, you'll never be able to provide a normal family life, life will never be the same for you, might as well give up now, you're helpless and hopeless."

Unfortunately, Anonymous has attempted suicide twice and thought about it more times that she can count. She has also self-harmed by cutting for a couple years and became addicted to it. She mentioned, "It was a long hard journey to stop, but I am now more than a year clean!" Her relationship with others became affected because most cannot understand how she thinks or feels. She draws herself away from others because she feels ashamed, but through this hardship Anonymous has been able to create some of the strongest relationships she has today with her parents and best friend.

The turning point for Anonymous was when she had to drop high school. She explained, "I was making a decision to stop everything and focus on my recovery." She focused on learning about herself so she can manage and work. Anonymous also shared, "I have been at it for almost a year now, and I am still focusing on getting myself under control." The strategies she uses is to talk with those she trusts about her thoughts, she is also self-training a psychiatric service dog right now." Anonymous said, "Only 0.01% of Canadians that have service animals have successfully trained their own. This is the hardest thing I have ever done, but it is also the most rewarding. It keeps me going every day, gives me a reason to get out of bed, and gives me hope in the future that I'll be able to be independent. The dog will be able to bring me out of panic attacks, notify me of my mental state so I can recognize bad thoughts and behaviors, he will be able to bring me out of nightmares and pick me up when I'm down." Not only that, but she is also taking Tae Kwon Do for self-confidence and constructive physical activity. She surrounds herself with family, her best friend and boyfriend to boost her mood and give her advice when she needs it the most.

Anonymous has learned many things through her mental illnesses, she says:

"Life is not fair. It never will be. But that does not mean you give up. Some of us are born in perfect health, some are born with terminal illnesses, and some are born with something somewhere in between. We cannot choose our start in life, but we can choose how we proceed. Everyone makes mistakes and everyone faces the bad of the world at some point or another. Everyone has their struggles, some worse than others, but struggles nonetheless. What I learned most heavily from this is how much I should be relying on God. I found Christ through my ordeals and it is the best thing that has ever happened to me."

This is her advice for others dealing with mental illness:

"The first thing I would suggest is seek professional help. It's confidential, it's safe, and it's the first step to a brighter future. It's scary, I know. But it is worth it. Please just do it. The next thing would be to find community support from people you know. It could be at a church, a trusted family member or adult friend. But share your feelings and build confidence in yourself. I would also suggest to others to find Christ in their lives as well. It has changed my life for the better so drastically, I recommend it to everyone."

STORY # 67

GENERALIZED ANXIETY DISORDER & DEPRESSION

A aron is from the UK and he loves video games, music and movies. He likes things that are expressive, creative and different. Anything experimental interests him. Overall, Aaron would like to be a happy person. He said, "Within the next five years I would like to finish University with good results, get a job within the gaming industry, hopefully somewhere in the UK or Germany. Get into a nice stable and loving relationship, and get a mortgage on my first house."

Aaron was diagnosed with and still suffers from Generalized Anxiety Disorder (GAD) and depression, but thankfully he is slowly getting better. He believes his mental disorders were caused by several traumatic events. He shared, "A mixture of my grandma dying, unhappiness with my progress in life, a failing relationship with a partner who cheated multiple times; it's the lies that hurt more than the act of what happened." Not only that, but Aaron didn't have much of a happy childhood either, he hasn't seen or spoken to his father in over 10 years. Over time, his feelings got worse and he ended up seeing a doctor when his mother recommended it.

Aaron ended up taking anti-depressants and attended talk therapy sessions for approximately three months, before he dropped out. He added, "Honestly the therapy was the worst experience of my life; I have never felt as low as I did in those sessions, every symptom worsened each time I would attend. In the end I dropped out and I am currently 'winging it' and trying to get better." Aaron still deals with numerous symptoms. He mentioned, "I am constantly tired, but at the same time unable to sleep properly. Sleeping for one hour has the same effect as sleeping for ten, I still feel exhausted when I wake up." He also becomes irritable towards other people, even if it's in the presence of someone he loves. Most of the time Aaron wishes to isolate himself and have space to breathe. He dreads not trying out new things, but feels on edge when he does. Not only that, but he constantly has a dry mouth and is always thirsty. Aaron usually feels sick to the point where he doesn't eat at all.

Due to this Aaron's life became affected. He explained, "I feel a sense of dread that something is going to go wrong, like I am going to upset someone and cause a problem. I spend a lot of time each day over thinking conversations and interactions I have had with people." He also said, "Sometimes I get through a day fine and feel happy, sometimes it is the total opposite. It is really easy to slip into a thinking pattern that is only negative. Initially it was so bad that I couldn't go to work most days and when I did go into work I would end up breaking down in tears in a panic attack at least once throughout the day." Aaron often thinks about suicide, but thankfully has no intention of ever doing it.

He has had difficulty maintaining relationships with others. Aaron added, "Multiple romantic partners have told me that they can't deal with the emotional baggage that this brings. I think it is hard for someone who has never suffered with a mental disorder to understand the perspective of someone who has." It is hard for him to explain to friends how he feels or why he feels that way. He said, "I feel very guilty being depressed and anxious with no real reason. It becomes easy to just shut down and never express emotion." Because of this Aaron felt lonely and empty. He also stated, "It is hard to explain what it feels like to be empty. Somehow it feels like deep in my chest there is a chasm or a gap that somehow isn't filled. A lot of people have said that they have no idea what I mean by this and I don't really understand either."

Although, Aaron feels like he's made progress, he knows he hasn't truly overcome his mental disorders yet. Most of the time, he tries to keep himself busy by involving himself in coursework or revision, reading a book, playing video games or listening to music. Others have helped him by simply being there and giving him a hug when he needs it the most. The lesson Aaron learned from this ordeal is to listen to that voice in his head that is telling him to get help. He says, "Don't let yourself believe how you feel is normal and you'll just be okay by leaving it. Do something about it, you've got to take action and kick yourself up the arse. In words of Shia Labeouf: JUST DO IT."

Aaron's outlook in life has also changed. Now, he appreciates the small things in life such as, being a healthy and happy person. He values this much more than being successful and wealthy. This is his advice to those going through similar situations:

"Ask for help when you need it. There are people you can talk to. It is okay to not be okay, it is okay to ask for help. It is okay to be different and it is okay to be YOU."

STORY # 68

SOCIAL ANXIETY DISORDER, PANIC DISORDER & DEPRESSION

Christa is from Saskatoon, SK. (Canada) and she enjoys reading and anything space related. She is fond of watching movies at the theater and hanging out at the library. Her goal is to become an astronomist, but she sees herself in university or college. Christa was diagnosed with and still has social anxiety, panic disorder, and depression. She received daily medication and believes her mental disorders were caused by various events, such as childhood experiences, and how she's been treated by everyone in her life.

Christa felt a wide range of symptoms, she said, "[I felt] Lots of nervousness and always wanted to be secluded, and away from everyone and anyone." Not only that, but her life was affected as well. Christa shared, "I never got along with anyone and it was hard to even get out of my room for school or supper. I was very explosive and aggravated and I never liked talking to anyone." Although, she has self-harmed and considered suicide many times in her life, she thankfully has never acted upon it. Due to this her relationships will her family members became affected and Christa didn't have any friends. She also added, "It was satisfying because the only thing I ever wanted was to be left alone."

Even though Christa hasn't overcome her mental illnesses, she continues to maintain control over her situation by taking medication and attending therapy. She decided to straighten out her priorities and start her journey on the long road to recovery. This experience changed her outlook on life, Christa said, "It made me into a more social person, even though it's still hard for me to be around large groups of people, I still enjoy my favorite activities."

This is Christa's advice for others trying to recover:

"Always think about your priorities and know that you can always be doing something better."

STORY # 69

ANOREXIA NERVOSA

Amanda is from California and she loves reading. She's a big movie lover, especially horror movies and the occasional romance. She is also training in boxing. She wants to be successful in life, she said, "I want to become a psychologist and see myself in college studying for that in 5 years." Amanda was diagnosed by a psychologist and doctor with anorexia nervosa and has been 2 years clean.

She believes her mental disorder was caused by a buildup of events, but there was one particular event that really impacted her. She stated, "I do know my breaking point was in 7th grade. Physical fitness testing was coming up and I did well in most of the areas that we were being tested in. However, I was considered "overweight" according to the BMI scale. My PE teacher showed us a chart that showed where we were "supposed" to be weight wise. Looking back now, I see that it was inaccurate. But I was a very insecure 7th grader." This event impacted Amanda immensely because she was going through puberty and she cared deeply about her physical appearance and what the rest of her peers thought of her. Not only that, but she explained: "I was also never considered the pretty girl and that also lowered my self-esteem greatly.

I incorrectly thought that my appearance was all that mattered. I started paying more attention to the mirror and comparing myself to everyone. I started thinking I saw fat where there wasn't any and started nitpicking at all my flaws. I thought if I lost weight I would feel happier and that my life would be so much better. It started small, but soon spiraled out of my control."

Amanda ended up receiving weekly therapies and went to a specialized clinic for eating disorders to watch over her physical health. She ended up feeling a wide range of symptoms associated with anorexia. She said, "I had an unhealthy relationship and obsession with food. My whole life revolved around food and it was all I thought about. I thought of ways to hide food, ways to avoid eating, calories in everything, how long I needed to exercise if I wanted to eat, and anything food related. I worked out to the point of near exhaustion and I restricted myself." Amanda also dealt with physical symptoms such as, hair loss, dull skin, and her period stopped. She was constantly always cold, and felt irritated or annoyed at little things.

Her daily life became affected by her negative behaviors because she did not care about anything other than food and her physical appearance. Her school became affected as did her relationships with her loved ones. They could not understand why Amanda wasn't eating. Amanda turned to self-harm as a coping mechanism that she hid from everyone and she constantly thought about dying, but thankfully never attempted it. She ended up isolating herself from everyone because people could not understand why she was down all the time. Because of this Amanda felt hopeless and trapped, she said, "I felt like no one would be able to help me and that I didn't deserve the help. I felt like my eating disorder would always have a grip on my life and that I would never escape from its hold on me."

Amanda's road to recovery began when she saw the effect her situation had on her loved ones. She added, "My little sister started asking questions about weight and why I wouldn't eat. My mom and grandparents were losing sleep and I was all they thought and stressed about. I realized that I needed to change and get help if not for me, then for the people I loved." The strategies she used to beat her mental illness were to do everything her doctor and therapist told her to do. Amanda said, "I ate when I was supposed to, and stopped over-exercising. I also tried to find one thing I liked about myself every day. There were still times when it was hard to keep going, but thinking about my motivation and why I was getting better in the first place helped me to pull through."

This is the lesson she learned from this ordeal:

"My eating disorder taught me a lot, but the biggest lesson I would say I learned is that people are fragile. Always be careful about what you say to others and how you treat them because you don't know what a person could be going through or what can send them over the edge. People aren't as strong as they want you to think they are, so just be kind."

This experience has changed her for the better. Amanda is now more understanding of other people's situations and has a positive outlook in life; she tries not to dwell on the negative. She now keeps herself busy and is happier, she said, "I make sure that I am balanced in what I eat. I don't restrict myself at all. I also exercise and found a passion for boxing and it reminds me to take care of my body and my mind. I don't deprive myself from anything. If I want ice cream, I'll eat ice cream because there's no harm in having it every once in a while. And I just make sure to keep my confidence level up by doing what I love and what I am good at."

This is her advice for others struggling with anorexia nervosa:

"For anyone struggling with this, you are strong and beautiful and perfect and don't need to restrict yourself. You deserve a happy and healthy life free of this and are worth so much more than what you're going through. You can beat this! Stay strong and remember that you are capable of defeating this. I wish you luck, joy, and love in your life. Good luck on your road to recovery, you can do this. "My worst days in recovery are better than my best days in relapse."

STORY # 70

DEPRESSION, ANXIETY DISORDER &
EMETOPHOBIA

Maruša is from Slovenia and she is 22 years old. She loves animals, music, books, writing, blogging, nature and fitness. Her goal is to be happy, she said, "My top goal is to be healthy and happy. First, I want to finish school, and hopefully in 5 years I'll be able to work with animals and in a fitness or wellness industry. I also want to write books and help other people."

Maruša was diagnosed with depression, anxiety disorder and emetophobia (fear of vomiting). She didn't realize she had emetophobia until she was 16, but thankfully she doesn't have it anymore. Maruša is dealing with her depression really well, but she is having problems with her anxiety disorder. She believes her disorders were caused by various events in her life. Maruša shared, "I had a bad experience with a stomach bug when I was 8 and since then I was always afraid of being sick and vomiting and I would avoid EVERYTHING AND ANYONE. I felt so weird when I was 14, I felt like I didn't belong or fit anywhere… my dad is an alcoholic and I lived in violent environment. I don't want to blame anyone, but my home, my family caused my depression. I never felt safe or loved."

Because of this Maruša started using drugs and alcohol to feel normal. Unfortunately, her anxiety developed after she quit using drugs and her depression skyrocketed after her dog passed away 2 years ago. She explained, "She was everything to me, I never felt so much love and connection to any living creature. She made me happy no matter how awful I felt. Losing her was by far the hardest experience and part of me died with her." Currently, Maruša is visiting a psychologist every two weeks and is planning to stick with therapy. She is not on any medication, but is willing to take them if it helps improve her life.

Maruša has dealt with many symptoms, such as: extreme fear, feeling sick every day, no motivation, low self-esteem and feeling worthless. Not only that, but she also manifested physical symptoms like stomach problems, dizziness, shaking, sweating, weak legs, feeling light headed, vision problems and ringing in her head. She felt like she was losing control. Due to this Maruša's life was affected, and she couldn't live the life she wanted. She said, "In my worst times, I couldn't even sleep because I was too afraid. I was too afraid to leave my bad, let alone go out. A simple walk felt like hell to me. I missed so much and I regret it, I regret the fact that I let my mental illness control my life."

Maruša thinks about suicide, not because she is suicidal, but because of intrusive thoughts. She started to avoid everyone and lost connections with most of her friends because she felt worthless and ashamed. She shared, "I thought they were better off without me. I wanted to be alone, I felt better when I was alone and invisible." Due to this Maruša felt trapped, angry, sad and desperate. Her road to recovery began after her 17th birthday, when she decided enough was enough and met a person who inspired her to get healthy.

Maruša decided to quit high school, although she feels like it was a mistake, but she had to put her health first. She mentioned, "I started eating healthy and clean, working out, reading self-help books, listening to music. I had support from my family and friends. The combination of that was positive for me. It was a long and slow process and no matter if I have anxiety disorder now, I can live quite normal."

This experience change Maruša's view in life, she said, "I think different. I feel different and I understand people more. I know what's really important in life and I don't waste energy on useless and stupid things. I want to live – as simple as that. I want to make something out of my life, something meaningful." She also shared, "I believe in a healthy lifestyle and I experienced it by myself. I think it's important to take care of yourself, nothing can destroy a healthy body and a healthy mind."

This is Maruša advice for those struggling with similar situations:

"Take your time. It's a slow process. Don't feel guilty or ashamed because you're having a bad day again or you had anxiety attack in a store (again). In fact, I had one just one hour ago and it was awful but nothing lasts forever. It will pass and it will come back and I know it's not what you would like to hear, but don't let these feelings control your life. Don't give it that power. Write down when you don't feel like yourself, write whatever is on your mind, even if you delete it afterwards. You will feel better. I'm not 100% cured, but I'm going in the right direction and if I can do it, you can do it too."

STORY # 71

BORDERLINE PERSONALITY DISORDER

Laura grew up in a tiny rural town in New Brunswick, Canada. The things that she loves in life are art and philosophy. What's more, she is health conscious and reveals, "I eat a gluten free and vegetarian diet and I am very passionate about eating clean and caring for your body. You would be surprised to know how badly food can affect your mind and mentality!" Laura further discloses, "After taking on a Buddhist perspective towards many things, 'striving' or 'goals' are words meant to be removed from our vocabulary." Nonetheless, 5 years from now, she hopes to be manifesting a successful career in tattooing. She intends to continue her personal growth: to grow to embody love and compassion.

When Laura was younger, her unrelenting anger led her to believe that she was Bipolar Type II. A professional agreed with her, but at that point she was influenced by her own research and perception of herself. She confides, "I was desperate to put a name on it so that I could stop feeling like I was a wild, bad thing. If a doctor tells you you're sick, then it isn't 'wrong' any longer to feel the weight of any mental illness." When she became a little older, Laura had a breakdown that led to the emergency room. There, she met a doctor who introduced her to Borderline Personality

Disorder (BPD). She explains, "I had heard of it once before, another doctor had mentioned it, but I had been too convinced that I knew best, but when I read the information he gave me, it felt like someone had put all of the symptoms and reactions, that I couldn't explain to others into words, in a checklist in my hands." Laura asserts, "Borderline Personality Disorder means that people who have it react to negative stimulus with the part of their brain that uses impulse instead of logic."

When she was younger, the first symptoms that Laura experienced were unreasonable irritation, self-loathing, overwhelming guilt, invalidation, dissociation, impulsivity and months upon months of depression. As she got older, her impulsivity and dissociation caused her to take disastrous decisions. Laura remembers, "I didn't feel like I was the one doing all the crazy messed up things that kept landing me in trouble, and once I'd realized what I'd done, I would be so overcome with guilt, shame and bad thoughts about myself that I would have to dissociate to cope with how much I hated myself." She didn't want to be herself and this would circle right back to impulsivity. It was a vicious and exhausting cycle for Laura. She injured herself for many years by cutting, burning or hitting herself and when her blood would catch fire she couldn't control it. She recalls, "I started hurting myself because I was depressed and that was before anyone ever taught me what depression was, and I think there is just a natural curiosity for the link between physical and emotional pain."

The way she treated herself affected every relationship she had at that time, primarily her family, her parents especially, although her sister was always a very stable figure in her life. Laura's relationships, like everything else, were affected due to her own internal pain that made her feel weak, shameful, and undeserving of love. She confesses, "I hated myself for not being able to 'love correctly' and that only amplified the problem." During her second year of university, Laura lived in a house with five girls who were like a family to her and she was in a relationship with a boy who meant the world to her. But as the cycle would have it, her new relationship with her then boyfriend started turning sour and fights provoked emotions that were always running way too high. She describes, "One night a fight led to me impulsively punch a glass window in the house where I lived with my friends. As I was bleeding profusely and could see way too many of my internal structure, it felt as though I could feel everything that I'd caused others to feel throughout my life. I believed at the time of the accident that it was going to kill me and all I could do was apologize for my life." After this incident, Laura found Buddhism which gave her a new aspect on life and death.

Laura's relationship grew worse until she was completely manipulated by him. She laments, "I was so emotionally abused that I couldn't see what was happening. My friends began to resent me for not leaving him and eventually, I was completely isolated in my home. No one would talk to me, the love of my only friends was gone and the only person I had to turn to was my abusive boyfriend." She stopped leaving her room, became paranoid and was hurting herself again all the time, for which her boyfriend only blamed her. After many passive aggressive incidents, Laura ended up at a tattoo shop which gave her the confidence to finally leave. Laura reveals, "It only got worse when I did and he started to threaten my life. I lived with a stranger and had no friends or family to talk to." Laura was all alone and spent months like that. Eventually, the more time she spent alone, the clearer everything became. She stopped being angry at the world and started forgiving everyone who hurt her. She explains, "This made me see the importance of forgiving myself. Once I learned how to let myself off the hook, everything else fell in line right behind it. I actually learned how to love myself, everything about myself, for the very first time in my life. I had spent twenty years hating myself and once all of the noise from other people was gone, I could finally see myself. I knew I would dedicate the rest of my life to being happy and in love with every single day."

This is Laura's advice:

"This sounds harsh to say but the only people who helped me were the people who hurt me. You have to find meaning and lessons in everything, in every single little thing that happens to you! Coincidences and mistakes are lies you've been told about since you were born! Forget them, because everything is perfect. For me, the only thing I needed was to be by myself, so that I could get to know myself truly without the influence of anyone else. Me and I are best friends now, nobody can come between us and that is a phenomenal feeling! The worst thing I've ever been through ended up being the best thing that ever happened to me. Keep in mind that things are almost never what they seem."

STORY # 72

DEPRESSION, POST-TRAUMATIC STRESS DISORDER & BORDERLINE PERSONALITY DISORDER

Miranda is from Portland, OR. She enjoys the idea of Buddhism/Hinduism and her favorite animal is an elephant. Her goal in life is to be an elementary school teacher and five years from now she sees herself in school or doing what she loves to do in another country. Miranda has depression, Post-Traumatic Stress Disorder (PTSD) and Borderline Personality Disorder (BPD) and has not received therapy.

Miranda felt many symptoms: "[I had] nightmares daily; I find that there can be gaps in my day where I don't know what I was doing or thinking; I've scared myself because I didn't remember dying my hair a couple times; impulsiveness; splitting on my friends or family; jumping to the worst conclusion; feeling like I have no way out other than suicide." This affected her daily life because sometimes Miranda didn't even have the energy to get out of bed and she relied on others for reassurance. Moreover, she has self-harmed and has sadly attempted suicide four times.

Importantly, this has affected and still affects her relationship with others. Miranda confides, "I can't keep friendships afloat without shooting a few holes in it first and then frantically trying to fix it." This makes her feel like no one stays due to the way she is. Miranda colors, smokes, has sex and listens to music to maintain control. The children she works with help her and she also uses awareness. The lesson Miranda learnt from this ordeal is not to expect to receive trust and love even when you put it out there.

This is her advice for others going through similar problems:

"I can't say it gets better because I haven't reached that point, but you are worth something to someone and you are loved even if it doesn't feel like it. Whether it's an acquaintance, a friend, your mom, your aunt, grandpa, the love of your life, you are cared for, and would be missed."

STORY # 73

DEPRESSION, ANXIETY DISORDER, ATTENTION DEFECT DISORDER, EATING DISORDER, & ALCOHOL/DRUG ADDICTION

Anonymous is from Nashville, TN and is currently living in Newport Beach, CA. She has multiple interests such as yoga, music, art, animals, being around friends and family, anything outdoors, watching movies and learning. She is currently working in a drug and alcohol rehab center. She declares, "I plan to go back to school this year and do something in healthcare or social services." Anonymous was diagnosed with Attention Deficit Disorder (ADD), depression, anxiety, eating disorder and alcoholism/drug addiction. She explains, "I think I was born with all of these things but the alcoholism/drug addiction didn't present itself until later on in high school. I've always had an addictive personality that uses whatever it can to numb or escape whether it be exercise, drugs, sex, shopping, and so forth."

Anonymous has received therapy and counselling for about seven years and has been on several medications. She reveals, "I went to treatment for my addiction in November of 2012 and have been sober ever since." Unfortunately, she has dealt with several symptoms throughout her life such as feeling loss of hope, very low self-esteem, lack of motivation, feelings of panic and discomfort, inability to focus and disassociation. Anonymous confides, "I always felt defeated by all these problems. If it wasn't depression keeping me from leaving my bed, it was anxiety keeping me from going outside. It seemed like it was always something. I have very little motivation to do anything and, when I do have the motivation, I can't seem to stay focused. I feel anxiety in almost everything I do, especially in social situations."

Moreover, she experimented in self-harming throughout her teenage years. When her alcoholism and drug addiction were at their worst, she wanted to die but feared suicide. She confesses, "I just hoped maybe I'd eventually overdose and not wake up the next morning." Her behavior affected her relationship with others: she constantly let her parents down, worried her siblings and lost friends. Before anonymous went to rehab, she always felt so alone. She discloses, "I was living for drugs and was honestly convinced that I was only hurting myself. I wasn't aware of the impact that my disease had on anyone else." She continues, "I felt so indescribably miserable. I felt like I had no control over my life. I didn't understand that I have a disease. I remember thinking 'I'm so weak' every time I would try to regain some semblance of control over my life."

Her turning point was going to treatment. For anonymous, the past three and a half years have been full of ups and downs. She still struggles with mental illness today but has gained confidence. She explains, "I have overcome so many obstacles and I believe that if I keep fighting, this will be another thing I will conquer." She used different strategies to help maintain control, for instance medication, spirituality, therapy, meditation, writing, reaching out for help and taking suggestions. Anonymous also loves helping others in any way she can. She claims, "If anything good can come from all the bad stuff, it's carrying the message to other people in pain that there is a way to get better."

Through her experience she has learnt a great deal:

"I learnt to keep taking the next indicated step. When life gets too scary or overwhelming, I do my best to take little steps at a time and remember to be gentle with myself. I don't want to spend my life at war with myself. Self-pity has gotten me nowhere. I've learned to enjoy life in its purest form rather than drowning my feelings and numbing my mind. I've learned to enjoy the little things much more and accept life on its own terms."

In order to prevent herself from slipping back into her old behavior, she plans to keep herself honest and open to wherever her recovery takes her—even if it's challenging or uncomfortable. Likewise, she intends to put her recovery and spirituality first. She asserts, "I am determined to constantly improve myself and become a dignified recovered woman."

This is her advice:

"I would suggest, first of all, to be honest with yourself. If you think you may have any kind of problem with depression, alcoholism, etc. seek help right away. There's never any harm in trying different things that could potentially change your life for the better. Recovery is so worth it. Another thing I would suggest is to take suggestions from others. It's uncomfortable and humbling, but it has saved me time and again. Also, learn to separate yourself from your mental illness. If you struggle with the constant battle inside your head it doesn't make you any less of a person or any less worthy of a beautiful life. Doing bad things or being mentally sick doesn't make you a bad person."

STORY # 74

ANOREXIA NERVOSA, BULIMIA NERVOSA, PANIC DISORDER, OBSESSIVE-COMPULSIVE DISORDER & DEPRESSION

Anonymous is from The Netherlands and she loves animals, dancing and being active in general. Besides sports, she is grateful to be with friends and family and is always busy with music, baking and drawing. Anonymous wants a happy future: "In 5 years from now, I would hope to have finished my studies and have a job. I would really hope that my boyfriend and I will live together by then and have a dog together. Besides that, I hope that my mental illness will not affect my daily life anymore."

Anonymous was diagnosed with anorexia mixed with a tendency to bulimia. What's more, she has panic disorder which leads to many panic attacks. At times, she has obsessive compulsive behaviors and had depression in the past. She believes her disorders has been caused by a wide range of factors: "For one I have always been a very insecure child. I have been bullied all throughout elementary school, parts of high school and also outside of school. Besides bullying, there was my mother who was very conscious about her health and weight and, as a child, I grew up with that. I also got molested by a good friend and lost a really close friend."

Her depression kicked in when her eating disorder developed and her panic attacks started when she began treatment, affecting her even during social events. Anonymous claims that her obsessive compulsive behavior is linked to the eating disorder: when her anorexia skyrocketed, she obsessed that everything had to be perfectly straight on a table. Her treatment lasted for about 2.5 years. In addition to that, she asked for help at the university campus but got sadly denied and is now currently following an online program to get her life back on track.

She went through a wide range of symptoms: "I was weak, often dizzy and nauseous all the time. I had barely any energy. I was isolated and felt alone often. I was always very cold and trembling a lot. I had very bad joint pain and stomach cramps. I was always tired and often very moody." Anonymous was barely eating and had no social life since she focused on school so much. This would help her to forget about the next meal. She also lied a lot, hurting those around her. She explains, "I only wanted to be good enough. I wanted people to be proud of me and of what I had achieved, and I did not realize that I was destroying myself." The depression caused her to miss out on fun activities with friends because she isolated herself. Anonymous' panic disorder made daily life harder than it already was. She randomly had to leave places, would be late to appointments or cancel them at the last minute.

Moreover, she has unfortunately attempted suicide and has self-harmed in the past. She confesses, "I attempted suicide a couple of times, only to get too scared and stopped. Once, a friend saved my life as she was knocking on the door to tell my parents what was going on." Anonymous sadly lost many friends because they did not understand her. She also lost her boyfriend because he did not know how to deal with her. This led to her losing trust in everyone and she felt devastated. She recalls, "I felt trapped in a world that I couldn't get out of. Nobody could hear me and nobody could help me. It was a life where I was sort of brainwashed to do a certain thing and if I didn't do it right, it would get hellish inside my head."

The turning point for anonymous was when she broke her foot because her parents had discovered what she was doing and had sent her to treatment. She realized that the death of her friend affected her although she didn't care anymore; she stopped eating, taking care of herself and many other things. She remembers, "Her wish was to see me healthy. After a while, that motivated me but it wasn't enough. I relapsed multiple times and stayed at an okay weight with an okay daily life." With the passing of time, anonymous started to realize what life can offer and she decided to start a program. Her friends and family have helped her by simply being there for her when she needs it the most, it being to talk or simply a hug.

This is what anonymous has learned for her ordeal:

"I am much stronger than I think I am and no matter what the problem is, there is always a solution. As long as you feel that your voice matters and that you want to recover for yourself, you will get there. I learnt that it is impossible to recover on your own: you may get far but you will fall hard. I have learnt to talk about things, to say what is going on and to be honest to the people trying to support me."

Likewise, her outlook on life has changed. Anonymous feels more grown up and is happy to help others with her story. She is aware that she might not be able to stop her mental illness from taking over again, but she knows she can fight back.

This is her advice for everyone going through similar problems:

"Talk. You don't have to get treatment right away but talk to someone you can trust, someone you can fall back on. Be honest with that person, no lies, not keeping anything from them, and when you're ready, start talking to a professional, try to find your motivation and try to get some kind of treatment. If one treatment doesn't work, try something else. There will be something out there that can help you start living your life again."

She would also like to share this:

"I would like to give all my love to the people who read this story and feel the same way that I have felt and still feel it some days. Recovery is possible, I truly believe that 100% recovery is possible. I also believe that it is only possible when you want to do it for YOU. You are worth so much more than you think. You can be loved if you start to love yourself, and I know it is hard but that doesn't make it impossible.

STORY # 75

ANOREXIA NERVOSA

Anonymous is from Canada and she is a traveling writer. She shares, "The written word is my passion." She hopes to have a stable future: "When I am ready to settle down, I suppose that I would run and own a B&B. Though I am a long way from it." Anonymous was never officially diagnosed but she has struggled with different forms of mental illnesses to varying degrees. One of the most prominent mental illnesses that she had to combat was her minor battle with Eating Disorder Not Otherwise Specified (EDNOS). She doesn't know what caused her mental disorders but she suspects it might be different factors. She reveals, "I would say that I grew up having significantly low self-esteem, with a mixture of bullying and being a natural introvert. I spent the majority of my adolescence believing that I was disliked by everyone. Thus I stayed silent and turned to terrifyingly unhealthy ways to cope."

Those who spent time around her noticed her unhealthy eating habits, weight loss and overall behavioral changes. Anonymous developed disturbing symptoms such as restricting calories with days of binging and purging, weight loss, moodiness and irritability, hiding food, lying about what she had eaten, mirror obsession and social isolation. She recalls, "For the most part I put on a face around people but I kept interactions to a minimum with others. I started to become a loner." Anonymous' thoughts eventually revolved only around eating. She ended up researching tips and support for weight loss and staying strong on Pro-Ana websites, blogs, videos. She discloses, "Everything was calculated. Every bit of food and drink was portioned. Pro-Ana helped me find diets, tricks and exercise plans. Simply looking at food was distressing. At first, it was just fatty foods. However, after a while, all food looked disgusting to me."

She continues, " 'How many calories', 'Just another hour on my bike', 'Skip dinner, wake up thinner',… My life revolved around Ana and weight loss. It was almost like a voice in my head that would remind me of my appearance. It would tell me that everyone saw the little bits of fat on me, that I was a giant, unworthy of happiness until I succeeded to my goal weight."

Anonymous started smoking cigarettes more regularly to depress her appetite. She made a list of good foods vs. bad foods. This led to the creation of an internal dilemma: she would be devastated if she craved something from the bad food list, or worse, caved in. Anonymous wanted to be anorexic, she says, "I wanted to have a disorder so I forced it upon myself. It became an obsession. Nothing else mattered. It was like a secret affair." She ended up thinking about self-harm and suicide. During her recovery, she ended up making small gashes along her wrists because she was desperate to find a way to release her anguish.

Her relationships got affected since she stopped being social, even with her best friends. She confides, "At work I tried to stay/appear positive but everyone was noticing my weight loss, eating habits and less positive demeanor. I was short, irritable and harsh at times." At the beginning, anonymous felt strong and powerful like she was superior to the rest of the world by being able to resist, but it was toxifying. Ultimately though, she became depressed. Due to this, she felt a wide range of feelings: "I felt trapped, disgusting, damaged, ashamed and pathetic. The only thing that made sense at that time was to make my disorder stronger, to feel powerful within myself."

A major turning point for anonymous was noticing how her disorder was affecting her overall character. Her usual positive and optimistic outlook on life was slowly diminishing. She sensed that she was on the path to a place where she did not want to be. She realized that certain thoughts and feelings never really go away. Therefore, what helped her maintain control was moving in slow motion by taking each thought one at a time, and reminding herself that she is a more beautiful person without Ana. The strategies she uses for self-help is positive self-talk, placing health above appearance, making eating a priority and a lot of willpower. Since anonymous doesn't do well with lectures, she has surrounded herself with helpful people who listen to her.

The biggest lesson she learned was about being kind to herself. She describes, "Like for most people who have experienced some degree of an eating disorder, it was a form of punishment induced upon myself, restricting and distorting a basic human need for survival, death in slow motion." Nonetheless, she is now in recovery and has the strength to live positively, She asserts, "I am a big believer in the universe and have embarked upon a spiritual path, it is what keeps me in the present moment. Of course, I do still struggle with times of depression and anxiety, but being free of Ana had allowed me to focus on the root feelings I have, to heal, to be healthy." She is not sure of anything that will prevent her mental illness from happening again. But now, she does whatever she has to do to remain conscious when the feelings resurface.

This is her advice for anyone struggling with a eating disorder:

"When you are in it, it can feel like the loneliest place in the world. But the truth is just the very opposite. Everyone else is there hiding just the same. They are just camouflaged by their own monsters."

She would also like to share this:

"I just remember waking up every morning. Restless sleep. Starved and uncertain. Slowly my bones started to protrude from my skin. Everyday. More and more. Before getting out of bed I would caress my body. Only then could I feel at ease. Intoxicated by my success. I felt great because I looked great. I am now in shock of how far I have come."

STORY # 76

DEPRESSION & GENERALIZED ANXIETY DISORDER

Molly is from Australia and is into opera, theatre, cabaret and fantasy books. She is also a writer and is learning Welsh. What's more, she belly dances and is part of a youth theatre company. Her future goal is to have a degree in computer science and have a career that involves computer work that allows her to travel. Molly was diagnosed with major depression when she was 14 and has Generalized Anxiety Disorder (GAD). She says, "Looking back, I can tell I was experiencing symptoms frequently enough to be called depression when I was 11." At first, Molly informed her mother of her suspicions of mental illness and she was taken to the GP and received a referral to see a psychologist/ therapist. She recalls, "We started Cognitive Behavioral Therapy (CBT). CBT worked for quite a while: I got the all clear. However, I relapsed about a year later and ended up being medicated. Today I am still on the anti-anxiety meds and using CBT to cope with my depression."

Molly felt all kinds of symptoms: "The depression was extreme periods of glumness, unwillingness to do things and distancing myself from my day-to-day life and interactions. I would lose interest in things, then in getting up; to binge-eat then starve." In addition to that, Molly became really antisocial (not asocial) and amoral. She couldn't complete simple tasks and felt that she was right and that her experiences did not hurt her or anyone else around her. She also experienced symptoms from her anxiety disorder: "I felt lightheadedness, inability to answer questions or to ask them in class, inability to use public bathrooms or to eat in public/around others, panic attacks without definitive triggers, freaking out about being apart from my mum or my dog, freaking out if I was with them too and constantly fearing that I would hurt someone I love. I would panic about clothes and cancel outings just because I was so anxious about being seen in an outfit and having people know I chose it for myself."

She also felt irrational rage and needed to lash out: "I got really aggressive and curt with people. I would yell, cuss, and be incredibly impatient. I thought I was justified in how I treated others." Due to this, she lost some friends, nearly left some of her extracurricular activities and started failing her classes. She remembers, "When my depression relapsed, I missed a month of school and a full set of assignments, lowering my grade considerably since I had missed half of the exam content."

It got bad to the point that Molly considered suicide several times. She did try to end her life once but stopped due to a panic attack that was triggered by the fear that her body would be overlooked once she passes away, and thankfully she couldn't pierce her skin because she could not find a sharp knife. Molly also self-harmed. She confides, "I would also unconsciously scratch myself when my anxiety was really bad. I would just start scratching my arms, legs, etc. when I was really upset. I still have a few little scars hanging around from digging out chunks. I never noticed until after my anxiety had cooled and I could feel the motion. It wasn't intentional and I managed to start checking it and stopping, once I realized how bad a habit it was getting."

Molly's relationships got affected because it took her two years to let her friends know, "Hey, I'm depressed. I have crippling anxiety, just so you know." A lot of people really struggled to understand her behavior before she mentioned anything. Once Molly opened up to others, most people came back and her friendships grew solid again. She explains, "The hardest part about talking to people about my mental health was establishing that I, personally, don't mind what others talk about around me, and if it bugs my anxiety/depression I'll move off – trying to get them not to censor themselves around me was a bit tricky." She continues, "My family were fine. My sister didn't really understand it but she accepted it and all that came with it. My mum was fantastic – she's been depressed before too. She was coming out of eighteen years of it, so she was really helpful." Before Molly opened up, she couldn't understand why others weren't trying to help her: "I couldn't understand that they didn't know that I needed and wanted help. My behaviors damaged a lot of my relationships but once I was out with it, it was so much better."

The turning point for Molly was two years after being diagnosed. During CBT, she realized that she couldn't have a better life, relationships, and everything if she didn't want to be better, "I came to understand I need to work for it – seeing a therapist weekly or bi-monthly or however frequently was not an instant miracle cure. I had to put work into it and run some hard yards before I could get better. This understanding made it so much easier." The strategies that she used to help maintain control over her mental illnesses was using self-help resources. In addition to that, she searched online for other people's experiences and started yoga and going to the gym. But it was her mother who helped her the most. She proudly relates, "Mum was a champ and made sure I was okay. She let me take mental health days when I needed them, took me to my therapy, shared her experiences with me and joined the gym with me."

The lesson that she learned from this ordeal was that in order to help herself, she had to want that help first. She should be willing to seek help and she shouldn't be ashamed of her mental health. This experienced has changed Molly. She says, "I am much kinder and more relaxed now. I am less judgmental and more open to sharing and honesty than I was before. I'm far less proud, envious and cruel. I find much more pleasure in the simple things in life these days."

This is her advice for others struggling with similar situations:

"Never be scared to reach out for help. Never be ashamed of needing help, or having a condition. Don't let your pride get in the way of seeking help. Sometimes, there will be people in your life whom you cannot avoid or separate from, and they will not be good for your mental health – don't endure in silence. Tell them what causes you trouble and ask that they avoid those behaviors, opinions, etc. around you. If they don't, then it's time to take the extra step and force a separation. Sadly, that will happen. You cannot change if you do not want to change. The same goes for others."

She would also like to share this:

"Hope this has helped some people understand themselves or the people around them with mental health illnesses. Remember to put your health before anything else. Remember that you might feel content and safe in the bubble your mental health has created for you but just because you feel that way doesn't mean that you are actually well."

STORY # 77

BIPOLAR DISORDER

M olly is from Florida and will become an Air Force wife. She is a published author and shares, "My first novel was when I was 16. I'm currently working on my second one." She loves watching movies and reading books and basically anything that has to do with storytelling. Molly reveals, "My favorite fairy tale is Beauty and the Beast and my favorite book series is The Black Dagger Brotherhood by J. R. Ward." She has two cats and is fond of cooking and eating. Molly wishes to have a successful and happy future: she wants to publish her second book, get married and start a family. In addition to that, she would like to become a high school English teacher.

At the age of 11, Molly was diagnosed with depression. However, after a manic episode where she stayed awake for 74 hours straight, her diagnosis was changed to bipolar when was around 14 years old. She reveals, "I had more depression months than manic periods. But more recently, I've balanced out, though a new struggle with anxiety has emerged." Molly was put on medication and went to therapy. At first, she struggled with taking the medicine because she did not want to admit she was sick. And then there were years where she was off medication and didn't talk to anyone. She confides, "But, I'm taking my health more seriously now and I've accepted that I have a chronic illness. I'm currently on a 'mood-stabilizer' that also helps me sleep through the night."

Molly dealt with different symptoms such as sadness, tiredness, lack of motivation, lack of appetite and sluggishness. She discloses, "I didn't enjoy anything really, just slept a lot. I tried to commit suicide four or five times while I was in High School. On the few, rare occasions I had a manic period, I was quick to anger, had racing thoughts, couldn't concentrate, was a little paranoid, couldn't sleep, [had a] very big appetite and I really really wanted to spend money on frivolous things." Her anxiety made her go through overwhelming panic episodes where all she could do was lie on the floor.

Molly's daily life became a battle and everyday she had to tell herself this, "Okay, Molly, it's time to get out of bed!" and had to count how many hours she had slept to reinforce the idea that she had gotten enough sleep. When something bad happened, for instance if she broke a glass or something simple like that, she had to take a few breaths to simply realize that it's super fixable and not a big deal. Thankfully, her fiancé is helpful and talks her through how they can both fix the problem. Another issue she has been dealing with since the end of elementary school, is that she has to remind herself to eat because she never has an appetite.

Molly has thought about suicide a lot and got extremely close, four or five times in High School. The only self-harming she has done is biting her nails and the skin off her lips. She confesses, "When I wanted to die, it was because I wanted the darkness and the pain to end. But every time I wanted to do this, I thought of my family and my pets and I just couldn't do it. I didn't want to hurt anyone; I don't want to hurt anyone. I know what it's like to be hurt and depressed and abused and forgotten. I don't want anyone to ever feel the way I've felt."

Molly's family understood her. She explains, "My mom's battled depression on and off all her life, her father's mother was bipolar. And I recently found out that my dad's sister is bipolar. So my family understood... that it was sort of my brain attacking itself and it wasn't really me and I needed help, and wanted help." The first time Molly tried to kill herself was in 9th grade. Her mother was going away on a trip and the day before she left, she decided to leave Molly at her father's house instead of her best friend. For some reason, Molly felt that was the last straw and tried to kill herself. She laid a letter out, and her mother found it. Molly recalls, "All I remember is her getting angry. She still went on her trip, but she did leave me at my friend's house instead of my dad's." She continues, "My mom still went on her trip to see her boyfriend, I felt that much more alone. I remember staying at my friend's house, lying on her couch, unable to sleep for hours, just wishing she'd come check up on me." Due to this, Molly felt trapped even though her depression doesn't make her feel at all. She says, "I'm so used to the depression that I just sort of go 'oh, okay' and go about my day."

The turning point for Molly to control her mental disorder was when her fiancé was laid off and they were forced to move out of their first apartment together. She relates, "I remember feeling unsafe in my own skin. I called my dad while he was at work and asked if he could come over for the weekend. I told him what I was feeling. After he said yes, I called my friend to watch my cats. And then I went into work to tell my boss – I told him the truth, that I was suicidal and needed to be around family." By doing all this, she felt like she wanted to live and wanted to get better. Molly contacted her doctor, got meds, started eating better and regulated her sleep. Around the same time she began writing her new book, which has always been a tool for her survival.

Her strategy to continue her recovery is to remind herself of why she wants to live. She explains, "Every day I try to give myself a reason of why I have a good and happy life. Sometimes it's my kitties, sometimes it's a really good movie. Sometimes it's because I want to publish another book and I find such accomplishments in writing. Sometimes it's because I want to have kids. And with taking those few minutes to note even just one good thing, I can get up and keep going."

Molly also says:

"There is beauty all around us, there is reason to feel happiness everywhere. I smile when I see my ivy plant on my desk and I love the smell of the incense I burn. It's hard, it's really hard to find the light in the dark but that's all you need. Just to stare at that light no matter how small, and know that there's hope. There's always hope. There's always a reason to keep trying. Even if it's that you want to find the love of your life, or adopt three dogs, or have a rose garden, or eat at the world's oldest restaurant, or memorize every line of Harry Potter. There's always a reason to keep going."

Her family and friends have helped by giving her a safe place. Molly explains, "A place to go when I don't want to be myself, where for a few hours or a few days I can just sort of be on holiday from life., where I can eat and sleep and enjoy my time with people I like. They don't judge, they don't force me to talk, but they're there." Molly learned that her strongest attribute is her will: "I may feel small, I may feel broken, but I'm not. I'm still me, I'm still a person who was gifted life, who has the ability to help others. I don't want anyone to ever feel the way I've felt."

Her outlook on life has changed as well. Molly doesn't know a life without darkness: her parents got divorced, she had terrible health as a child, she has been in two abusive relationships, and much more. But through all that darkness, she has decided to focus on the light. She claims, "I know that life can be very beautiful and that happiness is all around it. I make a point to surround myself with good things to make my home a safe and happy place. And I work... I work very hard, every moment that I'm awake, to do something about my state of existence. I fight every single day, every single way, to make sure that I get the happiness I want and need and deserve."

This is her advice for those suffering with mental illness:

"Getting help is the best thing you can do for yourself. But the most important thing is accepting that there's a problem. It sucks and it hurts and you're going to be angry... maybe for all your life, but that's okay. Your health and safety and happiness is what matters. Do everything in your power to make your life exactly want you want it to be, exactly what you need it to be. Don't be afraid to change everything... keep going, keep fighting, until you find your safe haven."

Molly would also like to share this:

"I hope that this helps people to know that they are not alone. If I could reach out to hug every single person who's hurting, I would. 'Be the change you want to see in the world', even if it's just your own little bubble. Make those changes, fight for your happiness. And above all, be there for those who need you."

STORY # 78

DEPRESSION, ANXIETY DISORDER, POST-TRAUMATIC STRESS DISORDER, ATTENTION DEFICIT HYPERACTIVITY DISORDER

Vincent was born in Manhattan and has moved around a lot since he was a child. He loves to write in his free time and his musical interests are pretty broad, though he has always favored Classical over anything else. He declares, "The violin, piano, cello; it's all great in my opinion!" Vincent is also an avid reader and was on a high school level by the time he got to 5th grade. He doesn't know where he will be in the next 5 years but he would like to go to college or have some sort of career that will allow him to travel. He explains, "I've had to learn to be very flexible when it comes to planning anything in the future. My life has been prone to sudden and unexpected changes."

Vincent was diagnosed at an early age with depression and social anxiety. He relates, "Over time, the depression just grew worse. I'd battled self-harm and anorexia throughout high school. When I was 17, I was sexually assaulted by a man while I was heavily under the influence of something, though I'm not sure of exactly what. That incident set something off and reminded me that it might not have been the first time. So Post-Traumatic Stress Disorder (PTSD) and childhood trauma were added to the list." At 18 he was diagnosed with Attention Deficit Hyperactivity Disorder (ADHD), but medication has helped him a lot. His mother sent him to see a therapist around the age of 11 and ever since then Vincent has continued to see different professionals that combined the treatment of medication and therapy.

Since the age of 10, Vincent realized that he felt different from others. By the age of 11, he started self-harming. He explains, "I had started to self-harm in an attempt to use some sort of physical distraction to gain emotional relief. I've had panic attacks as far back as I can remember. A lot of times it would start with a feeling of nervousness in my stomach, like you know something bad is going to happen. I would sweat and shake and my heart would start to pound." Vincent's perception would become warped and a lot of times things would feel like they're moving in slow motion, yet too fast for him to catch up. His low self-esteem would cause him to constantly analyze everything that was wrong with him. He remembers, "I would convince myself that everyone was looking at the things I considered flaws." After the assault when he was 17, Vincent became so paranoid that he would run into him or someone who was at the party that night. He confides, "I remember being at a store with my mother and sister one afternoon. I thought I saw him outside walking towards me. I immediately had a panic attack and ran to the car, where I waited for my mother for about an hour, as low in the seat as I could go while still looking out the window. Eventually I realized he was wearing the same outfit from that night, so it couldn't have been real."

Vincent's daily life became affected because he couldn't leave the house and most days, he had a hard time getting out of bed. He ended up making excuses not to hangout with his friends. He reveals, "I did things like that for so many years that it became normal." At the age of 16, he forced himself to socialize, but after the assault, he decided to leave things as they were. He confesses, "I couldn't stand to be around people, including even my own family sometimes. Anyone who wanted to help me in any way was also someone I didn't want to deal with." He simply did not have the energy to eat or talk or even shower on some days. He didn't even get a haircut: any place where there were bound to be a lot of people was off the table.

At the age of 12, he sadly attempted suicide for the first time. He describes, "I suppose I didn't really know what I was doing, but I was decided. I took some pills one night after school. A lot of pills actually. It wasn't enough to kill me, I later found out, but it was enough to put me in an incredible amount of pain and vomiting constantly throughout the day. I said that it was the flu so that I wouldn't have to go to school, and I spent the day crying. Scratching and digging my nails into my hands and arms eventually turned into cutting and drug abuse in high school."

His relationships with others eventually got affected. He did not get along with his father and it only got worse throughout the years and his mother, who he did get along with, did not know how to handle the situation. Vincent adds, "In my efforts to try and fake my way out of depression and anxiety, I had developed a very large circle of friends in high school. By the time we graduated, that circle had really sunk down to just a few people. They became my best friends but the springboard for the relationship was that they suffered from depression as badly as I did."

Vincent felt all kinds of emotions except for happiness: "Eventually I just felt numb. I started to just go about my business, feeling nothing. Someone would get into an argument with me and they would give up when they saw that I just didn't have it in me to care." For a while he was okay with it but then one after another, his best friends started moving away and he ended up feeling alone and claustrophobic. He discloses, "I felt suffocated and trapped in my own life."

The turning point for Vincent was at the age 22 when he was living on his own. He somehow managed to land a great job making good money at a hotel downtown. In September of 2014, his doctor prescribed him Prozac. He reveals, "I was hesitant due to past experiences but I found myself at the point of willing to try something new." The medication helped but it wasn't enough. He explains, "I still felt like I was just barely hanging on."

Around November there was an incredible snow storm which had buried whole cars. Roads were shut down and people kept calling off of work. No one was coming into the restaurant anymore except the buildings' residents. Money stopped coming in and the bills were piling up. In December, Vincent started having moments when he would suddenly lose consciousness, which was provoked by a rare side effect of Prozac. He recalls, "I broke my glasses and had two black eyes. My social anxiety was in full swing because I felt like everyone was staring and wondering what was wrong with me." Vincent couldn't afford food anymore and didn't know if he would still have electricity the next day. Unfortunately, he got hit by a car while crossing the street one night and the driver drove away. He didn't go to the hospital because he couldn't afford another bill and couldn't miss the chance to make even a few dollars at work. His boss made him leave until he returned with a note from a doctor. He went to the hospital, and was held there for two days. Then he got the flu and took the bus home from the hospital, showered and went to bed on his twin size air mattress, because he couldn't afford an actual one. His family was having financial problems so he couldn't ask them for help.

Vincent lost his job due to a streak of tardiness and went back to his old job at 7-Eleven. He confesses, "I knew I needed help. I'd planned to kill myself and I think my roommates might have known it. They all kind of approached me in different ways, individually." Vincent continues, "I spoke to my mother regularly. She knew something was wrong too and she said that she wouldn't be able to handle it if anything happened to me and made me promise to take care of myself. I called her back the next night and I told her that I don't know if I can keep that promise. In that moment I decided that I would try one more time." In four days, he scraped together the rent to hold his roommates over, quit his job, announced his sudden departure and packed his things. On the 5th, day his mother picked him up.

The strategies he used to help control his mental illness was writing, even though it was very difficult for Vincent at first. He would spent months in his bed and barely moved. The room he stayed in had a glass sliding door, so he would spend his time watching deers, birds, foxes and a groundhog. He remembers, "They were all so full of life and I wanted that. It was an unexpected motivator and reminder of why I came here: to be able to feel alive again; and to feel life. I spent a lot of time watching them. I read plenty of books when I would start to feel like I was trapped in my own head." The hardest part of his emotional journey after moving back into his mother's house was that he mainly needed to be alone to work things out on his own. He explains, "I was afraid of what digging into the past would uncover. There was a lot that I would remember that I didn't even realize I'd forgotten. Working through one trauma would bring a flashback of another. It was painful, the worst thing I've ever gone through, but I knew that I needed to do it in order to get better and that it had to be done alone."

This is the lesson he learned from this ordeal:

"Do not be afraid of your past. Don't be afraid of who you are. You need to face yourself before you can face the world. Stop running from your problems or yourself or your past: it won't help. You aren't alone. If you have someone who cares, don't push them away. They can make their own choices and they want to help. LET THEM. Don't ever be afraid to share your story, it could help someone else who's silently suffering."

Vincent feels better now. He doesn't feel like he needs medication and he is less afraid of the world. He can go into a grocery store without having a panic attack. He says, "I can honestly say that for the first time in my life I'm happy. I've accepted myself."

This is his advice for others struggling through similar situations:

"Accept yourself and your condition. Pretending it isn't there won't make it go away, especially if you're doing it for the sake of other people. Don't ever be ashamed of who you are or the things you've been through. Everyone has a story to tell. Don't compare your suffering to other people. There is no 'scale from 1-10' where you aren't allowed to feel sad if you fall on a certain end of the spectrum. You are allowed to be sad or anxious or angry. Not everyone realizes this and will sometimes say things like, 'Well there's people in such and such country that have it so much worse. Be grateful for what you have!' You are allowed to feel your pain without guilt. AND PLEASE PLEASE PLEASE don't ever be afraid to seek help! Even if you feel like you aren't sure you need it, or like your situation isn't bad enough to need it, therapy or counselling is for EVERYONE."

STORY # 79

DEPRESSION, OBSESSIVE-COMPULSIVE DISORDER & SOCIAL ANXIETY DISORDER

Philip is from New York and he has a passion for learning. He says, "Anything that can be learnt, I want to know it." He enjoys listening to music or playing music of his own. Philip taught himself how to play the ukulele and wants to learn to play the cello. He is fond of playing video games and researches into why the characters in the games are the way they are. Philip doesn't have any huge future goals so he instead makes small ones. He expresses, "This coming December, I am going to try and build my first ever PC." He has been diagnosed and still struggles with depression, Obsessive-Compulsive Disorder (OCD) and social anxiety. Philip was originally forced into therapy after a failed suicide attempt. During the summer after his freshman year, he saw a psychiatrist and was prescribed medication, but he is still in the process to see which one works better for him. Unfortunately, he stopped therapy because it is terrifying, but, with a more solid support structure, he is willing to give it another try.

Philip has dealt with many symptoms. He describes, "My depression makes me feel lonely and I can seldom feel a connection between myself and my peers. I disconnect myself from my feelings and most of the time I just find myself feeling devoid of all emotions." Philip is constantly challenging himself just to shake someone's hand or touch something unfamiliar. He reveals, "I wash my hands way too many times to count throughout the day and patterns dominate my daily thoughts and actions. My OCD revolves around the number 8, so things must be done in multiples or add up to 8. My bed used to have two sheets on it so I would make my bed 4 times each morning. (2 sheets x 4 = 8)." At times, Philip has to turn on and off certain appliances if it doesn't feel right. He is an outgoing introvert and wants to meet people, but is constantly dreading that they will find his faults and hate him forever.

This has immensely affected Philip's life and he has resorted to self-harm to cope. He describes, "I used to cut the bottoms of my feet, and, being a student and an avid martial artist, I walked around a lot, causing a lot of pain. Once, my feet became too heavily scarred and I began to cut my hips. Wearing a belt for martial arts and just in general, I would purposely tie it super tight, inflicting more pain. Now I have moved onto my arms and chest. The reason I would cause my body so much pain is because when you can feel nothing, you can always feel pain."

Philip's relationships also got affected. He has a difficult time finding friends, and the friendships he has are strained. He says, "My family life is weird, coming from an adoptee, and my parents have NO idea how to help. They mean well and read a lot about how to help, however, it is still very challenging. I try hard, and I mean very hard, to make valuable friendships but it is very hard when all these personal things get in the way, especially when I have a hard enough time trusting and opening up to people." Due to this, Philip doesn't know what to feel and is now desperately trying to feel something.

The turning point for Philip was realizing how little he had left in himself. He feels that the poet Neil Hilborn traps this meaning perfectly in his poem The Future. At the moment, Philip doesn't have a strategy to overcome his mental illnesses and because of this he is considering to go to therapy again. He discloses, "For the most part, I am very passive about my disorders and do the bare minimum to get by. But keeping myself busy all the times can help me avoid overthinking." Philip has a hard time asking for help and accepting help from others. He confesses, "I hope to find someone who is stubborn enough to stick around and help me even when I refuse it. Maybe one day."

The lesson that he has learned from this ordeal is that:

"Treat everyone you meet with love and respect, try and make them smile, because you never know what type of war they are fighting."

Even his outlook on life has changed: "I've never really had a positive outlook on life, more of a realistic outlook. I know life isn't all sunshine and rainbows, but I also realized that it isn't all overcast and dreary either." Philip wonders what he would be like without these disorders, but he thinks he wouldn't recognize himself.

This is a poem Philip wrote about depression:

10 things I learned from dealing with depression

1. *F*** you depression. Who gave you the right to control my life? This is my story and I will write it how I want. I can be that lone alpha who's looking for his pack. Better yet, I'll be that rich CEO who don't need no help.*
2. *Actually.. It's okay to ask for help. Especially when you need it. And I know. I know that it may seem scarier than anything that has come before it. And that's okay. Let yourself be vulnerable.*
3. *Let yourself be vulnerable, in front of other people. Let the room fill up with mutual sadness, like our mutual hate for one Donald Trump.*
4. *It's okay to hate Trump. I hate him too. And your ex, it's okay to hate him as well. In fact. There are days where it's okay to hate*

every single being on this earth. But when you hit that point, know that I love you.

5. *Learn to love yourself. In a world dominated by hate crimes and hatred towards anyone who doesn't look like us. It is important and essential to love yourself. Even if you don't want to, or feel you deserve it. Learn to be accepting of love and give it back when you can.*

6. *When you feel down. Like all the water from all the major seas, oceans, lakes, and this specific glass of water are being thrust onto you from all directions, and it feels like your drowning in a room full of air. When you feel down, know it's okay to take time for yourself. Do not rely on food or friends, or season 4 of F.R.I.E.N.D.S, that will only make you lonelier when they're gone. Focus on yourself. You are the only constant in your life when all around you the only constant is change.*

7. *It's okay to fall in love. It's an inevitable fault of the universe. Let yourself. It's okay to beat this with someone. Some will. Some will not. But having someone who loves you certainly will help.*

8. *Let go of the things that don't matter. What happened five years ago doesn't matter. What happened yesterday you cannot change. What matters is that you learned from it.*

9. *So here you are. With me, and together we are here. Experiencing and clawing our way through this enigma we call life. And at the end, we don't get much out of it. But it's the experiences, and the pure act of touching someone else's life. That makes it all worth it. You are worth it.*

10. *Tomorrow is a new day. So I challenge you to live until the sunrise. Whether that's 4 seconds, 6 minutes, 12 hours, or 24. Live to the fullest. Because eventually the earth will rotate enough so that the sunlight falls perfectly onto our little town. And..I will see you.*

STORY # 80

PERSISTENT DEPRESSIVE DISORDER WITH MAJOR DEPRESSIVE EPISODES, GENERALIZED ANXIETY DISORDER, EATING DISORDERS NOT SPECIFIED, POST-TRAUMATIC STRESS DISORDER, ATTENTION DEFICIT HYPERACTIVITY DISORDER & BORDERLINE PERSONALITY DISORDER

Bailey is from Wisconsin, USA and she enjoys writing, doing special effects makeup and really loves space. She plans on having a bright future: "I plan on becoming a psychologist and moving abroad." Bailey was diagnosed with and still has dysthymia with major depressive episodes, Generalized Anxiety Disorder (GAD), Eating Disorders Not Otherwise Specified (EDNOS), Post-Traumatic Stress Disorder (PTSD), Attention Deficit Hyperactivity Disorder (ADHD), dyslexia, mood disorder unspecified and Borderline Personality Disorder (BPD).

Bailey believes her mental disorders was caused by a combination of different things. She explains, "It's a combination of genetics and my childhood. My mom's side has depression, bipolar disorder, and anxiety very prominently among them. My childhood wasn't the greatest so that had to do with the other conditions. My dad is a narcissist who was verbally abusive and possibly physically towards me (a lot of my childhood has been suppressed). He would yell at me for things like my interests, my weight, and my personality traits- things children really can't help. Also, at the ages of 15 and 17 I was raped by my ex-roommate's friend (15) and my ex-boyfriend (17)." She has received talk therapy, dialectical behavior therapy and group and family therapy.

Bailey has dealt with numerous symptoms: "I had severe bursts of anger. I was like a ticking time bomb at all times. I also had blackouts where I would become very destructive and would hurt myself or others. I had hallucinations and paranoia. My anxiety was constant and when a depressive episode would hit, I would stay in bed for days." Due to this, her daily life was affected. She skipped school, lost weight very quickly and lost a lot of friends due to her temper and destructive tendencies. Bailey confesses, "I became a foreigner to myself." She has attempted suicide four times and has been hospitalized three times. What's more, she has also self-harmed for seven years. Bailey relates, "I was an addict for two years. I've been in countless fights and have hurt those I love."

She ended up feeling all kinds of emotions. Bailey was full of rage because no one trusted her and she didn't know what was going on with her. She remembers, "I was confused because I knew something wasn't right because my friends didn't snap at little things or have scars up their arms, but at the same time I didn't care because I liked the rush of being the way I was." The turning point for Bailey was seeing how her loved ones suffered. She recalls, "It was hearing my friends cry over the phone asking me why I was acting like this. It was my grandmother's face when I woke up in the hospital from an overdose. It was hearing my mom cry out of happiness when I was baking again. It was my brother hugging me and saying 'I knew the old you was somewhere in there'.

It was ending a toxic relationship and being able to get help. All those little moments showed me that I can get better and people will support me."

The strategies that she used to beat her mental disorders was opening up. She also stopped lying to her therapist. She shares, "I told people when I wasn't okay. I told myself that I could make it through and it would be okay. I threw out my blades and wore short sleeves all the time. I used the coping skills I was taught in the hospital and didn't give up if one didn't work." Her friends and family respected her boundaries and listened when Bailey felt comfortable telling them what was wrong. The lesson that she learned from this ordeal is that happiness always wins. Even her outlook on life has changed; "I'm a lot more empathetic now. I'm always there for people. It makes me want to go into the psychology field in hopes that I can show another person that life isn't so terrible." She now tells herself how lonely she got and how much it hurt, whenever she feels like she is slipping back into her old destructive behavior.

This is Bailey's advice for others struggling:

"Happiness is achievable. It won't come overnight, but you can get there. You just have to fight against what your mind has been telling you. You have to remind yourself you are worth it and you deserve true happiness. It's hard, I'm not gonna lie, but if you can make it through this; you can do it. Keep fighting. I believe in you."

STORY # 81

MAJOR DEPRESSIVE DISORDER & ANXIETY DISORDER

Ryan is from Illinois and loves to read, write, draw, and play video games. He is also a fan of modern rock and techno. He is fond of movies that make him think. Five years from now he sees himself doing something he loves, although he is currently unsure of what that is, but he is willing to giving social work a try. He shared, "I'm hoping to be a counsellor and write or do other arts-y stuff." Ryan would like to be in a stable community with a loving partner.

On September 2015, he was diagnosed with Major Depression Disorder (MDD) and anxiety. At first Ryan stayed as an inpatient in a mental health facility for 10 days, then was on an outpatient partial program for 5 weeks, and is now seeing a therapist. He has dealt with various symptoms stating, "[I had] decreased appetite, extreme fatigue, negative thought patterns, irritability, anxiety, rumination, self-hate, and an increased need for sleep, among many others." These symptoms profoundly affected his quality of life. Ryan had no energy to do the things he enjoyed most. "If I tried, I would overthink and think of ways to get me out of enjoying the activity because I felt it wasn't worth my time", he confessed.

"I isolated myself and pushed all my friends away by not inviting them over or talking to them." Ryan viewed his body and other aspects of the world negatively. He added, "I constantly told myself that I hated my life and felt hopeless, worthless, useless, and everything I did was pointless. I told myself that I had no use for the world, that it would be better without me."

Ryan considered suicide and even wrote a note, disclosing: "I planned and planned, but I could never finish it due to complications that I couldn't resolve. I wasn't going to attempt without a foolproof plan, I wanted to succeed."

His relationships dwindled as he isolated himself further and didn't talk to anyone. He often acted irritable and this caused some disconnection and discord between Ryan and his family. He often felt lonely and useless. "I didn't know whether to tell anyone about how I felt or not, basically because I believed men should not show weakness or emotion. My viewpoints have changed since then", he mentioned.

The turning point for Ryan was when he was putting away his journal in a hiding spot, when his mother came in and confronted him. "She told me she can't take my behavior any more. The next day I got evaluated and put into inpatient care program." This incident forced Ryan's parents to evaluate their parenting. With help Ryan is managing his illnesses and is working towards recovery.

He now uses the skills he learned in the hospital and outpatient program to cope with day to day living. Cognitive behavioral therapy has been useful for Ryan. He reported, "I learned to recognize my negative thoughts, reality check them, and use neutral prompts instead." He now has better eating habits and exercises to stabilize his mood and energy levels. His parents and close relatives support Ryan by trying to understand what he was going through. "We had many talks on how things in the household would change for the better and now my parents are working harder to make sure my brothers and I live a happy life", he explained.

When asked Ryan said he has learned a lot from this experience:

> "I learned that if I work hard for what I love in life, it'll come. It may not come tomorrow, or the week after that, but my hard work will pay off one day. There's always hope, even in the darkest of times. There's always a sliver of hope to hang onto."

Ryan feels he is more insightful than before and can understand people better now. His therapy has brought him closer to his family and friends. Ryan can stay on top of things now and he makes sure his negative thoughts don't go unchecked. He also finds it easier to take care of his body and mind to stay healthy.

This is his advice for others battling mental illness:

> "Recovery from mental illness is a process. You will have ups and downs. Just because you fell down doesn't mean you can't get back up. Try to stay on top of things and vent to your friends and family that you trust and will support you.

Everyone has to deal with the cards they've been dealt. Try to make do with what you have and improve. Look at your life and see what things you could change. Work toward those goals with the support of your family and friends. A healthy balance of certain aspects in your life really does wonders for your mood."

STORY # 82

AUTISM, DEPRESSION & EATING PROBLEM

Felix is from Massachusetts and likes to knit, write poetry and fanfiction. His goal is to study literature and psychology in college. He is autistic and transgender, suffering from depression and an eating disorder. Felix reveals, "I am over the worst of my depression, and [I am] in the process of recovering from self-harm. I still have food problems though." At first, his diagnosis wasn't official because it came from a social worker. He adds, "My diagnosis [became] official when I ended up in a partial hospitalization program after attempting suicide and getting kicked out of Camp Aranu'tiq for writing concerning poetry." He also received group therapy, where he learned many coping skills and how to think more positively. Not only that, but Felix was prescribed Zoloft.

He had to struggle with numerous symptoms, constantly feeling tired and irritable. He hated himself and thought that he was annoying everyone around him. Felix explained, "Life didn't seem worthwhile. I had trouble concentrating, and procrastinated often, which made me hate myself more, and so I spiraled." He became dysphoric, and began to skip meals because he wanted to lose his curves to look less feminine.

Felix's life declined and was having trouble concentrating. His grades began to slip. Felix grew exhausted and stressed due to the lack of nutrients and calories. He confesses, "I was just negative the majority of the time, and so I missed out on a lot of opportunities I would have liked because I felt too tired or depressed to partake in them." Felix began self-harming by scratching, that led to cutting with scissors. Felix tried to kill himself using mouthwash on June 8th, after considering it on and off for about four months.

He had a difficult time with his relationships. "I would confide in my friends about the self-harming and meal skipping, they would try to get me to stop. I would, for a while, but then I'd be back at it again and I felt like I was disappointing them", he mentioned. The relationship with his parents suffered because of his irritability. Which led them to yell at each other a lot. Felix felt angry and desperate, he thought there was no way out of his cycle of self-hatred.

The turning point was after he got kicked out of Camp Aranu'tiq for writing unsafe poetry. His parents got him a psychological evaluation at Newton Wellesley Hospital and he was sent to Westwood Lodge's partial hospitalization program, where he learned how to properly cope with depression. The strategies he used maintain control is using the techniques he learned, called "reframe my thinking". This works by pausing in the middle of destructive thoughts and changing it into a positive one. He said, "If I start thinking that I'm selfish for having tried to kill myself, I reframe my thinking by telling myself that suicidal thoughts were just a struggle I had and it didn't make me a bad person. I am not selfish now because I know that hurting myself hurts others and I have a support system."

His friends helped him by being there or simply hanging out with him. His parents helped by putting him into treatment and being more empathic and understanding at home. Felix learned that people do care and situations, like getting kicked out of camp, can turn into experiences for growth. He asserts, "I also learned that the negative thought patterns that I thought were unchangeable aspects of my personality weren't, and they were just symptoms of depression." Not only that, but his outlook in life has changed, stating, "My depression made my outlook on life a whole lot darker, but it also helped me because before I suffered from depression and self-harm, I would judge people for self-harming because I thought it was for attention. I can't do that anymore because I know it isn't for attention. It was a coping mechanism. A bad one, sure, but it was one. I will prevent myself from going back [to them] by taking my medication and using my new coping skills, as well as telling someone if I start to get bad again. I will also continue to avoid self-harming and try to eat regular meals."

This is Felix's advice to those tackling mental disorders:

"Being found out or forced into treatment is not the end of the world. It sucks and feels unfair, but going along with it will usually be more beneficial in the long run. And, trust me, there is a long run. Killing yourself always leaves someone behind, and if you live, the people around you will not trust you anymore. Depression sucks, but with medication and/or therapy, it doesn't have to ruin your entire life.

Try not to judge people who relapse into self-harm two, three or four times before quitting. I was one of those people, and I always felt guilty afterwards, which led me to want to do it to get rid of the guilt, and so on. It's hard enough without other people's judgement."

STORY # 83

DEPRESSION, ANXIETY DISORDER & POST-TRAUMATIC STRESS DISORDER

Anonymous is from the Washington D.C., and she loves art and reading. She doesn't know where she will be 5 years from now, but reveals, "I'm just hoping I'll be in a better place than I am now." Anonymous was diagnosed and still battles with depression, anxiety, and post-traumatic stress disorder (PTSD). She believes her mental illnesses were caused by different factors. Stating, "The depression and anxiety were genetic with other family issues I'd like to remain private, but the PTSD was caused by a very close family and private friend of mine who molested me while I was at a sleepover. I have a feeling it had happened before, and possibly gone further. At this point, I honestly don't know if I'm a virgin."

Anonymous saw a psychiatrist and therapist regularly for 3 1/2 years and took different medications until recently, when a medication caused severe hallucinations and side effects that would have been fatal. She was put in a mental hospital for a short time, then a partial hospitalization program for a while, but it didn't work out. "Now I'm seeing a new therapist with new medication and it's working well". She had to deal with various symptoms throughout her day. The depression at first made anonymous feel empty, but it eventually turned into despair and sadness. The anxiety caused multiple panic attacks. "The PTSD is still around with the anxiety, but after the molestation, I wasn't able to sleep and would freak out if anyone ever touched me" she confesses.

Anonymous felt lost, explaining, "After the molestation, I actually lost a whole year of my memory. It's now starting to come back in bits and pieces, 3 years later." This situation made her feel like everything was hopeless and meaningless. Anonymous considered suicide, but never attempted it. She did self-harm for about a year. "I would cut my wrists and tell myself I deserved it. I also starved myself for about a year as well. I would sometimes go up to 48 hours without eating."

Not only that, but her relationships became affected. "I lost many close friends because I pushed them away. I felt like they didn't understand what I was going through", she added. Anonymous hasn't overcome her mental disorders, she is learning how to cope and live with them. She now goes to therapy, disclosing: "I never believed talking to a stranger would help, I fought it for a while, but I always feel better after I have a session." Her family have supported her the whole time, even when anonymous pushed them away. Her outlook has changed. She said, "I'm more realistic now. I see things for how they are. I still dream, yes, but not as often as I used to."

This is her advice for those struggling:

"For you individually, I have no idea how your mental illness will work out, because every case is different. You just have to be brave and face it. Don't hide from it. Face, it head on and don't let it consume you."

STORY # 84

BIPOLAR TYPE I & ANXIETY DISORDER

Martha is currently living in Mexico City. She considers herself a reading addict (science fiction, real science) and enjoys writing fanfiction. Martha is fond of progressive rock as well as OST classics. Martha loves to cook, is a Trekkie, and enjoys mystery/horror movies. She tries not to think about future goals explaining:

> "The last time I thought in that way, was before the big earthquake in September 19, 1985. I'm a survivor. In one minute, I lost dreams, house, plans, everything. The best you can do, is prepare for life, just like you prepare for a mountain expedition; with the best of your resources and in all your capacities. But conditions in an expedition could change, from better to worst...to better again."

Martha was diagnosed by a psychiatrist with bipolar type I and anxiety. She received cognitive behavioral therapy (CBT). She doesn't know what caused her mental illnesses, but her doctor suspects it could have been caused by a medical reason. Martha said, "I was supposed to be born on a Wednesday, but wasn't till Saturday. My

Mom suffered from placenta and a very serious hemorrhage. It is assumed that I had fetal distress and lack of oxygen. Doctors said I should have cerebral palsy or more lesions."

Sadly, Martha battles with serious bipolar symptoms. During the depressive cycle of her bipolar disorder, she had four suicide attempts and in the high (manic) cycle she changed her kitchen completely. "Yes, the entire kitchen, as in take out from the walls the shelves, racks, doors, fridge, stove and oven. Disarmed it all and put every piece in perfect order" she reveals. This has affected her life and relationships.

Unfortunately, this is what Martha thinks about every day:

"I think that suicide is the best solution. Every day, I cope with the thought that my daughter, her dad, and even my kittens, need someone better."

Her most serious suicide attempt was when she took 95 pills of phenobarbital and a half liter of whisky. Martha was in a coma for 72 hours. She said, "In México, to attempt suicide is a crime (attempted first-degree murder), so if you 'fail', you go to jail. Unless someone takes care of you. In my case, my dad and one of my brothers signed a document for me to receive psychiatric treatment." She was placed in a clinic for 3 months.

Many people in her life fear Martha, making it difficult for her to get and keep a decent job. She is a chef, a writer, and a motorcycle mechanic, but she has to lie about her mental illness. "I lost my last work for this cause. So, I work by myself in a bakery and catering." She sells her cooked goods in the street and hates pity from others. "As a BP, I lost my right to be angry for real reasons" she added, and because of this she feels sad. Martha also shared, "Therapy taught me to get out of my mental closets. Let me explain; I'm lesbian, mother, writer, and an activist. My family, employers and friends know this. And even though it's 'Martha against the world'. I have a very lovely family, and a few, but very real friends."

Her turning point was when she was placed in the psychiatric clinic after failing to commit suicide. Martha could not see her daughter and she felt guilty. Her family would call her every day and she did not want to disappoint them. "I cooperated with doctors and took medication. Also, I prepared my healing in the same way as a mountain expedition; I ran in the hospital garden to exercise. Meditated and wrote a lot." Her doctor, brother, daughter, best friends, ex-husband, and parents helped Martha along the way. The lesson she learned from this ordeal is 'Vivir, mata' (to live, kills). This means to live in all possible ways before you die.

This is her advice those battling mental illness:

"Seek help and professional advisement. RIGHT NOW. [If] your psychologist doesn't help you? Change them. [If] your meds cannot help you? Try others. DON'T STOP EVER. Many people depend on you. If someone doesn't love you or understand you, LEAVE THEM BEHIND. It sounds rude, but it is for the best.

STORY # 85

DEPRESSION

Anonymous is from Houston, TX and loves music. "I listen to it almost all day, every day. All types of music from rap to R&B to soul, even some indie rock." He enjoys art and grew up drawing and painting. Five years from now he would like to have a career he loves, that will keep food in his stomach and gas in his car, with new Ralph Lauren threads here and there. He said, "I see myself as a freelance Web designer taking piano lessons with the love of my life."

Anonymous self-diagnosed himself with depression and addiction. He shared, "I think that they both fed off each other, which created a terrible monster inside of me that I couldn't shake. I still fight with addiction, as anyone will tell you it's a day to day process, but I try to keep the depression at bay." His addiction started as a way to cope with life. "I'm very sensitive to things and when I start to feel too much, I go straight to my medicine cabinet. Originally, I started taking Vicodin for a bad back, then of course I started taking them to feel better about the situation I was in. Before I knew it, I was hooked" he explained.

He had to battle depressive symptoms, including; sleeping all day, feeling lethargic, pessimistic, and on some days anonymous would feel upset because he didn't die in his sleep. He stopped going to social events and not only that, but he began stealing and pawning things. Anonymous was borderline suicidal. He confessed, "I didn't want to wake up in the mornings, and would sleep until 3 pm. This was a cycle I was stuck in for about 3 years."

Even though Anonymous felt suicidal he never followed through it because he still had faith that one day, things would work out. He reveled, "I could always see my Mom crying at the funeral of her oldest child and I couldn't give her that pain. Although one day the pressure got too much to bear and I sat in my closet, cried, called the National Suicide Hotline, hung up and swallowed 9 Xanax. I'm still here by the grace of God." His relationships with others were a little affected, due to the lack of trust. "Friends would call to check on me to make sure I wasn't dead, other friends stopped checking up on me altogether. But it also brought me closer to God than I have ever been in my life."

Anonymous felt trapped, angry, desperate, and sad. It was a vicious cycle. His depression didn't allow him to leave drugs alone because it was his only way to cope with it at that time. "I was upset due to the fact that I had helped people every day from the age of 16 when I first got a car, but no one would come near me with a 10 foot pole. I felt stagnant because I couldn't even find a job. It was just horrible." The turning point for Anonymous was back in 2013 when he ended up in jail. That moment made him think that things may not be so bad after all. In jail he found a book called The Purpose Driven Life by Rick Warren which greatly impacted him spiritually.

The strategies he used to help maintain control over his mental disorders is to pray every morning, keep a routine throughout the days, getting out of the house and keeping mind over matter. Not only that, but anonymous had friends who heard him out when he needed to speak. He also had friends who showed him how they coped with their depression that didn't involve drugs.

This is what he learned from his ordeal: "The storm doesn't last forever and there are others going through the same struggles as you. The grass isn't always greener, sometimes it's astroturf (an artificial grass surface)."

This experience changed him, "It showed me who my real friends are and what real friends do. I'm still as pessimistic as I was the day I was born, but now I'm happy to wake up at 7 am again and see the sun rise and get some work done during the day." Anonymous is not sure if he can stop any of this from happening again, but he plans on going to therapy once he gets a job.

This is his advice for those who are also battling with mental disorders:

"As cliche as it sounds, try not to give up. I'm not the type to say suicide is selfish nor do I advocate for it, but if you feel you are close to the edge, pick up the phone and call a friend. Text a friend. Tweet your feelings, maybe someone will hear your cries. Write in a journal. Find a new hobby to pursue. Pursue an old hobby. Do something that will keep your mind at ease and keep you calm whether it's depression, addiction or anxiety that has a hold on you."

Mind over matter. All of those old cliches your parents, grandparents and English teachers used to tell you in school, they start to make sense after you turn 24, 25. There's light at the end of the tunnel. You have people who love you, and if you don't have anyone who loves you, love yourself."

STORY # 86

ATTENTION DEFICIT DISORDER, BI-POLAR DEPRESSION, GENERALIZED ANXIETY DISORDER, BINGE EATING DISORDER & SELF-HARM/SUICIDAL TENDENCIES

Madeline is from Cincinnati, Ohio, and is pursuing a BFA in Acting at Wright State University. She enjoys acting, drawing, painting, and crafting. She also loves music, saying "My taste is all across the board, but I especially love listening to pop-punk/ alternative and indie music." Madeline watches a lot of TV and movies because she doesn't have any friends in Tennessee. She added, "When I'm home, I'm all alone, so I often go to the movie theatre by myself to see films. I don't read as much as I wish I do, I have Attention deficit disorder (ADD) and so it's very hard for me to concentrate and my mind wonders frequently, but I love stories which is why I watch as many films as I do."

Five years from now Madeline sees herself as happy. "Cliché I know, but plain and simple I would really like to have some balance in my life, wake up happy, and not spend all my time sleeping to get away." She'd also like to be emotionally stable enough to find herself in a relationship.

She was diagnosed with ADD, Bi-polar depression, general anxiety, with a history of binge eating disorder, self-harm and suicidal thoughts/tendencies. She reveals, "I've had severe body image issues that resulted in a sort of body dysmorphia type condition." She also suffered from insomnia and abused alcohol for some time. 18 years passed until she told anyone about her mental state. She became fearful that she wouldn't make it to her 18th birthday. She confesses:

"After a huge argument with my mother where she angrily asked if I had any plan to do anything with my life, I broke down, asked her for help and told her what had been going on. She took me to see my general doctor, but what she had to offer me didn't work. I instead saw a psychiatrist and a therapist."

Unfortunately, Madeline's medication caused more harm than good. She explained: "I had so many side effects from the medications I actually went crazy. It gave me terrible insomnia, I didn't eat, I began to hallucinate and sometimes I would even speak in Spanish instead of English."

In college, she flushed all her medication down the toilet because they still weren't working. Madeline went half the year alone again when things got bad. "I had a depressive episode nearly every night. I went back to cutting and for the first time even slit my wrists. I knew there was something terribly wrong. I starved myself for a short period and lost about 15 lbs. I felt sick, tired and trapped constantly." Madeline decided to see the college therapist when she asked, "Why are you even here? What are you hoping to get out of it?" So, she went go back home for the summer.

Madeline has dealt with debilitating symptoms, sharing:

"I was always sad. But not sad like when you see a puppy get run over by a car, the kind of sad that sticks to you and won't go away. The kind where it takes away all your good thoughts and makes you think that you're better off dead simply so you won't have to feel this way anymore. When I was 15 I began to feel nothing. Completely and utterly nothing which is why I began to cut, so I could feel something."

Not only that, but she felt angry all the time. She would cry herself to sleep every night and take breaks at school to cry in the bathroom before rehearsals for theatre, orchestra, and class. Madeline body image issues spiraled out of control. She said, "I actually locked myself inside and refused to leave the house because the thought of anyone seeing me made me want to die. I didn't even want to see me. So, for about a month I covered all my mirrors. I didn't even look at them when I brushed my hair or teeth. I couldn't or else I would break down and cry on the floor and hurt myself."

This affected her relationships because Madeline wouldn't go out with people. It was challenging to make friends and she has never been in a romantic relationship. "It's mainly because of how I look and I always worry that they'll hurt me or get hurt. I hate this because I crave attention and a relationship so much, but I can't even get myself to be alone with a boy and feel safe."

The turning point for Madeline was the argument with her mother and the realization that she couldn't do it alone. The strategies she used to beat it were taught by her therapist. "I learned to separate what thoughts were results of my illness and then countered back with something logical. The best one I had was when I felt like killing myself and realized "No, I don't. I want to kill what is making me feel this way. I want to kill my mental illness. I want to kill that so I can be happy. That's what I want. I want to metaphorically kill myself, not actually end my life."

Madeline now is understanding and caring. She also has decided not to push people away, because people don't have to be bad to do a bad thing. "There is theory where I believe that hardship builds better people, understanding people, caring people, strong people, and these people will go on to teach their children how to be the same...The world will be much fuller of these kinds of individuals when our generation starts having children and it can only grow from there too."

This is her advice for those passing through similar situations:

"GET HELP. I know people say this all the time, but take it from someone who waited 18 years to even tell someone they had a problem...get help. Tell a friend, family member, counsellor, teacher, SOMEONE. It is the hardest thing to do in that moment, but it is only a moment and you will be so thankful...but remember if you aren't ready to, it's okay... Help can be a whole other journey and struggle on its own and you really have to be willing to go through hell to get better."

Madeline would like to also share this:

"No good book ever started with a happy beginning, and you are the protagonist of your own story. But, you are also the writer, and the day you find the courage to pick up the pen and accept that responsibility is the day you start to write a happy ending."

STORY # 87

DEPRESSION & ANXIETY DISORDER

Hailee is from Augusta Georgia and she enjoys music. "This past week I've been in marching band, I love playing my flute and I am currently reading the Game of Thrones series." In five years Hailee should be 3 years into college. She hopes to have good grades. She shared, "I hope to have a social life with a whole bunch of friends I trust." Hailee was diagnosed and still struggles with depression and anxiety.

Hailee believes her mental disorders were caused by different situations. "A mixture of my life at home, switching between my Mom and my dad's house. It felt like my Mom did care, but my dad had just moved in with his girlfriend who he spent more time with than me. Also, I started high school and my grades were dropping. At this point I had two friends and my boyfriend to depend on. I became extremely emotionally dependent on my boyfriend who moved away 1 year ago. My two friends kind of ignored me and didn't include me in anything, which made me feel really bad about myself." When her Mom found out she was cutting, she took Hailee to a family counsellor, but unfortunately every time she went the counsellor made her feel worse. Hailee convinced her mother to take her to another therapist. Stating, "She finally got me into GRU with a really nice therapist. I don't remember the treatment exactly, but we didn't use antidepressants and worked on my skills to cope with my surroundings."

She had to battle with various symptoms each day including feeling useless and unwanted. Hailee hated herself and couldn't handle it. She wanted to die so much and cried every day. It was a terrible existence. Hailee stopped being social and confident. "I wore pants every day, I have a birthmark on my leg that I didn't care about until this started." Sadly, she attempted suicide once and no one found her. She believed if she told her mother, she wouldn't believe it. Her relationships also suffered and Hailee lost friends. "When I told one of my friends that I was depressed, she tried to convince me her life was worse and I didn't have it so bad."

Hailee's turning point was when she went to her therapist and used realizing she wasn't the problem. "My Mom helped by actually realizing that this was a real thing. She never listens to me until she hears a professional opinion. My boyfriend helped by staying in touch with me and knowing how to calm me down in bad times."

This is her advice:

"It may seem like life will never get better, but it really does. 3 years ago, when people told me it would get better I never believed them. I know it's hard to believe that but it's really is true. There is help out there and with the rising global awareness, it should be easier to get help for anyone with any kind of illness."

STORY # 88

SCHIZOAFFECTIVE DISORDER, POST-TRAUMATIC STRESS DISORDER & LEARNING DISABILITIES

Heather was born in Illinois and now lives with her husband in the Tampa Bay area. She loves to write. "I have co-authored a post-apocalyptic book with my husband and I am currently working on writing an epic science fiction book." Five years from now she would like to work as a social worker with children who have disabilities or have a history of trauma, or with adults with disabilities and mental illnesses.

Heather was diagnosed with and still has Schizo-Affective Disorder, Post-Traumatic Stress Disorder (PTSD) and learning disabilities. She believes her mental disorders were caused by different situations. Stating, "With the schizo-affective disorder, it's been suggested to me that my father who died when I was 7 was schizophrenic, so genes may have played a part. I also have a family history of learning disabilities, so there is a high genetic component there. The PTSD was caused by repeated childhood abuse, physical, psychological and sexual in nature."

Heather wasn't diagnosed until she was in college and living with her husband. "I received accommodations for my learning disability (dyscalculia) and for PTSD symptoms that were very useful. I could not have graduated with my Bachelor's degree in Anthropology without them. For Schizo-affective disorder, we are still searching for the right combination of medicines. I'm currently taking Wellbutrin, Effexor, Zyprexa and Seroquel. I also have intensive therapy twice a week", Heather revealed.

She also struggled with many symptoms. Her dyscalculia does not allow her to compute mathematical problems in her head and is unable to read an analogue clock, cannot make change, and can't read a bus schedule. Her PTSD made her fear crossing the street, driving, motorcycles, large trucks, vans, toy rains and several songs. Her schizo-affective disorder provoked paranoid delusions, auditory and tactile hallucinations, disorganized speech and thoughts.

Heather's life became immensely affected, "The PTSD made me jumpy, easily startled and afraid of having people walking behind me, as well as an inability to drive or cross streets by myself. It means that I spend most of my time at home, avoiding triggers. My schizo-affective disorder makes me very paranoid and untrusting. I commonly think that there are cameras in my home, that helicopters in the area due to the close by airport is there to follow and spy on me. I often think that I am being experimented on by the government and that they are using listening devices and special mind control drugs to keep tabs on me" she admits.

When Heather was 18, she was very depressed and afraid. She reports, "I was convinced that the college I was attending was being inhabited by malevolent spirits and demons after my aunt and uncle told me that the nuns on campus were worshipping the devil. I felt trapped and scared and attempted suicide. My friends on campus intervened, saving my life and flushing my pain pills." This also affected her relationship with others. After Heather's suicide attempt, her friends grew distant immediately after.

Heather felt sad and lonely. She felt like she had no one other than an abusive family to turn to. The turning point in her life was getting away from her abusive family and moving over a thousand miles away to South Florida with her soon to be husband. Heather explained, "The second turning point occurred after I re-enrolled in College and sought help for my mental health. I was soon diagnosed and was given accommodations to use in quizzes, tests, exams, group activities and when taking notes in class. I wouldn't have been able to graduate in spring 2014 without my accommodations and the support of my husband and my little sister."

Heather used lots of therapy, medication, and support from the people in her life. She also vowed to prove the abusers and naysayers wrong by excelling. "When I graduated with a 3.5 GPA in Anthropology, it was a huge accomplishment that took every ounce of determination and anger at my abusers to completing college." Her therapist gave her numerous exercises and tools and her psychiatrists provided medication. While her husband, little sister and friend that she met online provided their unconditional love and support.

This is the lesson heather learned:

"With the right support and accommodations any goal is possible for those of us with schizo-affective disorder."

This ordeal has changed Heather's outlook in life. She became more positive and began to be able to encourage others which makes her genuinely happy. In order to prevent this from happening again, she keeps taking her medications, even if her symptoms have gone away. She goes to therapy and keeps up with her friends and family. She also creates smalls goals to achieve each day.

This is Heather's advice:

"Don't give up. There is hope. Read about others who have our mental conditions and see for yourself. This pain is not permanent."

STORY # 89

DEPRESSION, ANXIETY DISORDER & POST-TRAUMATIC STRESS DISORDER

Patience is currently living in Nebraska, but has moved around a lot. She has many hobbies. "I really enjoy writing, in fact I've even self-published a couple of books, and I love to spend time with my loved ones. I also enjoy driving, shopping, going on road trips, cooking, baking, and even cleaning. I love rock music, but I'll listen to nearly everything. I love hundreds of movies, from Disney to horror, but my all-time favorite has to be The Perks of Being a Wallflower, and I love reading books." Patience would like a successful career and to travel the world, have a family of her own and learn to follow her dreams. She said, "I see myself either living on my own or still with my family as I attend college, do recreational dance and act in community plays while I work a part-time job to achieve the objective career I want, which is to be a criminal profiler."

Patience was diagnosed and still has depression, anxiety, and post-traumatic stress disorder (PTSD). She believes her mental illnesses was caused by different situations. She mentioned, "My depression is clinical as well as generic, which came from my Mom's side of the family. It started to grow when I had to move from Texas at age 11 to California. At the time school had already started and I struggled making friends. I was also bullied a lot and my grades were slipping. I would actually cut myself a lot because it was a way to escape the emotional pain and I felt like I needed to punish myself. As for the anxiety, that came with my paranoia. I constantly worried about everything and when things started getting worse in my life I would have severe panic attacks and had difficulties for a long time talking to people, even waiters at restaurants. My PTSD was caused by my ex-boyfriend. He mentally and emotionally abused me as well as sexually abused and raped me."

She receives therapy once every two weeks and is on two different medications. Patience has to deal with difficult symptoms, such as hopelessness and self-anger. She projected her angers towards her family and friends. "I felt worthless and weak and pathetic and there are still some days where I feel like people would be better off without me" Patience disclosed. She would cry every day and have negative thoughts. Patience has attempted suicide a lot, and would hurt herself by cutting, scratching or punching her legs. Due to this her relationship with family and friends became negative. She shared, "I did feel trapped, angry, depressed, and desperate, but I also felt isolated, broken, weak, tired, and resentful sometimes towards my mom and dad for wanting to have me. I also felt like everything was always my fault even though things clearly weren't my fault."

The turning point for Patience was to move with her Mom, and started seeing a therapist and psychiatrist. She moved because her father did not believe her and didn't think she needed help. The strategies she used to move forward in life was to talk to her loved ones while taking medication. She would also go out and try new things or stayed indoors and did things she loved. Patience said, "I also downloaded some apps like 7 Cups and Calm to help me keep control of myself when I felt like I was losing it."

This is what she learned from this ordeal:

> "I learned that there are going to be times where it gets really hard and it gets really tough and ugly, but there are also times that life is beautiful and precious and that we need to enjoy it while it lasts."

Her experience changed her outlook in life. She grew up a lot faster, and even though there are days she hates everything, she understands and sees the beauty in things. Patience is in constant communication with people she loves in order to get support and keeps herself busy with school or work.

This is her advice:

> "Talking to people, even if it's difficult, is definitely a good start. It doesn't even have to be people you know. There are so many support groups out there now that can be anonymous when you need them to be. It's also good to look into yoga or some other form of exercise and to take a step back and breathe when you begin to feel like everything is getting bad again. I would also recommend 7 Cups and Calm for those who can get apps on their smartphones. It costs nothing and it's incredibly helpful."

STORY # 90

POST-TRAUMATIC STRESS DISORDER

Blaire is from Kentucky and she enjoys learning Spanish, ASL, watching One Tree Hill and riding horses. Her goal is to become a Mounted Police Officer. Blaire still battles with mental illness. She added, "I have Post-Traumatic Stress Disorder. I am currently still dealing with it from day-to-day." She believes her disorder was caused by different situations. Sharing, "Aside from anxiety running in my family, a large fistfight broke out in front of me pulling me into the situation. This was all while I was at a school function. This event threw me into a whirlwind of problems." She was diagnosed by a mental health professional and was put on medication, and goes to therapy.

She felt stressed out in public. Reporting, "I constantly have an uneasy feeling when going in public or to large events with a lot of people where another fight could break out at any second. At night, I lost many hours of sleep worrying about the next day and what was going to come with it." This ended up affecting her daily life, because Blaire would feel sick, and her stomach would get irritated. Not only that, but she could not sleep if someone was in her room. She felt having to take her medication was a big responsibility and was unable to return to her school for the rest of the year.

Blaire did fear the side effects her medication might have given her. Her PTSD affects how she perceives others, for instance "Because of the yelling during the fight, now when I hear loud voices I begin to go into panic mode. Slight changes in tone of voice can make me think someone is angry with me and send me into a full-blown panic attack." Her parents both dealt with the situation differently, she said, "My mother and I had trouble together. She would try to force me to get over things faster and my dad would take the time to try and understand my thoughts without any pressure." Blaire felt trapped, angry, sad and desperate because she had difficulties expressing her thoughts. "It made me feel like I was an alien who nobody could understand", she confessed.

What helped Blaire to gain control over her life, is her service dog Jazz. "She [Jazz] has gotten me out of the house, back into the car, in school, and into more public places." The strategies she uses in her journey through recovery is to distract herself when she is anxious and her dog helps by alerting Blaire when she is about to have a panic attack. She also has conversations about different things other than her reality to distract herself.

Blaire is trying to figure out what lesson she has learned from this ordeal and this is her advice for others struggling through similar situations:

"It isn't the end of the world and you aren't alone!"

STORY # 91

BORDERLINE PERSONALITY DISORDER, ATTENTION DEFICIT HYPERACTIVITY DISORDER & GENDER DYSPHORIA

J ason is from Ontario, Canada and he is transgender. He enjoys many things. "I play a lot of video games. I love sushi, soccer, basketball, and volleyball. My favorite band is Twenty One Pilots, and I have a love for The Maze Runner, and Harry Potter." He also has a girlfriend in California. His goal is to either go to university for Biomedical Engineering, or college for Game development or Computer Programming.

Jason possesses various mental disorders, he shared, "I am currently diagnosed with Borderline Personality Disorder (BPD), ADHD, and Gender Dysphoria." Additionally, he was diagnosed with Chronic Suicidal ideation, and has attempted suicide 10 times in a 4-year span, with a few instances of self-harm, but thankfully he is in the final stages of overcoming this disorder, after not having a crisis in almost a year.

Jaon's BPD was most likely caused by the bullying and harassment he got from his peers as a child, as well as the trauma of his teacher locking him in a closet when he was six or seven years old.

Jason's mental disorders were diagnosed by a psychiatrist and he is currently visiting a counselor, and meeting with his doctor on a regular basis. Unfortunately, Jason has been dealing with numerous symptoms.

He reported, "Frantic attempts to avoid real and/or imagined rejection, recurrent suicidal or self-harming behaviors, unstable moods, chronic feelings of emptiness, difficulty controlling anger, "black and white" perception of mood and/or reactions, unstable or intense interpersonal relationships characterized by alternating between extremes of idealization and devaluation."

This ended up affecting his daily life. He struggled to maintain relationships, and felt rejection when he pushed others away. Because of this he would either lash out more to push them away, or try everything he could to make them happy and keep them close. He says, "This didn't always work, which then made my mood plummet, and make me want to die. This would start a violent spiral."

Jason was alone most of the time, because people didn't want to interact with him, which was a hard situation for his parents, because they felt scared. This made him feel all kinds of emotions. "My moods were very difficult to define in any one moment. They could, and still sometimes do, change within a split second. The main emotions were anger, depression, and like I was being abandoned."

Jason's turning point was when he was hospitalized. There he received his diagnosis for BPD, and began taking the proper medication, and counselling he needed in order to recover and be healthy. The strategies he used to gain control over his mental illnesses were getting support from friends and family, who helped by listening and understanding why his brain worked the way it did. He also used techniques he learned in counselling to gain more control over his life and emotions.

Jason learned a significant lesson from this:

"You can gain control of anything. It may take a while, and it may not be easy, but it is possible. Just put in the effort, and constantly expect more from yourself. Understand your limits, and know when to push them, and when to let things lie. Do your very best, and you will succeed."

Even his outlook in life has changed. Jason is no longer suicidal, happier, and getting increasingly stable each day. He has become positive to the point where he can see a future for himself. Jason knows he can't fully prevent a relapse, but if he keeps working on his health, both mental and physical, he can reduce the chances. He added, "If I take care of myself, and make sure I'm being safe, and that I'm in a safe environment, I can keep this from possibly ever happening again."

This is his advice for those struggling:

"Don't be afraid to ask for help. Be honest with your doctor and parents. Remember that they are here to help you. Most importantly, get the help you need. There is very little one can do on their own. Just be true to you. Stand up for yourself, and keep yourself and your environment healthy. Don't be afraid, but also be smart. Educate yourself on your health, and your mental state."

STORY # 92

BURNOUT

S umiyah is from the Kingdom of Saudi Arabia, and is aspiring to be a writer and poet, hoping to be able to publish her own written works in the future. Her current goal is to graduate from medical school, with an outstanding GPA. She shared, "Five years from now I see myself as an Ob/Gyn (obstetrician-gynecologist) resident at Queen's University".

"I've put myself under a lot of pressure in the past three years to get into medical school and it may have backfired." She was diagnosed with and still suffers from burnout, as a result of academic stress, and believed she had everything under control. "I had a hard time coming to terms with it, let alone talking to anyone about it" Sumiyah says.

"I couldn't get myself to get out of bed in the morning. Falling asleep was effortless, but waking up was extremely difficult. When I wasn't sleeping, I was in trance. I did most things absentmindedly. I felt apathetic towards almost everything that was going on in my life. The more colorless my days seemed, the more futile I felt."

Before she started college, Sumiyah was content with life, and was appreciative about everything. The lack of sleep made Sumiyah tense and angry, lashing out over the smallest things.

She explained, "I tried to limit the effect of the negative energy I was radiating, so I avoided friends and family members. I stopped working out and began to make unhealthy choices, which made me feel worse about myself." She started to question if medical school was worth her physical and mental health. She reported, "I've thought about dropping out so many times but since I was skipping college, I couldn't even execute my decision."

Although Sumiyah never had suicidal thoughts, she did have thoughts about her own death. She even hoped to get into a car accident on her way to university. She disclosed, "I always thought about how it would all be so much better, to everyone, if I weren't alive. I no longer feared the idea of death."

Since Sumiyah isn't an expressive person her family believed everything was normal. When she skipped class, she would tell her family that class was cancelled. When Sumiyah wasn't with them, they thought she was studying. According to her, "Everything seemed just fine. I was at a strange place with my friends, since I wasn't seeing them nor talking to them about it. Even though I was deliberately detaching myself, I still felt so distant and alienated." This made Sumiyah feel confined and helpless.

Unfortunately, she hasn't reached a turning point yet, but tries her best to keep herself busy and distracted so she doesn't have time to dwell on those things. She is also grateful for someone in particular. She shared, "Although I isolated myself from everyone, one person's presence has helped me greatly. They were the reason I got out of bed on my good days. Their company was the one thing I looked forward to. They made me want to be better. They were both my purpose and my audience."

Sumiyah has learned to appreciate the smallest things, and works alongside her feelings, instead of resisting them. She learned to express her feelings in a way that does not involve vocalization, by writing three things she was grateful for at the end of each day.

This has helped her become more patient with other people and herself, but most importantly, she has learned to have hope.

This is her advice for those in similar situations:

"Don't resist. The sooner you come to terms with it, the sooner you can start to recover. Baby steps. Take it one day at a time. Progress is not a straight line. Don't be afraid to reach out and ask for help."

STORY # 93

ANXIETY DISORDER & DEPRESSION

Bryce Evans was born in Edmonton, Alberta and now lives in Vancouver, BC, Canada. He is an artist, introvert, entrepreneur, and loves expressing himself in creative ways, as well as helping others. She shared, "I started The One Project, which is a photography community for people who suffer from depression and anxiety. It began with my own story and how my photos were what helped me to better understand and eventually work towards breaking my silence. Once I made my story public, I saw how common these issues were and how many other people could benefit from using photos in this way."

Bryce teaches people the exact techniques that he used to overcome his own issues, with online courses and a free, private online platform. His goal is to further his project and help over 100 million people change the way they think about mental health, through photography. He explained, "In 5 years, I see myself leading and empowering a strong organization of incredibly passionate people who have already served 10 million people through our work and that we have helped to bring therapeutic photography into normal conversation."

Since his teens, Bryce has struggled with severe depression and anxiety, with suicidal thoughts. Amazingly, he has overcome it, but has to stay on top of his tools, habits and routines that prevent him from regressing back into getting overly anxious or into a depressed state. He said, "In the times where I've fallen back into it, the way that I experience and deal with it is much different, likely because I'm a much different person now."

He believes the cause of his mental illnesses is that he wasn't aligned with himself. He disclosed, "I allowed my anxiety and depression to control my actions and silence my voice and I just continuously retracted more and more. I didn't listen to my gut or inner voice and I eventually felt out of touch with myself and began to hate myself." Bullying, social pressures, and the environment were also major factors that affected Bryce. He reported, "It was also partially existential depression and as I'm mature for my age, I felt I was not able to relate or connect with people who I was surrounded with at the time."

Bryce has dealt with various symptoms. His social anxiety made him nauseous and resulted in vomiting before social events. Additionally, he had negative thought patterns, with low self-worth and energy. Due to these issues, his life became disastrous. He recalls, "Constantly second guessing and overthinking. I would isolate myself from others and always be thinking that they were out to get me, making fun of me, or about to turn on me. It kept me from building strong relationships with people and building social 'muscles' and experiences during that important time of development." Fortunately, he never acted upon his suicidal thoughts.

Bryce said he felt, "Worthless, trapped, broken, desperate, hopeless, wrong and all the things I don't have words for. That's why I used photos". He also added. "I took one photo specifically, that was a moment when I started to listen and take action on that gut instinct and inner voice that I had ignored for so long. I felt a shift happen within me and it was the start of my process to start expressing and working to overcome these issues with my photos." Bryce even spoke about his full story in a TEDx talk.

He now has a strong daily routine and set of tools that he consistently uses:

1. Meditation
2. Daily journaling / free writing
3. Working out / exercise
4. Photography
5. Quality connection with friends (or people in general)
6. wim hof breathing
7. Positive affirmations
8. Proper eating &; drinking lots of water
9. No caffeine and no/very low sugar intake

In a way, Bryce is grateful for his depression because it helped him learn so much, including the importance of being in connection with and living true to his authentic self. It forced him to look deep within himself to discover the answers that he was looking for. He confessed, "I am a completely different person than I was during my struggles in the best way possible. It pushed me at a very young age to start a journey of self-development and figure out things that sometimes take half a lifetime for people to work through. It also put me in touch with my true calling and purpose, which I am eternally grateful for."

This is Bryce's advice for anyone going through similar situations:

"Do not look outside of yourself for the answers, look within. And if you're struggling in silence or don't have the words to express what you're going through — try using photos. You can sign up for free to our online platform. We welcome you with open arms!"

STORY # 94

POST-TRAUMATIC STRESS DISORDER

Aislinn - who likes to go by Ax – was born in Indiana, but has moved around throughout her life, and now resides in California. She loves to crochet, sing and dance to any music that speaks to her. She is also fond of reading, watching fantasy and mystery shows, and has a huge sweet tooth. Her goal is to get her driver's license, and to study psychology to help others. In five years from now she sees herself as either genuinely happy or dead. She explains, "I'm preparing for both, because the universe is chaotic and I have no idea what's gonna happen. Infinite possibilities".

Aislinn was diagnosed and still battles with post-traumatic stress disorders (PTSD), with symptoms of depression and anxiety. A traumatic childhood caused her mental illness.

Aislinn's mother had tried to abort her, but was not successful, so she mentally and emotionally abused Aislinn throughout her life because she did not want her. Her father was also mentally ill, and used to physically abuse her and her mother, before her mother divorced him, and remarried. Her relationship with her brother was also very troubling. They both have tried to kill each other on multiple occasions, until the police got involved, and recommended she seek help. Three months later she went to a therapist who was not trained well, and left therapy feeling worse. Fortunately, she is now with a good therapist and has been able to make progress.

Aislinn dealt with horrible symptoms throughout her life. She reported, "I wet the bed until [I was] 12 years old, I flinch if people move too fast, if someone seems even slightly upset or are super focused on doing something I get hyper aware of everything, making me anxious and shaky. I get panic attacks on a regular basis, and I have severe social anxiety. I can't go into my full list of symptoms, but those are the big ones." She has attempted suicide in the past, and became apathetic just to get by until she received help. Aislinn also became aggressive and on edge looking for fights as an outlet for her feelings.

She had few friends because of the walls she put up to protect herself. Everyone else left her alone because they felt intimidated by her. She says, "At the time I didn't give a sh*t, I was almost completely apathetic to everything as a survival mechanism".

Aislinn's turning point was learning how to take care of herself through grounding exercises to properly handle situations, and leaving toxic environments. She uses tips she finds on Tumblr, and stays close to supportive friends. Aislinn is now more positive than ever, and feels a bit more freed.

This is her advice:

"It's cheesy but - you will make it. You are stronger than you think you are. Listen to me: You Can Do This. Just go find your happy place and put a death grip on it, use it to claw your way out of whatever situation you're in and DON'T GIVE IN TO IT."

STORY # 95

GENERALIZED ANXIETY DISORDER, INSOMNIA & SUICIDAL TENDENCIES

Anonymous is from Poland, but has lived half her life in France. She loves to write, listen to music, and watch television shows. She is also very fond of reading. She shared, "Some of my favorite books include: Harry Potter, Game of Thrones, Percy Jackson, and Lord of the Rings". Rugby and jiu jitsu are other activities she enjoys. In the future, Anonymous pictures herself with friends, and would love to become a psychologist one day to help people, but she doesn't think she will able to become one. She believes, "I'm not good at school, can't really see a future for myself, at least, not academically."

Anonymous has and still struggles with generalized anxiety disorder & insomnia with suicidal tendencies. Her suicidal thoughts & tendencies sprung up after she came out to her family, who were not accepting and treated her badly for it. She believes her anxiety and insomnia is due to the stress and pressures of finishing her last year of high school with good grades, getting into a university, and passing her exams in a language she is still not familiar with.

She suspects she also has depression, attention deficit hyperactivity disorder (ADHD), and anger management issues. Her anger issues stem from pushing her feelings aside, and not expressing herself. She suspects ADHD because she is hyperactive and has difficulties concentrating. Anonymous believes she has depression because she has long periods in which she feels numb. She said, "I really don't care about what happens to me, can't see a future, I skip meals & just try to find happiness but in vain."

Anonymous has tried to treat herself, by looking online for tips to sleep better, but nothing has worked. Unfortunately, she is still dealing with numerous symptoms such as an inability to concentrate, bad memory, difficulties following instructions, however her parents dismiss these symptoms as normal. She explained, "I mean, my parents told me that's just the teenage rebel phase, but I don't think so".

Some other symptoms of hers include panic attacks, insomnia, over analyzing things, and constantly feeling exhausted. She also struggles to find motivation for things, due to her negative thoughts. She shared, "I don't wanna do anything, I think life is pointless and I might as well just die." Anonymous feels like she can't enjoy anything. She struggles with intense anger, that she believes is more intense than other people's, and admits that she wants to "... Punch people in the face. On my worst days, I can imagine just physically torturing some of them". Anonymous has outbursts of anger, verbally hurting those she loves the most. Sadly, she also struggles to sleep more than three hours per day.

She explained, "I just wanted a way out. I still do. I feel so hopeless & helpless but at the same time, I've lost people to suicide & I don't want those who love me to go through the same y'know?"

Even though her academic and personal life became affected, she was able to get help from friends. "Some people noticed my anguish and reached out to me, and I'll be forever grateful. I can call them my friends now". She also said, "They manage to make me feel a bit better about myself & inspire me to go on."

Anonymous believes her mental disorders have also helped her, she added:

"I guess in some twisted ways these disorders helped me. Anxiety pushed me to work when my depression would rather stay in bed all day long. My anger issues helped me find my jiu jitsu class & in all honesty sometimes we box & it's super therapeutic. Thanks to my insomnia I could explore the parts of my brain I don't usually hear, and could enjoy the beautiful view of a starry night… the scars I have remind me I've gone through a lot already & can go on."

This is her advice for anyone struggling with mental illness:

"Asking for help isn't a sign of weakness, and the right people will be willing to help you with whatever you're going through." Those who like metal (music genre) & often feel isolated but don't know how to reach out, listen to "Don't Go" by Bring Me The Horizon. It's relatable and a great song. I also love Get Scared or Motionless in White."

STORY # 96

DISSOCIATIVE DISORDER, BIPOLAR DISORDER WITH PSYCHOTIC FEATURES, DELUSIONAL DISORDER, GENERALIZED ANXIETY DISORDER, SCHIZOTYPAL & PERSONALITY DISORDER

Carissa is from the U.S state of Kentucky. She enjoys things in the fantasy genre, like Harry Potter and Lord of the Rings, and is fond of anime and video games, her favorites being Non Non Byori and Destiny. Carissa also loves various foods, particularly chocolate. She disclosed, "I literally eat chocolate in some form for nearly every meal of the day. Breakfast: Chocolate protein shake. Lunch: Greek vanilla yogurt with chocolate on top as a side. Dinner: Fiber One brownie as a side. Snack: Granola bar with chocolate chips. Not to mention an occasional Ghirardelli Chocolate square with caramel. Mmmm."

In five years, Carissa sees herself married to her wonderful boyfriend, Zach. She would also like to teach elementary schoolers English in Japan. She shared, "I hope to have grown and matured as a person, broadening my world views and continuously learning new things from different cultures. Maybe

I'll even make a difference [with the] little girls or boys I'm teaching."

In October 2013, Carissa was diagnosed with numerous mental illnesses, such as dissociative disorder, bipolar disorder with psychotic features, delusional disorder, generalized anxiety disorder (GAD), schizotypal (STPD), and personality disorder. She still battles these mental disorders, but fortunately, leads a functional life. Carissa believes various things triggered these illnesses.

She explained, "I'm adopted, and my birth mother did an unknown amount of drugs while carrying me, which made me quite the different child for my reserved, God-fearing parents. It's not that they were bad people, but they had another, "neurotypical" daughter who was quiet and well behaved. I couldn't sit still and had some violence issues due to the chemicals in my brain already mixed with the fact that I was severely neglected for the first two years of my life. Right off the bat I was clearly different, and all my parents knew was "do not spare the rod." Swats on the hand turned into spankings, which turned into the belt until I had bruises I couldn't show anyone, which turned into slaps in the face (including a time where dear mom knocked out my front tooth in the process), finally climaxing with my father, hate in his eyes and his hands around my throat when I was 16 or 17."

Carissa ended up looking for comfort in boys, and in the process got molested in high school, and raped by her first boyfriend. At the age of 18, Carissa ran away from home, moving into an ex boyfriend's family house. She worked a minimum job, starving, and eventually her ex boyfriend's family turned on her. Carissa walked back to her parent's house and was put in the hospital. After being discharged she started group therapy, then received weekly therapy. What most helped Carissa was hypnosis, art therapy, eye movement desensitization and reprocessing (EMDR). She also received medication, although it took her three years to find the right medication and dose.

Carissa also struggled with terrible symptoms, she said, "I felt utter worthlessness and detachment from reality. I was under so much stress that my only friend was someone the world said didn't even exist and that was heartbreaking for me." Because of this she felt alone and unloved. She dsclosed, "I was starving for a kind word or touch from anyone." When the world was too overwhelming, there were voices in Carissa's head, and felt she was being split into seven different people, and none of them were happy.

Her social awkwardness also affected her relationships. Carissa had a difficult time making friends, and felt like everything was out of control. She confessed, "I wanted so badly to go to college and make something of myself, move away and just start over. But I had to take a year off and work on my inner self before I could be a real part of society." She never hurt anyone, but was suicidal, becoming addicted to cutting to get closer to her mom. Since Carissa had many broken relationships, she became paranoid and pushed them all away. Later on, when things were getting better, she met Zach and they developed a strong relationship. "I've grown to love him very deeply and healthily. We are very strong, and he has helped me form stronger relationships with other friends."

Carissa felt all kinds of emotions throughout her journey, she added:

"At first, I felt utterly alone, like who else out there is like me? How many other people are seven different people at once? Aren't I some sort of freak? I began to wonder if my life was even real. I considered theories of nothing being coincidental and my whole existence was a poor game of Sims. I was terrified of everyday things. If someone set the groceries down too hard, I flinched. Are they going to hit me again? Will this pain ever stop?"

Carissa didn't have an actual turning point. She started to change after much affirmation and visualization of her issues, and began to have less symptoms. She mentioned, "Some of my visualization techniques included picturing bad scenarios as nasty bubbles bursting out of my ears and mouth. They would hover and I would use my will to make a pin and I would pop each of them. I listened to relaxation hypnosis before bed each night to practice 'mindful relaxing on purpose.' This helped me in the heat of the moment." Additionally, her parents got support from her therapist, and Carissa's medicine helped her maintain control of herself.

"As for my seven personalities, I went into hypnosis from my therapist and visualized all but the one who was my protector and best friend, Desi". What helped her the most was having a good support system, and wanting to help others who are suffering.

The biggest - and happiest - lesson she has learned is that she is strong. She confessed, "I had been violated, abused, neglected, and broken and yet here I am fighting every day and finally, after 20 years I have moments of peace where I am comfortable with who I am". Carissa now strives to surround herself with positive people who do not have intentions of hurting her.

This is her advice for anyone struggling:

"In the moment, practice being calm, try taking 7/11 breaths (breathe in for seven, out for eleven). Then when the terror has passed, be proactive. Stick close to your good friends. Cut off relationships that are dangerous or toxic to you. Talk to your protector if you have one. If you can't believe in the power you have, believe in those who believe in you. If no one you know believes in you, know that I believe in you. And if I'm too distant for you, look to social media support groups like the "spoonies" tag on Tumblr or the DID tag on Reddit. There is always someone out there who will care for you. You absolutely can overcome anything.

You are not broken or a freak. You are a beautiful human being who has been forced to see the world in a different way. You are special."

"Also, when humans fail you, stick close to pets. They will love you unconditionally."

STORY # 97

DEPRESSION, ANXIETY DISORDER & POST-TRAUMATIC STRESS DISORDER

Diana is from Colombia and enjoys reading, watching movies, and listening to music. She has also found a love for cooking and baking. She confessed, "I recently discovered that passion of mine and hopefully I'll be able to pursue higher education [in that field]." She wants to graduate and finish studies in Gastronomy, and in five years, hopes to be living by herself, successful and happy.

She was diagnosed with and still is battling depression, anxiety, PTSD and believes her disorders were caused by various situations. She believes, "My diseases were initially triggered by the need to be perfect or at least appease my mom and her image of who I should be. I guess I wanted to be the intelligent, talented, and kind daughter she wanted, but her expectation was too high and I could never get there as much as I tried. I just didn't want to disappoint her."

As well as her family's financial issues, her parents had an unhealthy relationship with each other, and states that "Instead of divorcing they just made my brother and I suffer with their fighting until my dad would leave and then come back a few days later." Her relationship with her brother was also affected by her parents, and sadly, her brother blames her for not accepting and loving their father. She reported, "Basically, my parents unconsciously put my brother and I against each other by comparing us, and what not, so that affected me a lot."

Diana identifies as an ambivert, but inclines more towards introversion. Due to this, it is difficult for her to make friends. She shared, "My thoughts, actions and ideas were always different from my fellow classmates, and they rejected me often." Diana also developed self-esteem issues, and fell into an eating disorder. Her health was affected, and she suffered from migraines, and low brain oxygen. She explained, "My relationship with friends and family was a disaster, so I had to get new friends and fix family issues." Diana also said, "I have trouble believing in what I am capable of and often sell myself out short or disaster like. I ended up being insecure and self-conscious."

Diana ended up receiving therapy once a week for a couple of months and was prescribed medication, however, it just made her drowsy, so she stopped taking it. Eventually, she could not go to therapy because she could not afford it. Diana used free online certified services and hotlines when she was feeling particularly blue. She also battled many terrible symptoms:

> "Insomnia, eating disorders, cutting, I was suicidal, social withdrawal, fatigue, loss of interest, turned [me] into a disorganized person, I took refuge in dark rooms, rejected any help, had nightmares, stopped going out, kept to myself, body pain (real and imagined), breathing difficulties, forgot everything and anything, loneliness, hopelessness, constant crying, I developed obsessive compulsive behavior too, I was defensive all the time, weight issues, I was easily irritable."

Her symptoms have caused her attempt suicide a couple of times in the past, and engage in self harm. She explained, "I did cut,

and when that became noticeable I started damaging the surrounding area of my nails and made it constantly bleed. [I]
would purposely get bruises that seemed [like a] fall or accident.
[I] would burn myself with the straightener or curler, and would
make myself sick."

Diana's recovery was slow and gradual, and didn't really have
a turning point. She mentioned, "I didn't feel determined to get
rid of it; I just slowly realized little things. I still have breakdowns.
Just yesterday I had one and up till now I have been experiencing
a major low, but I guess it did get better."

She now tries to go out and maintain control of her life. She
believes that "… it's just a matter of knowing yourself and recog-
nizing you're not okay. I may not tell my friends or family, but I go
online and seek help from people who work for that and help me
get better by just listening to my rants and then suggesting books
or movies or sites for me to feel better. I may never get over it, but
I learned how to live with it and accept it."

She also listens to songs that make her feel better and focuses
on one day at a time. Diana also had help from others around her.
Sharing, "I had help from certain people, whether they're still here
or not is not important because they were there when I needed it
and that's enough and I will forever be grateful. Some would let
me call them and cry until I fell asleep, some would be silly and
make me laugh, others would b*tch with me, it all depended on my
moods and reactions. They were just there for me however it was
and didn't judge or ask unnecessary questions."

Diana outlook in life has changed, despite all her down moments:

"I'm still lonely, I'm still depressed, I am still anxious and
I still imagine my abuser is everywhere, but I can hold my
head high now. I am not living in shame now. I can actually
live free because I embrace my illnesses and know how to

make them work for my advantage or just how to control it. I still have trouble with my future, but I know if I've made it this far I'll make it further."

Her suggestion for those struggling:

"Breathing techniques helps. Battling negative thoughts with positive ones works. As for PTSD, having someone who you feel safe with is good. Whenever I feel cornered I call my someone, meet them, Skype them or just make sure I get in contact with them so that I won't feel so helpless and alone. Listening to instrumentals, classical music or instrument music is good for nightmares and insomnia too. During daytime blast the damn volume up and jump or dance around until you have no energy anymore. One of my long-term solutions is keeping a diary. Not a "dear diary" more like a record kind of diary. I usually take notes on my emotional and physical development. It's actually a very good method to track your mental health and it also helps keep track of triggers and eventually you learn to avoid bad situations. It also helps me keep track of school, life and finances. You can use it to have a peaceful state of mind."

STORY # 98

POST-TRAUMATIC STRESS DISORDER, ANXIETY DISORDER & RAPE SURVIVOR

Veronika is from Sacramento, California. She is into anime and cartoons, and has been cosplaying more frequently. She is also fond of outdoor activities like hiking, and looking for mushrooms and flowers. Veronika is interested in taxidermy and entomology, and hopes to finish college with mostly A's in Psychology. Sharing, "In five years from now I hope to already have my masters and be on my way to getting my PhD. hope to be teaching or still working for the county/state, and living with my current partner - hopefully married - with lots of dogs."

She was diagnosed with post-traumatic stress disorder (PTSD) and anxiety, and still struggles with it today. Veronika shares that "Before I started therapy I was sure that the cause for my PTSD and anxiety was due to being raped by a group of boys in high school while also being in a long term abusive relationship with another (unrelated) boy. This relationship was so abusive my therapist told me the feelings and thoughts I was describing sound very close to Stockholm syndrome." She received therapy for a year and began to discover the reasons for her anxiety. Stating, "I realized that the anxiety I suffer has been due to lifelong stress, because literally every household I have lived in was physically and/or emotionally abusive."

Veronika would have flashbacks due to triggers and dreams, and had hypervigilance of her surroundings. She would get anxiety attacks daily, but the frequency of them has decreased. Veronika said, "Closer to the time of my trauma I was genuinely afraid to leave the house. Nowadays I can, but I still feel better when someone accompanies me." She became suicidal and engaged in self-destructive behaviors like cutting and over drinking. Veronika was very jumpy, and nervous, to the point that if anyone flirted with her or did something she considered to be a red flag, she would go home and hide.

She shares that, "I did attempt suicide a few times, however my ex had such strong control over me, he could order me not to commit suicide and I would obey. I did cut myself frequently until my ex ordered me to stop that as well." Since Veronika had no outlet for her emotions, she would occasionally burst out in anger. "I would take it out on inanimate objects or scream at strangers who didn't deserve it, like phone representatives or servers" she confessed.

This also affected her relationships. Veronika was obsessively devoted to her ex, and he encouraged her to push people away. She ended up with only the friends her ex approved of. Fortunately, her brother was a huge support in her life. "The only exception was my brother, who will always be my best friend. He was consistently patient with me throughout the whole ordeal. He never told me what to do, only that he wished the best for me. I really think it was due to his patience and support that I was able to hang onto a reality that my ex didn't create."

Veronika felt angry and trapped, and often victim-blamed herself. "I felt incredibly guilty about being gang raped because I truly felt it was my fault. I felt myself constantly daydreaming about having a time machine so I could go back and change everything" she mentioned. For Veronika, obeying the wishes of her ex was the only thing she found comfort in, as he had convinced her that he was the only person who had her best interests at heart, which was not true.

Veronika's turning point was when she started hanging out with her current partner. She recounts, "I was having a panic attack and essentially cried and yelled out my entire life story to him. He is the first person I have ever told that story to who said, 'I don't know how to help you.' He suggested I seek out therapy, but was willing to offer emotional support too."

Now Veronika meditates daily, and practices the grounding methods her therapist shows her. She is thankful for cognitive behavioral therapy, because it's teaching her how to react to stressful and scary thoughts or memories. Veronika now surrounds herself with supportive people, such as her brother and her partner's friends, who understand when she is triggered, and don't ask for an explanation.

She doesn't know if this experience changed her life, but knows she wants to help others who also experience these types of struggles. She says, "I want to help those who have been through abuse too. I want to talk to teens who don't feel wanted, and lead people like me towards help. I want to be a kind and compassionate person despite what I've been through. I feel like if I keep healing and assisting those around me in positive ways, it would almost be like revenge against my past."

This is her advice for anyone out there who have been through similar situations:

"Honestly cognitive behavioral therapy is the best thing ever and they should check it out. It's not easy since you're literally training your brain to change its knee-jerk reactions. But it is worth it. If your job is giving you anxiety - get a different job. If your family is making you feel panicked - choose a new accepting family. The things in life that do not allow you to grow are not as important as they claim to be."

STORY # 99

MAJOR DEPRESSION DISORDER

Courtney is from New Jersey, but lives in Cape Cod, Massachusetts with her 2-and-a-half year old Yorkshire Terrier named Lobo, meaning 'wolf' in Spanish. She is a big fan of all things sci-fi, and Disney. She usually goes to Disneyland once a year, and describes herself as "pretty geeky", and says she loves Star Wars, Doctor Who, and other sci-fi things, as well as shows like NCIS and Criminal Minds. She also engages in many creative hobbies such as knitting, crocheting, and coloring.

Currently, Courtney is studying for a Bachelor of Arts in Psychology online, but at the moment, she is unsure of where she will be in 5 years, and just lives life day-to-day. "I work with children with Autism, so I'd love to keep going on the path to a good rewarding career in this field" she shared.

Courtney was diagnosed with major depressive disorder (MDD) during the sixth grade, after she told a friend about her suicidal thoughts. Her friend told his mom, who then told the guidance counselor, leading to Courtney being put into an in-patient adolescent mental hospital, followed by therapy sessions and daily medications. Courtney still struggles with her MDD, and says "I would say I still have it, but it's pretty well maintained. I have worse days than others, and different parts of the year are harder than others. But I do recognize I have come a long way."

Courtney believes her mental disorder was caused by different tragedies throughout that year. She added, "Part of what triggered it (her MDD) was the death of my sister when I was 11. She was my older half-sister, but had Down Syndrome so mentally we were basically equal. Six months later my grandfather passed away, followed by my closest aunt 4 months after that. Rule of 3 I guess you can say. Life was turned upside down and I don't think my family dynamic was ever the same again."

Due to this, she has experienced very troubling symptoms, such as insomnia, exhaustion, hopelessness, and numbing. During this time, Courtney had no interest in anything. She isolated herself and developed panic attacks. Her schooling was the most affected. Courtney said, "I think I was just a horrible student. I had no concentration and because I was always so tired I just seemed to float through my freshman and sophomore year of high school." When she got to college her depression wasn't as bad, until she transferred schools, and had to leave college mid semester. She explained, "When I had to leave college and had a part time job, my anxiety could get so bad that I would throw up mid shift."

Since Courtney always isolated herself, she never developed good social skills, and now has a difficult time creating friendships. During romantic relationships, if her boyfriend did not understand her mental illness, the relationship would become hard to maintain. She confessed, "My most recent (now ex) boyfriend understood everything and I've actually come a lot farther in recovery because he was so supportive."

The turning point for Courtney was after the third hospitalization, when she didn't want to keep putting her loved ones through that ordeal. When Courtney became an adult, she went into an intensive two-year outpatient therapy. There she received cognitive behavioral therapy (CBT) and dialectical behavior therapy (DBT).

Courtney was given other alternatives, such as electro cranial stimulation, with a device called the Fisher Wallace Stimulator. She explains that, "It helps my brain create serotonin and dopamine naturally with electric pulses through my temples. I still go to therapy on a mostly regular basis and occasionally use meds for anxiety. I also discovered medical marijuana to help manage everything too. I live in a state that actually now has recreational marijuana and I'm a believer that it helps different medical problems."

Along with this professional help, Courtney has received support from her friends and family. Even the outpatient program became a second family to her. Courtney is not sure if she has learned any lessons from this, but has realized that things DO get better, and that she is stronger than she used to be. Her outlook in life has also changed. She reported, "I think I've always been more mature for my age because of [my diagnosis]. Recently, I realized that I deserve to be happy and if things aren't working then there needs to be a change".

This is her advice to anyone struggling with MDD:

"I'd say not to give up, as cliche as that is. As much as there are things out there to help, it's like addiction, you really need to want to change what's going on. Until then just manage everything as best you can. Depression becomes like a shadow following you everywhere, then you end up becoming comfortable with it and it can make it harder to overcome. Once you realize you want to change and be a happy person, it makes everything seem easier."

STORY # 100

PERSISTENT DEPRESSIVE DISORDER

Isa is from a small village near Munich, Germany, and her main goal in life is to be happy. She wants to appreciate what she has already achieved, and pictures herself in another country studying psychology. Her love for reading is something that helps her survive. She explains, "I want to exceed my self-created borders, live a healthy relationship with food, have a full functioning body and just to be content with myself and my environment."

Isa was diagnosed with recurrent depressive disorder. However, she chooses not to identify with the name of the disorder, as she believes that a person's being can't be defined by just a disorder. She states, "You can't say a person has this or that, just by knowing specific symptoms... there's so much more that constitutes a human being." Isa has a problem with eating, and her relationship with her body. However, she can recognize negative thoughts early enough to control it. She says, "One of my biggest problems is the depressive episodes that sneak into my life, mostly unseen and expand so much that my whole life consists of them." Isa also has specific symptoms of a post-traumatic stress disorder (PTSD), that appear during her depressive episodes. "I think the worst [part] is that I never know how long [it'll] last. Sometimes for just one week, sometimes it extends for months."

A traumatic experience triggered her mental disorders a few years ago. She now recognizes that it's also due to not reaching out for help on time, because she did not acknowledge that she had a serious problem. Isa is currently receiving behavioral therapy and treatment for her bad eating habits. She also shares, "On some days I just feel the overwhelming urge to stay in bed and never get up while on other days I feel like I could do anything." Her other symptoms include panic attacks, chronic fatigue, the feeling of constantly having a cold, concentration issues and sleeping problems.

Due to this, Isa struggles with daily situations like going to school or going outside. She reports, "It's very hard to attend school regularly and meet my own requirements. I often think that I'm not good enough for any [friendship] or relationships, leading me to isolate myself from people who care."

At times Isa is filled with self-hatred and self-confidence issues. She has self-harmed through cutting, but thankfully she has been self-harm free for about a year now. Isa has thought about suicide, and has never attempted it. "I think I wouldn't have the courage to do it... somehow I love my life too much to do something like that."

Isa has struggled to maintain relationships with friends or family, due to her symptoms. She disclosed, "People couldn't handle my extreme mood changes and the never fading trust issues." This made her feel sorry, for hurting those who wanted to help her. For Isa, there wasn't an actual turning point, it was - and still is - a long and slow process of learning, realizing, and changing.

"I think the most important insight for me was regardless of how bad I feel, I DESERVE to be happy. Not just to be alive, but to appreciate and to enjoy the privilege of many things. I've learned to cherish the small things in my life, to value everyone as much as they deserve and especially to value myself. To treat me like I would treat anyone I love and to see myself as a friend, not as an enemy." She also shared, "I can't say that I've overcome those illnesses and that I'm completely recovered. I think it's worthy to say that I am fighting, even though I'm close to giving up on some days."

One of the ways Isa helped herself was allowing herself to feel the emotions and thoughts she had suppressed, by observing them and identifying the negative thinking patterns. She admits that, "Sometimes they were hard to identify because they came in disguise, but once I've got to know myself better I could see them clearly."

Another important strategy that aided her recovery was accepting the help and support from the people around her. She went out with her friends on weekends, and her parents learned to deal with her mood swings, and let her stay at home on her bad days. She also allowed herself to open up to her therapist who taught her how to start all over again, and how important it is to seek formal support, saying "I've underestimated professional help and now I notice how much it can help you."

Through this ordeal, Isa learned an important lesson:

"I've learned that even if life hits you harder than you thought it ever could, it still goes on. Even if you feel like dying one day, it will get better. It will always get better. There are bad things, but life consists of so much more than the negative."

This is her advice for those battling with mental illness:

"After something bad has happened, do whatever makes you feel better. Bury and isolate yourself for days, don't talk to anyone, cry as much as you want to, read 1 or 100 books, watch sad movies, listen to sad music and just feel. Feel the things you need to feel and don't make the mistake of suppressing them. There's nothing wrong with crying for two hours straight. But even while you do those things, never forget this: There's a life. A life that waits for you. And even if you don't feel like it, never give up. Never stop hoping and believing in things. Nothing lasts forever and neither will these feelings. The only person who it starts with is you. Only you can change your life. Challenge yourself but don't expect too much, change comes in small steps, but if you never start, it never will. No one can save you, learn to realize that you're your own savior. And most importantly: Never, NEVER forget, that you're worth it. You're worth every bit of this life. You're strong, you're enough and every part of you deserves to be alive."

Made in the USA
Lexington, KY
09 May 2018